AMERICAN PRISONS

AMERICAN PRISONS

An Annotated Bibliography

Compiled by
Elizabeth Huffmaster McConnell
and Laura J. Moriarty

Bibliographies of the History of Crime and Criminal Justice, Number 1

GREENWOOD PRESS
Westport, Connecticut • London

Library of Congress Cataloging-in-Publication Data

McConnell, Elizabeth Huffmaster, 1949–
   American prisons : an annotated bibliography / compiled by
Elizabeth Huffmaster McConnell and Laura J. Moriarty.
      p.   cm.—(Bibliographies of the history of crime and
criminal justice, ISSN 1099–6370 ; no. 1)
   Includes index.
   ISBN 0–313–30616–8 (alk. paper)
   1. Prisons—United States—Bibliography.   2. Corrections—United
States—Bibliography.   3. Prisoners—United States—Bibliography.
I. Moriarty, Laura J.   II. Title.   III.   Series.
Z5703.4.P75M33   1998
[HV9471]
016.365′0973—dc21   98–25566

British Library Cataloguing in Publication Data is available.

Library of Congress Catalog Card Number: 98–25566
ISBN: 0–313–30616–8
ISSN: 1099–6370

First published in 1998

Greenwood Press, 88 Post Road West, Westport, CT 06881
An imprint of Greenwood Publishing Group, Inc.

Printed in the United States of America

The paper used in this book complies with the
Permanent Paper Standard issued by the National
Information Standards Organization (Z39.48–1984).

10 9 8 7 6 5 4 3 2

In order to keep this title in print and available to the academic community, this edition
was produced using digital reprint technology in a relatively short print run. This would
not have been attainable using traditional methods. Although the cover has been changed
from its original appearance, the text remains the same and all materials and methods
used still conform to the highest book-making standards.

CONTENTS

FOREWORD

This book, written as a supplement to the *Encyclopedia of American Prisons (1996)* contains annotations for selected references in the encyclopedia. Selection of references for annotation was based on the following criteria: (1) sources in the subject bibliographies which are generally recognized as the classic or substantive sources of the respective subjects, (2) sources that are readily available through university libraries, and (3) sources which the authors were able access. In the development of annotations, the authors used original articles and books, abstracts, indexes, and book reviews when possible.

The authors' purpose in writing the annotated bibliographies is to assist students and practitioners who are researching subjects in the encyclopedia. The annotations provide summary information on references, an overview of the source. This unique supplemental information is valuable to students and researchers because (1) it is useful in making decisions about whether or not to obtain the source for research projects, (2) it contains information about sources that are readily available through university libraries, and (3) it contains bibliographic entries for each subject in the encyclopedia, subjects which are integral in the research of corrections.

Students will find this annotated bibliography easy to use because the book's design has purposely mirrored that of the encyclopedia. For example, the subjects are presented in the same alphabetical format as the encyclopedia. Included in the book is an extensive index of authors, cases, and subjects. The index contains not only subject headings from the encyclopedia, but also "known as" subject titles; for example, capital punishment is also indexed as death penalty and executions.

ACKNOWLEDGMENTS

The authors are deeply appreciative of the invaluable assistance of Marilyn McShane and Trey Williams. Their advice and support have lightened the burden of this project, making it almost an enjoyable endeavor. We are also indebted to Michael Brooks, Bill Pelfrey, and Jay Albanese for their encouragement and administrative support. Librarian staff, especially the interlibrary loan personnel at Odom Library, Valdosta State University, and James Branch Cabel Library, Virginia Commonwealth University, are recognized for their unwavering assistance in obtaining reference material from other libraries. Special recognition is accorded Tom Dover for his help with library research. John McConnell, our technical expert, is acknowledged for the endless hours he spent on word processing, editing, and resolving all the technical problems associated with producing a camera-ready document.

Annotated Bibliography

A

ACCREDITATION

A.00001 American Correctional Association. (1966). *Manual of correctional standards* (rev. ed.). Laurel, MD: American Correctional Association.

Contained in this manual is an explanation of the standards of the American Correctional Association (ACA). Of particular interest are acceptable objectives, organizational structure, functions and operations of state correctional systems.

A.00002 Briscoe, K. & Kuhrt, J. (1992). How accreditation has improved correctional health care. *American Jails 6*(4), 48–52.

In this article the authors recognize that correctional administrators cannot control the rate of incarceration or the cost of inmate health care. However, they suggest that accreditation of the institution is an avenue for controlling or reducing unnecessary costs associated with frivolous lawsuits.

A.00003 Czajkowski, S. M., Nacci, P. L., Kramer, N., Price, S. J. & Sechrest, D. (1985). Responses to the accreditation program: What correctional staff think about accreditation. *Federal Probation 49*(1), 42–49.

Contained in this research article are the results of a survey of corrections' staff employed at accredited correctional facilities. The researchers measured the staff's perceptions of accreditation programs.

A.00004 Farkas, G. M. & Fosen, R. H. (1983). Responding to accreditation. *Corrections Today 45*(7), 40, 42.

Presented in this article are the results of a survey of correctional practitioners. The data were collected to determine practitioners' reactions to formal accreditation.

A.00005 Logan, C. H. (1993). *Criminal justice performance measures for prisons.* Washington, DC: National Institute of Justice.

Logan conducted a survey, supported by the National Institute of Justice, to identify performance measures in prisons. Described in the study are empirical indicators of the following eight dimensions of performance: security, safety, order, care, activity, justice, conditions, and management.

A.00006 Miller, R. (1992). Standards and the courts: An evolving relationship. *Corrections Today 54*(3), 58, 60.

Discussed in this article is the impact of American Correctional Association (ACA) standards on judicial decisions in corrections cases. The author argues that judges' decisions reflect a broader interpretation of the standards than was the intent of the ACA. It is recommended that the ACA continually review court decisions to identify trends in judicial views and to ensure that ACA standards change to reflect those established in court decisions.

A.00007 Reimer, E. G. & Sechrest, D. K. (1979). Writing standards for correctional accreditation. *Federal Probation 43*(3), 10–15.

The development of standards in correctional accreditation is examined in this article. The authors analyzed the following: existing standards, techniques of drafting standards, field testing standards, the approval process, and the use of consultants in the accreditation process.

A.00008 Reynolds, E. F. (1992). An auditor's view of accreditation. *Corrections Today 54*(3), 44, 46.

Presented in this article is a step-by-step explanation of the accreditation process, beginning with the initial call to the American Correctional Association and ending with submission of final reports. Accreditation is described as a process of continuing growth and education for corrections practitioners.

A.00009 Saylor, W. G. (1989). Quality control for prison managers: The Key Indicators/Strategic Support System. *Federal Prisons Journal 1*(2), 39–42.

Described in this article is the Federal Bureau of Prisons' Key Indicator/Strategic Support System, a personal computer based program.

Saylor suggests that the program aids corrections managers and administrators in two ways, it can be used to evaluate agency operations and develop operational strategic plans.

A.00010 Sechrest, D. K. & Reimer, E. G. (1982). Adopting national standards for correctional reform. *Federal Probation 46*, 18–25.

Sechrest and Reimer present arguments for the support of national standards for correctional reform. In particular, the researchers suggest that standards should include: sound administration and fiscal controls, an adequate physical plant, adherence to legal criteria, and the provision of basic services.

A.00011 Washington, J. (1989). Accreditation opinion poll update. *Corrections Today 51*(5), 160–161.

Washington discusses the results of an accreditation opinion poll. Reported in the article are the reasons why accreditation is viewed as having a positive impact on correctional facilities. Three positive by-products of accreditation are also noted, improved training, professionalism, and good morale.

ADMINISTRATION

A.00012 Archambeault, W. (1983). Management Theory Z: Its implications for managing the labor intensive nature of work in prison. *Prison Journal 62*(2), 58–67.

The author argues that Management Theory Z identifies and addresses the for general types of labor performed in correctional institutions. It is suggested that this theory is useful to managers and administrators who are characterized by decreasing budgets and are attempting to create an efficient work climate for front line correctional employees.

A.00013 Benton, F. W. & Nesbitt, C. A. (eds.) (1988). *Prison personnel management and staff development.* College Park, MD: American Correctional Association.

This edited volume contains several entries about a variety of prison personnel programs which have been successfully administered in the United States. Recommended are ways to improve education, recruitment, orientation, supervision, compensation, training, and career development of correctional staff.

A.00014 Cohn, A. W. (1987). Failure of correctional management: The potential for reversal. *Federal Probation 51*(4), 3–7.

Contained in this article is an examination of pedestrian and progressive management strategies that are employed in correctional facilities. The researcher describes and evaluates the differences in these two approaches.

A.00015 Farmer, J. F. (1988). A case study in regaining control of a violent state prison. *Federal Probation 52*(1), 41–47.

This study is based on data collected at Walpole State Prison in Massachusetts. Examined is the nine-member multi-disciplinary unit management team's approach to violence. Because of excessive violence in the institution, the multi disciplinary unit management approach was implemented to facilitate a positive change in the prison. Results indicate that success of this new management policy depended on continuous communication between the various prison groups.

A.00016 Simonsen, C. E. & Arnold, D. G. (1994). Is corrections ready for TQM? *Corrections Today 56*(4), 164, 166, 168–169.

Simonsen and Arnold provide a detailed description of Deming's 14 Total Quality Management model. They also evaluate its applicability in correctional management.

A.00017 Stojkovic, S. (1986). Social bases of power and control mechanisms among correctional administrators in a prison organization. *Journal of Criminal Justice 14*(2), 157–166.

The researcher presents the results of an analysis of the social bases of power among correctional administrators. The study was based on data collected from administrators in a maximum security correctional facility.

ADMINISTRATIVE SEGREGATION

A.00018 Adams, K. (1983). Former mental patients in a prison and parole system: A study of socially disruptive behavior. *Criminal Justice and Behavior 10*, 358–384.

Adams presents the results of a study of socially disruptive behavior of prisoners who had been mental patients. Comparisons were made between subjects' socially disruptive behaviors while incarcerated with their socially disruptive behaviors after release from institutions. The researcher also evaluated the use of administrative segregation as a behavioral management strategy.

A.00019 Buchanan, R. A. & Unger, C. A. (1988). *Disruptive maximum security inmate management guide.* Washington, DC: National Institute of Corrections.

Provided in this book are guidelines for correctional professionals who must deal with disruptive maximum-security inmates on a day-to-day basis. The authors discuss administrative segregation as a behavioral management strategy to control disruptive inmates.

A.00020 Henderson, J. D. (1990). *Protective custody management in adult correctional facilities.* Washington, DC: National Institute of Corrections.

Henderson addresses the necessity for protection, segregation, and surveillance that characterize protective custody. Of particular note is the relationship between protective custody and its increasing use for inmates characterized by aggressive activity, drug trafficking, and high profiles. The author reports that protective custody is encompassed in administrative segregation.

A.00021 Hodgins, S. & Cote, G. (1991). The mental health of penitentiary inmates in isolation. *Canadian Journal of Criminology 33,* 175–182.

Presented are the results of a study which was conducted to evaluate the mental health of penitentiary inmates in the Special-Handling Unit (SHU) and the Long-Term-Segregation Unit (LTSU) in the Quebec region of Canada's Correctional Service. These units are characterized as isolation or administrative segregation units.

A.00022 King, R. D. (1991). Maximum-security custody in Britain and the U.S.A.: A study of Gartree and Oak Park Heights. *British Journal of Criminology 31*(2), 126–152.

Presented in this research article are cross-cultural comparisons of custodial conditions at two institutions and an evaluation of the impact of custodial conditions on prisoners. The data were collected in two maximum security prisons: Oak Park Heights, a new-generation last-resort facility in Minnesota, and Gartree, a maximum-security dispersal prison in Leicestershire, England. Results indicated that both prisons contained substantially similar populations and that segregation from other inmates was a characteristic of each program.

A.00023 Olivero, J. M. & Roberts, J. B. (1990). The United States federal penitentiary at Marion, Illinois: Alcatraz revisited. *New England Journal of Civil and Criminal Confinement 16*, 21–51.

This article stems from an inmate class-action suit which was filed against the Federal penitentiary at Marion, Illinois. One issue being challenged is that conditions in the institution's isolation and segregation unit violate the Eighth Amendment protection against cruel and unusual punishment.

A.00024 Toch, H. (1982). The disturbed disruptive inmate: Where does the bus stop? *Journal of Psychiatry and the Law 10*, 327–349.

Toch presents arguments which support the necessity for stable settings for inmates who manifest both disruptive behaviors and mental illness. The researcher demonstrates that this type of inmate is frequently shuttled back and forth between prisons and mental health facilities, thus enhancing mental disturbances in these inmates. The author also recognizes that these inmates are often assigned to isolation or segregation unit, which enhances their mental problems.

Cases

A.00025 *Bruscino v. Carlson*, 854 F.2d 162 (7th Cir. 1988)

This case is based on administrative actions taken at the federal prison in Marion, Illinois. Because of widespread violence, the warden initiated a lockdown of "lifer" inmates. The prison lockdown consisted of confinement to cells, body cavity searches, the use of shackles for discipline, and a ban on group activity. The Supreme Court determined that these conditions were"sordid and horrible" but did not say they constituted "cruel and unusual punishment."

A.00026 *Graham v. Willingham*, 384 F.2d 367 (10th Cir. 1967)

In this case, an inmate alleged his confinement, at Leavenworth Prison in Kansas, constituted cruel and unusual punishment because of "prolonged and unreasonable segregated confinement in the maximum-security prison." The Court denied relief, stating that the control and management of penal institutions lies with the Attorney General and is not subject to judicial review unless it constitutes "clear arbitrariness or caprice upon the part of the prison officials."

A.00027 *Hewitt v. Helms*, 459 U.S. 460 (1983)

Inmate Hewitt argued that his constitutional rights were denied when he was placed in administrative lockdown. After a riot occurred, the inmate was ordered to administrative segregation until his role in the riot could be determined. The Court found that prison officials had not violated Hewitt's constitutional rights when it acknowledged that, "administrative segregation is the sort of confinement that inmates should reasonably anticipate receiving at some point in their incarceration, and does not involve an interest independently protected by the Due Process Clause."

A.00028 *Hutto v. Finney,* 437 U.S. 678, 98 S.Ct. 2565, 57 L.Ed.2d 522 (1978)

In a previous case, the Arkansas State Prison system was found to constitute cruel and unusual punishment and the Court outlined specific remedies to these violations. The present case is an appeal of two of the remedies identified by the Court: a maximum limitation of 30 days in solidary confinement; and an award of attorney fees to be paid by the Department of Corrections. The Court found these remedies to be valid.

A.00029 *Knuckles v. Prasse,* 435 F.2d 1255 (3rd Cir. 1971)

The Court ruled that prison officials did not have to provide Muslim periodicals and books requested by inmates practicing the Muslim faith. The Court reasoned that such literature in the hands of untrained Muslims would promote disrespect and disobedience among the inmates.

AIDS

A.00030 Aboulker, J. P. & Swart, A. M. (1993). Preliminary analysis of the Concorde trial. *The Lancet 341,* 889–890.

The authors report on a controlled study, administered in the United Kingdom, France and Ireland, to determine if symptom-free HIV-infected individuals would benefit from receiving zidovudine rather than waiting until the onset of AIDS symptoms to receive the drug. The results did not indicate any significant benefits of receiving early medication.

A.00031 Belbot, B. A. & del Carmen, R. V. (1991). AIDS in prison: Legal issues. *Crime and Delinquency 37*(1), 135–153.

The article contains a discussion of current statutory and case law relating to AIDS in correctional institutions. A review of relevant court cases is provided.

A.00032 Brien, P. M. & Harlow, C. W. (1995). *HIV in prisons and jails, 1993,*

Bureau of Justice Statistics Special Report. Washington, DC: U.S. Department of Justice.

This is a comprehensive report which contains statistics regarding inmates housed in prisons and jails who are infected with the human immunodeficiency virus (HIV) that causes AIDS. The statistics are current as of June 30, 1993.

A.00033 Centers for Disease Control . (1992). HIV prevention in the U.S. correctional system, 1991. *Morbidity and Mortality Weekly Report 41*(22), 389–397.

In 1990, 2.4% of the total U.S. adult population was under correctional supervision. By the end of November 1990, 4,519 cases of AIDS were reported among inmates in all federal and 45 state prisons. Moreover, 2,466 cases were reported by 25 city/county jail systems. HIV counseling and testing was being conducted in a few institutions in an effort to provide inmates with information about the disease, while assisting administrators in identifying persons who required medical treatment.

A.00034 Coughlin, T. A. (1988). AIDS in prisons: One correctional administrator's recommended policies and procedures. *Judicature 72*(1), 63–70.

Coughlin presents a description of the AIDS policies and procedures used by New York State corrections administrators. Special attention is directed at how procedures can overcome accompanying legal and budgetary constraints.

A.00035 Dubler, N. N., Bergmann, C. M. & Frankel, M. E. (1990). Management of HIV infection in New York state prisons. *Columbia Human Rights Law Review 21*(363). 392-396.

Outlined in this article is the plan used by the New York State Department of Corrections (NYSDC) to manage inmates with HIV. Education and counseling are the core elements of the NYSDC' AIDS/HIV policy.

A.00036 Freudenberg, N. (1989). *Preventing AIDS in prisoners: A guide to effective education for the prevention of HIV infection.* Washington, DC: American Public Health Association.

This guide provides information about the social and political forces that influence AIDS educators. The author offers advice on how to assess a population's needs, build coalitions, develop educational materials, and evaluate program effectiveness. Guide recommendations are supported by a study of case histories of successful and unsuccessful AIDS policies as well as interviews with more than 130 AIDS educators from around the United States.

A.00037 Glaser, J. B. & Greifinger, R.B. (1993). Correctional health care: A public health opportunity. *Annals of Internal Medicine 118*(2), 139-145.

According to the authors, approximately 1.2 million inmates have some type of communicable disease. The researchers argue that it is in the best interest of local health care personnel to test and treat inmate ailments while health care personnel have the opportunity to do so. It is pointed out that because many of the inmates are characterized by risky lifestyles and limited access to health care, without treatment while in prison their release from prison is expected to result in an escalation of communicable these diseases. Providing health care for inmates is regarded as a protective measure for society.

A.00038 Hammett, T. M. & Moini, S. (1990). *1989 Update: AIDS in correctional facilities: Issues and options.* Washington, DC: U.S. Department of Justice, National Institute of Justice, U.S. Department of Justice.

This report on AIDS in correctional facilities contains discussions of research developments in the epidemiology of HIV infection and AIDS in correctional facilities, tuberculosis and HIV infection, AIDS education and training, precautionary measures, HIV antibody testing, counseling and notification policies, housing and correctional management, medical care and psychosocial services, and the legal issues of AIDS in correctional facilities.

A.00039 Hammett, T. M., Harrold, L., Gross, M. & Epstein, J. (1993). *1992 Update: AIDS in correctional facilities, issues and options.* Washington, DC: U.S. Department of Justice.

This report is an update to one of the most comprehensive examinations of AIDS in correctional institutions. In this update, the authors provide the most recent statistics available and present the most recent court cases (prison/prisoner litigation) on AIDS related issues in correctional facilities.

A.00040 Lawson, W. T., Jr. & Fawkes, L. S. (1992). HIV, AIDS, and the female offender. *Federal Prisons Journal 3*(1) (Spring), 27–32, or In W. Lawson & L. Fawkes' *Female offenders: Meeting needs of a neglected population, 1993.* Baltimore, MD: United Books.

The authors indicate that HIV/AIDS is increasing at a much greater rate in American women than in American men. Within the female population, low income African American and Hispanic women are characterized by the highest increases in HIV/AIDS. Additionally, female offenders, because of their frequent sexual victimization and minority status, are predicted to be at greatest risk of heterosexual disease transmission.

A.00041 Lillis, J. (1993). Dealing with HIV/AIDS positive inmates. *Corrections Compendium 18*(6), 1–3.

In this survey the author explores how the U.S. and Canadian Corrections systems address the need of HIV/AIDS inmates. On average, 5.7% of the inmates have HIV/AIDS or AIDS related illnesses. The highest frequency of inmates with these illnesses is in the District of Columbia (20%). It is reported that prison operational expense is increasing because of health care costs associated with HIV/AIDS illnesses.

A.00042 Lurigio, A. J., Petraitis, J. & Johnson, B. (1991). HIV education for probation officers: An implementation and evaluation program. *Crime and Delinquency 37*(1) (special issue, January), 125–134.

Presented is a discussion of the reasons why HIV education is important. The researchers support their suggestions from an evaluation of a HIV education program that was implemented at the Cook County Adult Probation Department in Chicago, Illinois.

A.00043 Martin, R., Zimmerman, S. & Long, B. (1993). AIDS education in U.S. prisons: A survey of inmate programs. *The Prison Journal 73*(1), 103–129.

Past research has shown that prisons are an ideal setting for the development and study of AIDS education and prevention programs. The authors present their findings from a nationwide survey of AIDS programs in United States prisons. They present information about available programs and address many of the more common issues surrounding the problem.

A.00044 Nacci, P. L. & Kane, T. R. (1983). The incidence of sex and sexual aggression in federal prisons. *Federal Probation 47*(4), 31–36.

Contained in this article are the results of a research project based on a representative sample of federal inmates. The data were collected through personal interviews. Specifically, the researchers examined the extent of homosexual activity in Federal prisons, problem behaviors associated with homosexual activity, sexual aggression and sex acts, and inmates' sexual identity problems.

A.00045 National Academy of Sciences. (1988). *Confronting AIDS: Update 1988.* Washington, DC: National Academy Press.

The authors discuss their findings and make recommendations pertinent to HIV infection, modes of HIV transmission, and the prevalence of HIV/AIDS infection in the United States.

A.00046 National Commission on Acquired Immune Deficiency Syndrome. (1991). *Report: HIV disease in correctional facilities.* Washington, DC: The Commission.

The National Commission on AIDS conducted site visits and hearings in an effort to identify and understand the issues and impact of prisoners with HIV on federal, state, and local correctional facilities. The commission explores how HIV infected prisoners impacted three major areas of prison life: health care, human rights, and education.

A.00047 National Institute of Corrections. (1993). *Advisory board hearing report.* Washington, DC: U.S. Department of Justice, Prisons Division.

This is a report based on hearings which were convened in every region of the United States. Correctional officials provided data about critical issues in correctional facilities. The consensus of correctional officials is that prison health care is the most critical issue in the corrections.

A.00048 National Institute of Justice. (1990). *Drug use forecasting: 1988 drug use forecasting annual report.* Washington, DC: U.S. Department of Justice.

Reported are the results of the Drug Use Forecasting project. Data are presented for many types of drug users including drug usage among incarcerated populations. The drugs of choice for men, women, and teenagers are reported. The relationship between drugs and crime is also presented

A.00049 Snell, T. L. (1995). *Correctional populations in the United States, 1993.* Washington, DC: Bureau of Justice Statistics, (NIJ-156241).

This comprehensive document, based on national 1993 statistics, contains bivariate tables many topics including; jail inmates, offenders on probation, jail census, offenders on parole, and capital punishment.

Cases

A.00050 *Botera Gomez v. U.S.*, 725 F.Supp. 526 (S.D. Fla 1989)

In this case the inmate sought relief from the Court when denied medical treatment for AIDS. The Court determined that inmates with AIDS are entitled to treatment the same as inmates with other diseases. As a result, denying treatment on the basis that the disease is AIDS constitutes discrimination.

A.00051 *Cameron v. Metcuz*, 705 F.Supp 454 (N.D. Ind. 1989)

The plaintiff filed a complaint stating that the Westville Correctional Center acted in an indifferent and callous manner when they failed to protect the plaintiff from a bite wound inflicted by an another inmate who had tested positive for AIDS. The inmate claimed that such inaction was a violation under the civil rights act (42 U.S.C. Section 1983). The court found that the defendants' behavior did not violate any constitutional rights of the inmate.

A.00052 *Casey v. Lewis*, 773 F.Supp. 1365 (D.Ariz 1991)

The Rehabilitation Act was passed to protect handicap persons from discrimination. Federally funded programs are not allowed to discriminate against the handicapped out of stereotypes or fears regarding the handicapped individuals. This Act also applies to some discriminations against inmates with AIDS.

A.00053 *Cordero v. Coughlin*, 607 F.Supp 9 (S.D.N.Y. 1984)

In this case inmates objected to being segregated after testing positive for HIV. The prison administrators segregated the inmates even though they preferred to be in the general population. The Court found the prison policy of segregating inmates with HIV constitutional in some situations.

A.00054 *Doe v. Coughlin*, 696 F.Supp 1234 (N.D.N.Y. 1988)

Segregation of inmates who test positive for HIV is constitutional in some circumstances as established in *Cordero v. Coughlin*. In the present case, however, the court found that the segregation of such inmates furthered "legitimate interests" but did so in a "constitutionally impermissible manner." This case demonstrates that some instances of segregation based on HIV are unconstitutional.

A.00055 *Dunn v. White*, 880 F.2d 1118 (10th Cir. 1989)

In this case the prisoner Dunn refused to take an AIDS test. He argued that being forced to take an HIV or AIDS test violated his 4th, 8th, and 14th Amendment Rights to privacy. The court found that requiring inmates to take HIV/AIDS tests does not violate inmates' constitutional rights to privacy.

A.00056 *Estelle v. Gamble*, 429 U.S. 97, 97 S.Ct 285, 50 L.Ed.2d 251 (1976)

In this case an inmate alleged that his constitutional rights were violated when the correctional staff refused to provide medical treatment. The Court agreed when it recognized that failure to provide medical treatment to prisoners is a violation of the 8th Amendment.

A.00057 *Farmer v. Moritsugu*, 742 F.Supp 525 (W.D. Wisc. 1990)

An inmate challenged the correctional institution's policy of excluding HIV inmates from assignment to jobs that involved food and health services. In this case, exclusion was deemed constitutional.

A.00058 *Feigely v. Fulcomer*, 720 F.Supp 475 (M.D.Pa 1989)

In this case, inmates who had been voluntarily tested for AIDS and did not test positive, wanted mandatory testing for AIDS for all inmates. The court did not support mandatory AIDS testing. In fact, the Federal Bureau of Prisons does not automatically test each inmate for AIDS. It tests inmates prior to release from the institution, tests random samples of inmates, and tests certain groups of inmates, for example, pregnant females.

A.00059 *Glick v. Henderson*, 855 F.2d 536 (8th Cir. 1988)

Inmates at the Arkansas Department of Corrections alleged that the prison administration failed and refused to protect inmates from exposure to AIDS. The inmates sued for mandatory testing of all inmates for HIV/ AIDS, the court denied the inmates' appeal.

A.00060 *Harris v. Thigpen*, 727 F.Supp 1564 (M.D. Ala. 1990)

Inmates objected to being segregated because of their HIV status. The inmates argued that segregated inmates should have equal access to institutional programs that were suitable to their situations. The court found that such access caused management problems for prison officials. Therefore, segregation policy that resulted in inmates' inability to participate in institutional programs was not found to be unconstitutional. Management needs of the institution were deemed to have a greater interest than the ability of individuals to participate in institutional programs.

A.00061 *Hawley v. Evans*, 715 F.Supp 601 (N.D.Ga. 1989)

The general rule of medical care is that the care be "minimally adequate." An inmate is not entitled to seek alternative treatment even if the inmate is prepared to pay for it. Inmates may not receive AZT, treatment from non-prison doctors, or experimental treatments for AIDS if the inmate is already receiving treatment from prison personnel.

A.00062 *Jarrett v. Faulkner*, 662 F.Supp 928 (S.D.Ind 1987)

Three inmates at the Indiana State Prison filed a complaint for all present and future inmates of the institution. The plaintiffs asked the court to order the "screening of all inmates for the AIDS virus and the segregation of all homosexuals." The inmates were unsuccessful in their attempts to obtain mandatory testing and segregation.

A.00063 *Judd v. Packard*, 669 F.Supp 741, 742 (D.Md. 1987)

Inmates who tested positive for AIDS/HIV objected to being segregated from the general population. In this case the court found the circumstances of segregation to be constitutional.

A.00064 *Maynard v. New Jersey*, 719 F.Supp 292 (D.N.J. 1989)

In this case an inmate sought relief from the court when denied treatment for AIDS by the correctional system. The court found in the inmate's interest when it deemed that failure to treat an AIDS inmate is a violation of the 8th Amendment.

A.00065 *Myers v. Maryland Division of Corrections*, 782 F.Supp 1095 (D.Md. 1992)

Inmates from a Maryland prison, who had not tested positive for HIV, filed actions pro se requesting mandatory segregation of inmates with HIV. The issue was whether the policy used by the Department of Corrections violated the 8th Amendment. Using a two pronged test, the court said the plaintiffs must show (1) "pervasive risk of harm to DOC inmates exists under the current DOC policies and programs, and (2) defendants are being deliberately indifferent to that risk." Although the court found evidence supporting only the first prong, it entered a favorable judgement for the defendants.

A.00066 *Powell v. Department of Corrections*, 647 F.Supp. 968 (N.D. Okla. 1986)

The prison segregated inmates who tested positive for AIDS/HIV. The rational for such segregation was based on the premise that it protected the other inmates from the spread of AIDS/HIV. The court upheld the policy of segregating AID/HIV inmates because prisons are characterized by many at-risk behaviors, thus prison officials are allowed to segregate to limit the spread of the disease.

A.00067 *Traufler v. Thompson*, 662 F.Supp 945 (N.D. Ill. 1987)

Plaintiffs from the Stateville Correctional Center filed pro se civil rights actions charging the defendants with "conspiracy to commit genocide." The inmates alleged that prison officials were intentionally spreading the AIDS virus in and effort to eliminate minorities, thus reducing the welfare burden to the public. The allegations of a complaint generally must be accepted as true. The court ruled that in this case, the facts alleged are "so fantastic as to go beyond the belief of any reasonable person." Therefore, the case was dismissed.

A.00068 *Woods v. White*, 689 F.Supp 974 (W.D. Wis. 1988)

In this case the court determined that inmates have a protected interest in keeping their HIV status confidential. The court ruled that the unnecessary disclosure of positive HIV status violated inmates' rights to privacy.

A.00069 *U.S. v. Moore*, 846 F.2d 1163 (8th Cir. 1988)

After learning that he had tested positive for the HIV virus, inmate Moore bit two correctional officers during a struggle. An indictment was filed charging Moore with use of a deadly and dangerous weapon, his mouth and teeth. Moore claimed that the evidence at the trial was insufficient to sustain a finding that his mouth and teeth were a deadly and dangerous weapon and that AIDS can be transmitted by a bite. On appeal, the court agreed with the lower court and maintained that the bite in and of itself is deadly and dangerous, regardless of the status of the inmate's medical circumstances.

ALCATRAZ FEDERAL PENITENTIARY

A.00070 Fortunate Eagle, A. (1992). *Alcatraz! Alcatraz! The Indian occupation of 1969–1971*. New York: Heyday Books.

In this book the author provides a comprehensive and personal account of the Native American occupation of Alcatraz from 1969 to 1971. Although the book is primarily about the Native American occupation, the author also provides an informative overview of Alcatraz when it was a maximum security federal prison.

A.00071 Hurley, D. J. (1987). *Alcatraz island memories.* Petaluma, CA: Barlow
Printing.

Hurley, whose father was a Federal correctional officer, lived on Alcatraz
Island from the time the author was seven until he was eighteen. The
author provides a history of the island from its discovery to the present,
with particular emphasis on the 29 years it was a Federal Penitentiary.

A.00072 Hurley, D. J. (1989). *Alcatraz island maximum security.* Petaluma, CA:
Barlow Printing.

The author, son of a federal correctional officer who worked at Alcatraz
when the author was a child, discusses the mysteries and myths about
Alcatraz Federal Penitentiary. Presented is a brief history of Alcatraz's
most famous inmates and a discussion of the fourteen attempted escapes.

ALCOHOL TREATMENT PROGRAMS IN PRISON

A.00073 Armor, D., Polich, M. & Stambul, H. (1978). *Alcoholism and treatment.*
New York: John Wiley and Sons.

This book contains the results of a quasi-experimental evaluation of treatments for alcoholism. The researchers collected data on alcoholics in
treatment, as well as a control group who did not receive treatment.
Evaluation results for the various alcoholism treatments are reported as
well as the etiological implications of alcohol treatments.

A.00074 Bureau of Justice Statistics. (1993). *Survey of state prison inmates, 1991.*
Washington, DC: U.S. Government Printing Office.

Contained in this article is a compilation of data obtained in face-to-face
interviews with state prison inmates. This data can be used to examine a
variety of issues including: the roles of drug and alcohol use in crime, gang
membership as an element of crime, sentences, and time served as it relates
to turnover of prison populations.

A.00075 Gottfredson, M. & Hirschi, T. (1990). *A general theory of crime.* Palo
Alto, CA: Stanford University Press.

The authors argue that the essential element of criminality is the absence
of self control. They further argue that an analysis of the nature and
causes of criminality demonstrate that sociological, psychological, bio-
logical, and economic theories do not provide adequate explanations of
criminal behavior. The authors focus on the lack of self-control that is

characteristic of people under the influence of alcohol and also the number of crimes that are committed by people who have been drinking.

A.00076 Rossi, J. J. & Filstead, W. J. (1976). "Treating" the treatment issues: Some general observations about the treatment of alcoholism. In W. J. Filstead, J. J. Rossi and M. Keller (eds.), *Alcohol and alcohol problems: New thinking and new directions* (pp. 193–227). Cambridge, MA: Balinger Publishing Company.

The authors begin with the premise that individual reactions to a phenomenon are shaped by their thoughts about that phenomenon. Examined are the social and cultural forces of alcoholism, how the concept of motivation is involved in developing and implementing services, the selection of service personnel, and the sociopolitical effects of evaluating treatment services. Recommendations are also provided.

A.00077 Welte, J. W. & Miller, B. A. (1987). Alcohol use by violent and property offenders. *Drug and Alcohol Dependence 19*, 313–324.

Welte and Miller compare alcohol and drug histories of incarcerated property-crime offenders with those of violent-crime offenders to determine the degree to which alcohol or drug use were factors in committing crime. The researchers found that a higher proportion of violent crimes than property crimes were preceded by alcohol or drug use except in the case of offenders with lower educational levels.

AMERICAN CORRECTIONAL ASSOCIATION

A.00078 ACA Committees Caucus. (1988). ACA annual report shows growth in membership and programs. *Corrections Today 50*(6), 24–26.

The article contains an explanation of the Standards Committee of the American Correctional Association (SCACA). It indicates that the SCACA was organized to continually review correction standards and to evaluate whether its standards are relevant to current trends in correction management. The Committee consist of 20 members who serve six year terms. The members are knowledgeable of all levels of corrections management, including adult, juvenile, courts, jails, probation and parole. The SCACA suggests standards revisions and solicits comments from concerned parties before making decisions.

A.00079 ACA Committees Caucus. (1989). ACA moves to new heights for the 90s. *Corrections Today 51*(6), 90–92.

Presented is a description and an explanation of how the American Corrections Association (ACA) functions. It indicates that the ACA conducts studies on how its standards affect court decisions. The writer acknowledges that although ACA standards should meet court stipulations, court decisions should not always serve as a basis for setting ACA standards.

A.00080 ACA Committees Caucus. (1990). ACA's women's task force enjoys growth and success. *Corrections Today 52*(4), 18.

The ACA's Women's Task Force is developing a pool of training materials, seminars and workshops for women in corrections. It encourages more women to become involved and join the Women's Task Force.

A.00081 ACA Committees Caucus. (1992). Two dynamic leaders of the National Prison Association. *Corrections Today 54*(1), 96.

The authors outline the history of U.S. Federal Corrections and discusses the National Prison Association, which is the modern day American Correctional Association. Also highlighted are the two prominent leaders within the field of corrections.

A.00082 American Correctional Association. (1991). *Public policy for corrections*. Waldorf, MD: St. Mary's.

Presented in this handbook are the ratified public correctional policies of the American Correctional Association. Included is a brief history of why these policies were adopted, the process of how they were adopted and what the future holds for the American Correctional Association.

A.00083 Cerquone, J. (1987). CAC realignment with ACA complete. *Corrections Today 49*(1), 86.

The Commission on Accreditation for Corrections (CAC) was absorbed into the American Correctional Association's (ACA) division of Standards and Accreditation. The merger is designed to improve the efficiency of the accreditation process and to allow continuing improvement in the monitoring of accreditation costs.

A.00084 Cerquone, J. (1988). Corrections yesterday. *Corrections Today 50*(1), 70–74, 82.

The author provides a brief history of the American Correctional Association and of *Corrections Today*. Included are articles and cartoons from past editions of *Corrections Today*, some of which are as relevant today as when they were originally published.

A.00085 Huskey, B. L. (1988). Tracking critical issues in corrections, Committee refines program for 118th congress. *Corrections Today 50*(1), 40.

In this article the author discusses the programs that the American Correctional Association's Program Committee has proposed for the 118th Congress of Corrections meetings.

A.00086 Irving, J. R. (1992). ACA standards committee: Supporting a vital process. *Corrections Today 54*(3), 62,

In this article the author provides an explanation of the Standards Committee of the American Correctional Association (SCACA). It indicates that the SCACA was organized to continually review correction standards and to evaluate if its standards are relevant to current trends in correction management. The SCACA announces suggested standards revisions and asks comments from all sectors concerned before making decisions.

A.00087 Keve, P. W. (1991). *Prisons and the American conscience: A history of U.S. federal corrections.* Carbondale, IL: Southern Illinois University Press.

Contained in this book is a historical analysis of Federal imprisonment from its establishment, by the Continental Congress, through 1987, when Norman Carlson was the director of the Federal Bureau of Prisons. Key occurrences that impacted policy changes through the years are discussed.

A.00088 Miller, R. (1992). Standards and the courts: An evolving relationship. *Corrections Today 54*(3), 58, 60.

In this article is a discussion of the standards of the American Correctional Association (ACA). Miller explains the role of ACA standards in the decision-making process of the courts. The writer suggests that the ACA continues to review how its policies influence court decisions and vice versa.

A.00089 Pippin, K. (1989). Rutherford B. Hayes: America's 19th president was also a founder of the National Prison Association and its president for 10 years. *Corrections Today 51*(5), 112–116.

Rutherford B. Hayes attended the first meeting of the National Prison Association in 1870 and was its president from 1883 until his death in 1893. His obituary characterized him as the one man who did the most to give stability and character to the Prison Reform Movement.

A.00090 Travisono, A. P. (1990). Standards: A true reflection of ACA's membership. *Corrections Today 52*(4), 4.

The author explains the procedure the American Correctional Association follows when rewriting standards and the accreditation process.

A.00091 Travisono, A. P. & Hawkes, M. Q. (1995). ACA and prison reform. *Corrections Today 57*(5), 70–73.

The authors chronicle the American Correctional Association's prison reform efforts, from its founding in the 1870s until the present.

A.00092 Tyler, V. R. & Smalley, E. A. (1989). The ACA's diverse professional affiliates. *Corrections Today 51*(2), 185–188.

Tyler and Smalley discuss ways the American Correctional Association and its professional affiliates help one another. These affiliates must meet certain standards and their bylaws and constitutions must coincide with those of the ACA. These professional affiliates are national organizations that are dedicated to serving a particular sector of correctional professionals, i.e., the American Jail Association, and the North American Association of Wardens and Superintendents.

ANGOLA (Louisiana State Penitentiary)

A.00093 Butler, A. & Henderson, C. M. (1990). *Angola: Louisiana State Penitentiary, a half-century of rage and reform.* Lafayette, LA: Center for Louisiana Studies, University of Southwestern Louisiana.

This book contains the case histories of several inmates who were incarcerated at Angola. Described are the commission of crimes, the judicial process, and experiences in the Louisiana prison system. These personal accounts introduces the reader to the criminal as well as the victims. Solutions to solving some of the problems are offered.

A.00094 Carleton, M. T. (1971). *Politics and punishment: The history of the Louisiana State Penal System.* Baton Rouge: Louisiana State University Press.

Presented is a historical analysis of the development of the Louisiana State Penal System.

A.00095 Foster, B., Rideau, W. & Wikberg, R. (Eds.). (1989). *The wall is strong:*

Corrections in Louisiana. Lafayette, LA: Center for Criminal Justice Research, University of Southwestern Louisiana.

The Louisiana State Prison System is discussed by various authors in this volume. Included are discussions of the history of Angola, correctional administration in Louisiana, prison life in Angola and correctional institutions are administered in present day Louisiana.

A.00096 Rideau, W. & Wikberg, R. (1992). *Life sentences: Rage and survival behind bars.* New York: Times Books.

The authors, two inmates at Louisiana's Angola Prison, discuss the inhumaneness of capital punishment, various methods of execution, life without parole sentences, and the brutality of inmate power games. The book is based on a thorough review of literature and personal interviews with inmates.

ARCHITECTURE

A.00097 American Correctional Association (1983). *Design guide for secure adult correctional facilities.* Laurel, MD: American Correctional Association.

Presented in this book are design guidelines for secure adult correctional facilities which meet the standards developed by the American Correctional Association, the Commission on Accreditation for Corrections, and the U.S. Department of Justice.

A.00098 Barnes, H. E. & Teeters, N. K. (1943). *New horizons in Criminology: The American crime problem.* New York: Prentice Hall or (1951) revised edition, Englewood Cliffs, NJ: Prentice-Hall.

A comprehensive discussion of crime, criminals, punishment, and prisons is presented in this book. The authors also offer suggestions for future reforms in the repression of crime and the treatment of criminals. They document the evolution in the architectural design of prisons.

A.00099 British Home Office. (1985). *New directions in prison design: Report of a Home Office study of new generation prisons in the USA.* London: Her Majesty's Stationery Office.

A working group was appointed to study and evaluate current prison design in the United States and determine if there were any lessons or innovations that could aide the prison system in England and Wales. The focus of the report was new-generation facilities.

A.00100 Johnston, N. (1973). *The human cage: A brief history of prison architecture.* New York: Walker.

Johnston presents a historical analysis of prison architecture from its church–inspired European beginnings through the developments made in the United States.

A.00101 Nagel, W. G. (1973). *The new red barn: A critical look at the modern American prison.* New York: Walker.

The author provides a comprehensive overview of the state of the art in the physical design of correctional facilities. Included is a critical discussion, by architects, psychologists, social scientists and correctional administrators, of how the physical design meets the needs of treatment, rehabilitation, and security.

ARGOT

A.00102 Busic, J. E. (1987). Time and life. *Verbatim: The Language Quarterly 14*(2), 8–9.

The prison population is a highly specialized subculture that has a language all its own. Conclusions about prisoner mentality, perception, and philosophy are presented in this examination of prison language.

A.00103 Cardozo–Freeman, I. & Delorme, E. P. (1984). *The joint: Language and culture in a maximum security prison.* Springfield, IL: Charles C. Thomas.

Research conducted at Washington State Penitentiary at Walla Walla provides the basis for this book. The researchers collected data through taped interviews with inmates to test the hypothesis that language shapes and is shaped by culture.

A.00104 Clemmer, D. (1940). *The prison community.* New York: Holt, Rhinehart, and Winston.

This book results from a classic study of imprisonment from a sociological perspective. The researcher conducted this study in an average American state prison which housed over 2,300 inmates. The author describes the prison subculture and addresses language norms that are specific to the penal setting.

A.00105 Fishman, J. F. (1934). *Sex in prison: Revealing sex conditions in American* prisons. New York: National Liberty Press.

The author, the first Inspector of Prisons for the United States, has written the first book about sex in American prisons. He reports how wardens and administrators deny that sex activity exists behind the walls, explains what prisoners do about sex, conditions in coed prisons, what happens to homosexuals in prison, and if the administrators can control or handle sex in prison. Also discussed is the language of prison sex.

A.00106 Fox, V. B. & Stinchcomb, J. B. (1994). *Introduction to corrections.* Englewood Cliffs, NJ: Prentice-Hall.

Fox and Stinchcomb present an overview of corrections. The authors detail the nature, scope, and function of corrections and examine current and future issues in corrections.

A.00107 Little, B. (1982). Prison lingo: A style of American English slang. *Anthropological Linguistics 24*(2), 206–244.

This article contains a general ethnography of prison language which the researcher developed from data collected at a Southern 'county farm.'

A.00108 Maurer, D. W. (1974). *The American confidence man.* Springfield, IL: Charles C. Thomas.

Presented is an examination of the methods, personality, language, and characteristics that combine to form the subculture of the con man.

A.00109 Sykes, G. M. (1958). *Society of captives: A study of a maximum security prison.* Princeton, NJ: Princeton University Press.

The author presents the results of one of the classic studies of a maximum security prison from a sociological perspective. The researcher examined the prison's organizational dysfunctions and their consequent effects. One of the consequent effects is the prison subculture and its attendant language norms.

A.00110 Sykes, G. M. and Messinger, S. L. (1977). Inmate social system. In R.G. Leger and J.R. Stratton (eds.), *Sociology of corrections: A book of readings.* New York: John Wiley and Sons. Also in R. Cloward, (ed.) *Theoretical studies in the social organization of the prison, 1977.* New York: Social Sciences Research Council.

This edited book chapter contains a discussion of the norms, attitudes, and beliefs found in a social system within prisons, i.e., prison subculture. The authors provide a thorough explanation of the categories of social relationships that exist among inmates in penal systems. The categories of social relationships are described using inmate argot.

ASHURST-SUMNER ACT

A.00111 American Correctional Association. (1986). *Study of prison industry: History, components, and goals*. Washington, DC: National Institute of Corrections.

This report is based on data, collected by the American Correctional Association, from 39 federal, state, and Canadian jurisdictions through mailed surveys. The study was conducted to examine the evolution, goals, components, and organizational approaches of prison industries.

A.00112 Auerbach, B., Sexton, G. E., Franklin, C. F. & Lawson, R. H. (1988). *Work in American prisons: The private sector gets involved*. Washington, DC: National Institute of Justice.

This report contains a description of the historical, as well as, current developments in private-sector prison industries. Primary emphasis is placed on the prohibitions against prison industry, analyzing costs and benefits, and suggestions for future strategies.

A.00113 Callison, H. G. (1989). *Zephyr products: The story of an inmate staffed business*. Laurel, MD: American Correctional Association.

This publication contains the results of a study of a private sector-prison industry project. The researcher concludes that the project was successful and offers recommendations for corrections officials and business people who are planning a prison-based business.

A.00114 Cullen, F. T. & Travis, L. F., III. (1984). Work as an avenue of prison reform. *New England Journal of Civil and Criminal Confinement 10*, 45–64.

Work ethic in prison is the primary focus of the present article. The authors propose that the prison social order could be changed by employing inmates in regular jobs at decent wages, thus emphasizing the work ethic. The authors suggest that a work ethic approach could secure broad-based ideological support and could be conducive to both inmates and the custodial staff.

A.00115 Flanagan, T. J. & and Maguire, K. (1993). A full employment policy for prisons in the United States: Some arguments, estimates, and implications.

Journal of Criminal Justice 21, 117–130.

Flanagan and Maguire report the results of an examination of employment policies in prisons in the United States. The authors support a policy of full employment for prisoners, recommend several models for implementing full employment, and discuss the implications of dramatically increasing prisoner employment.

A.00116 Flynn, F. (1950). The federal government and the prison labor problem. *Social Science Review 24(March-June)*, 19–40 ff.

A discussion of the prison–labor acts that were passed by Congress from 1929 to 1940 as well as state imposed restrictions are presented. According to the author, prison industries have been severely handicapped by these restrictions and will continue to be until prison-labor laws are changed.

A.00117 McKelvey, B. (1936). *American prisons: A history of good intentions*. Chicago: University of Chicago Press. (Reprinted, Montclair, NJ: Patterson-Smith, 1968, 1977).

McKelvey presents a historical analysis of the American prison system from 1835 to 1977. Specific issues addressed are changing standards, reform movements, criminological theories, and confrontations in American penology. Also noted is the impact of legislation which prohibited the manufacture of goods to be sold to the public.

A.00118 Sexton, G., Furrow, F. C. & Auerbach, B. J. (1985). *The private sector and prison industries: Research in brief*. Washington, DC: National Institute of Justice.

This summary research report provides an overview of a survey on private sector involvement in prison industries. The researchers provide examples of how private businesses are participating in prison industry and make recommendations for consideration by prison officials in planning prison industry programs.

ATTICA

A.00119 Badillo, H. & Haynes, M. (1972). *A bill of NO rights: Attica and the American prison system*. New York: Outerbridge and Lazard.

Contained in this book is the results of an examination of the conditions that led up to the prison riot at the Attica correctional facility. The authors also provide a day-by-day analysis of the events that occurred during the riot and the days that followed.

A.00120 Clark, R. X. (1973). *The brothers of Attica*. New York: Links Books.

Clark provides "a first hand look" at the riot at Attica Correctional Facility which occurred in September 8, 1971.

A.00121 Deutsch, M. R., Cunningham, D. & Fink, E. M. (1991). Twenty years later: Attica civil rights case finally cleared for trial. *Social Justice 18*, 13–25.

The Attica civil rights case took 20 years to get to trial. Over the years the State of New York tried to cover-up what really happened during the retaking of the prison, for example, the use of excessive force which resulted in the deaths of correctional officers and instances where inmates were tortured by state personnel.

A.00122 Glaberson, W. (1992, Feb 6). Unanswered in Attica case: High level accountability. *New York Times*, B5, 1.

Addressed in this article are some of the concerns which emerged after the jury returned a mixed verdict in the Attica riots civil law suit. The jury found the former deputy warden liable on two claims and rejected the claim that the former corrections commissioner specifically failed to provide adequate medical care to the inmates. Raised in this article are some concerns over the accountability issue of administrators.

A.00123 Gould, R. E. (1974). Officer-inmate relationship – Its role in the Attica rebellion. *Bulletin of the American Academy of Psychiatry and the Law* 2(1),34–45.

The results of intensive informal interviews with staff and inmates at Attica correctional facility are presented. The purpose of the research was to evaluate the officer-inmate relationship and the degree to which the relationship contributed to the 1971 riot.

A.00124 New York State Special Commission on Attica, NY. (1972). *Attica: The official report of the New York State Special Commission on Attica.* New York: Bantam Books.

Provided in this is a description of the New York prison system, the correctional facility at Attica, and of the inmate's life inside the insti-tution. There is a summarization of the conditions and events leading to the uprising, with particular emphasis on how the inmates seized control on September 9, 1971. Discussed in the report is the assault, its aftermath, and several recommendations for major changes in the New York prison system.

A.00125 Oswald, R. G. (1972). *My story.* Garden City, NY: Doubleday.

This book, written by the New York State Prison Commissioner at the time of the Attica riot, is autobiographical. It provides a comprehensive discussion of the Commissioner's role in the Attica riot.

A.00126 Unseem, B. & Kimball, P. (1989). *State of siege: U.S. prison riots, 1971–1986.* New York: Oxford University Press.

Presented is a discussion of five significant prison riots in the United States, including the 1970s' riots at Attica and Joliet and the 1980s' riots in New Mexico, Michigan, and West Virginia. The authors offer their analyses of causes, variation, and effects of prison riots.

A.00127 Weiss, R. P. (1975). The order of Attica. *Social Justice 18,* 35–47.

When groups have unequal power the "order" dictates the process used to control the other groups. Because of unequal power and hierarchical distance, the prisoners of Attica felt that using power was the only means available to them to force the issue of basic humanity.

A.00128 Wicker, T. (1975). *Time to die.* New York: Times Books.

Wicker, a prominent writer, provides an eyewitness account of the negotiations between prison authorities and inmates during the riot at the Attica correctional facility during September of 1971.

A.00129 Yarrow, A .L. (1972, Feb 5). Jury renders mixed verdict in Attica case. *New York Times,* B1, 5.

The author reports on the verdict in a civil law suit regarding the Attica prison riot. Twenty plus years after the riots occurred at Attica, a jury decided in a civil law suit that the former deputy warden was liable on the basis of two claims. The jury rejected the claim that the former corrections commissioner specifically failed to provide adequate medical care to the inmates.

AUBURN SYSTEM

A.00130 Barnes, H. E. (1930). *The story of punishment.* Boston: Stratford. (2nd Edition, Montclair, NJ: Patterson Smith, 1972).

The author discusses the various methods of punishment used by modern man to punish criminals. He proposes that punishment should be discarded since there is no empirical evidence that punishment produces noncriminal behavior. Instead, Barnes suggests that psychiatry is the more appropriate method for the treatment of criminals.

A.00131 Crawford, W. (1969). *Report on the penitentiaries of the United States*. Montclair, NJ: Patterson Smith.

Crawford was commissioned in the early nineteenth century by the British government to study the innovations in penal regimen and architecture that were being made in the United States. This is the report that inspired changes in prison systems throughout the world.

A.00132 de Beaumont, G. & de Tocqueville, A. (1964). *On the penitentiary system in the United States and its application in France*. Carbondale, IL: Southern Illinois University Press. (Reprint of the 1833 original publication).

Contained in this book is a descriptive assessment of the penitentiary system of the United States. The authors visited prisons in the United States to determine if the American system used any principles or programs that would be applicable in French prisons. The authors proposed that France establish a model prison based on the Pennsylvania System, however, they recognized that because of legal, religious and administrative obstacles, the French government would only be able to utilize a few principles from American corrections.

A.00133 Hall, B. (1829). *Travels in North America in the years 1827 and 1828, Volumes I of III*. New Edinburgh, Scotland: Cadell & Co. (Reprinted New York: Arno Press, 1974).

The author and his family toured North America in 1827 and 1828. During their tour they visited Sing Sing Prison in New York. The author extolls the virtues of the Auburn system and recommends its adoption in Great Britain.

A.00134 Hall, H. (1869). *The history of Auburn*. Auburn, NY: Dennis Brothers and Company.   .

In this book, the author describes the town of Auburn, New York. Included is a history of Auburn and an explanation of how the Auburn Prison System developed in Auburn, NY.

A.00135 Lewis, O. F. (1965). *The development of American prisons and prison* *customs, 1776–1845.* Montclair, NJ: Patterson Smith. (Originally published in 1922).

The author present a historical analysis of the development of American prisons and prison culture, from the colonial period to 1845. Contained in the book are extensive discussions concerning the design, operation, and problems of early American penal institutions.

A.00136 Lewis, W. D. (1965). *From Newgate to Dannemora: The rise of the penitentiary in New York, 1796–1848.* Ithaca, NY: Cornell University Press.

In this book, Lewis provides a history of penology in the state of New York. Included is an explanation of how the New York prison system evolved, from mild correctional practices to a harsh and repressive system.

A.00137 Melossi, D. & Pavarina, M. (1981). *The prison and the factory: Origins of the penitentiary system* (G. Cousin, Trans.). London: Macmillan.

In this book, the authors use a Marxian framework to trace and analyze the correlates of the rise of capitalism and the rise of the prison. They argue that the emergence of different types of punishment is related to economics.

A.00138 Osborne, T. M. (1916). *Society and prisons.* New Haven: Yale Univ-University Press.

Osborne, the warden of Sing Sing, contrasts the results of the traditional methods of punishing prisoners and the results attained when inmates are allowed some say about the operation of the prison. This is one of the earliest proposals for inmate participatory management.

A.00139 Rothman, D. J. (1971). *The discovery of the asylum: Social order and disorder in the New Republic.* Boston: Little, Brown and Co.

Contained in this book is a functionalist perspective on asylums and the social structure. Rothman proposes that society's institutions, whether social, political, or economic, cannot be understood apart from the society in which they exist. The author argues that asylums and society are interdependent, each supporting the other.

A.00140 Wines, E. H. (1910). *Punishment and reformation: A study of the penitentiary system.* New York: Thomas Y. Crowell Company.

This book, compiled from a series of lectures the author gave at the University of Wisconsin in the 1890s, chronicles the changes in law that reflect a reformation approach criminals during the nineteenth century. Discussed are, what constitutes crime, retribution and punishment, mental factors and delinquency, treatment programs, inmate self-government, and what will evolve in the future.

B

SANFORD BATES

B.00141 Bates, S. (1936). *Prisons and beyond.* New York: Books for Libraries Press. (Reprinted 1971, New York: Macmillan).

Bates, the first director of the Federal Bureau of Prison, presents a thorough discussion of the following: the structure and administration of the Federal Prison System, the administration of county prisons, negative features of the prison system, how the Federal system recognizing its deficiencies used science to build a model system, practical problems of administration, prisoners' opinions of the system, an evaluation of the parole system, functional characteristics of prisons, the price of good prisons, model for the future prison, and the fundamental importance of community efforts to prevention. The author's intent is to prove that a prison system utilizing rehabilitation provides the best protection to society.

B.00142 Bureau of Prisons. (1936). *United States prison service study course.* Washington, DC: Bureau of Prisons, Department of Justice.

This study course, a first of its kind, was developed for the express purpose to train new correctional officers at the time of their employment. It provided in-service officers opportunities to learn more about prison work. Sanford Bates was instrumental in its development.

BEDFORD HILLS CORRECTIONAL FACILITY

B.00143 Fletcher, B. R., Shaver, L. D. & Moon, D. (1993). *Women prisoners: A forgotten population.* Westport, CT: Praeger Publishers.

In this book the authors present the results of a longitudinal study of offender and institutional factors that promote recidivism in females. Data on female inmates were derived from two Oklahoma prisons through the use of surveys, interviews, and field observations.

B.00144 Freedman, E. B. (1981). *Their sisters' keepers: Women's prison reform in America 1830–1930.* Ann Arbor, MI: University of Michigan Press.

Presented in this book is an analysis of female inmates. The study is based on data from the mid-nineteenth century to the present and it addresses women's concerns for female inmates in the United States. The findings are presented in two sections: an analysis of white middle-class women's perspective on problems of female prisoners and a history of the first state prisons run for and by women.

B.00145 Harris, J. (1988). *They always call us ladies: Stories from prison.* New York: Scribners.

Harris, an inmate at Bedford Hills, provides an inmate's perspective on incarceration. From personal experiences, the author writes about the history and current conditions of the Bedford Hills Correctional Facility in New York.

B.00146 Pollock–Byrne, J. (1990). *Women, prison and crime.* Pacific Grove, CA: Brooks/Cole Publishing Company.

Included in this book are discussions of the following: the development of female criminality, a history of women's prisons, rehabilitative treatment of women inmates, legal issues confronting incarcerated women, and future directions of female criminality.

B.00147 Potler, C. (1988). *AIDS (Acquired Immune Deficiency Syndrome) in prison: A crisis in New York State Corrections.* New York: Correctional Association of New York.

Because the New York State prison system houses more inmates with AIDS than any other state system, it has developed standards and policies for the handling of AIDS related problems. This reports contains information on the following five issues: education and training for staff and prisoners, segregation for prisoners with AIDS, treatment and medical care for AIDS inmates, the cost of medical care for the duration of AIDS patients' incarceration, and AIDS and female offenders.

B.00148 Rafter, N. H. (1985). *Partial justice: Women in state prisons, 1888–1935.* Boston: Northeastern University Press.

The results of an examination of women's prisons in the United States, from the late 1800s through 1935, are presented in this book. The data were derived from a national survey of all institutions that contained only female prisoners. Retrospective data, for example, prison reports, legislative and archival documents, as well as prison registries in three states, were analyzed for demographic and offense data on 4,600 inmates.

B.00149 Ryan, T. A. (1984). *Adult female offenders and institutional programs: A state of the art analysis.* Rockville, MD: National Institute of Justice/National Criminal Justice Reference Service.

In this research report, the author presents the results of a national survey that was mailed to 65 correctional facilities in 50 states and the District of Columbia. Contained in the report is an analyses of incarcerated adult female offenders, available programs and services, and recommendations.

JAMES V. BENNETT

B.00150 Bennett, J. V. (1970). *I chose prison.* New York: Alfred A. Knopf.

The author, Director of the Federal Bureau of Prisons from 1937 to 1964, discusses the history of corrections in America and offers his views about contemporary prison reform.

B.00151 DiIulio, J. J., Jr. (1991). *No escape: The future of American corrections.* New York: Basic Books.

The author examines corrections policy in the United States and makes recommendations for organizational and managerial changes. These recommendations are based on 10 years of interviews and observations of hundreds of Federal, State, and local corrections personnel as well as a review of corrections research.

B.00152 Glaser, D. (1964). *Effectiveness of a prison and parole system*, Indianapolis, IN: Bobbs-Merrill. (Abridged edition, New York: Bobbs-Merrill, 1969).

Contained in this book are the results of a study on the rehabilitative effects of prisons and parole agencies. The primary focus of the study was differences in recidivism between inmates who had been incarcerated in federal prison and inmates who had been incarcerated in federal prison and then paroled.

B.00153 Keve, P. W. (1991). *Prisons and the American conscience: A history of U.S. federal corrections*. Carbondale, IL: Southern Illinois University Press.

The writer presents a historical analysis of Federal imprisonment from its establishment, by the Continental Congress, through 1987, when Norman Carlson was the director of the Federal Bureau of Prisons. Included is a thorough discussion of James Bennett's contributions to the Federal Bureau of Prison from 1937 to 1964 when he was its director.

B.00154 Roberts, J. W. (1994). Grand designs, small details: The management style of James V. Bennett. *Federal Prisons Journal 3*(3), 29–39.

James V. Bennett, Director of the Federal Bureau of Prisons for 27 years, was known as an outspoken proponent of rehabilitation programs and for his visionary philosophy of corrections. Although he had broad, wide ranging goals it was his ability to focus on minute details that helped him achieve most of his goals. The author examines Bennett's philosophy, goals, and how his attention to detail allowed him to achieve his larger goal of individualized treatment for inmates.

B.00155 U.S. Senate Subcommittee on National Penitentiaries of the Committee on the Judiciary. (1964). *Of prisons and justice: A selection of the writings of James V. Bennett*. Washington, DC: 88th Congress, Second Session, 16 April.

On the 25th anniversary of James V. Bennett's appointment as Director of the Federal Bureau of Prisons, the U.S. Senate published a collection of papers and articles written by Mr. Bennett. This document contains the articles with subjects that range from valuative to philosophical.

GEORGE J. BETO

B.00156 Crouch, B. M. & Marquart, J. W. (1989). *An appeal to justice: Litigated reform of Texas prisons*. Austin, TX: University of Texas Press.

Provided in this book is a description of how the Texas Department of Corrections was transformed by the decision in *Ruiz v. Estelle*, a class-action suit that is characterized as having the greatest impact on correctional law. Data for the study were obtained through agency records and personal interviews with hundreds of prisoners, administrators, and correctional staff. The authors acknowledge Dr. George Beto's contributions to the Texas Department of Corrections during the years he was director.

B.00157 DiIulio, J. J., Jr. (1987). *Governing prisons: A comparative study of correctional management.* New York: Macmillan.

> In this book the author presents a comparative analysis of the differing philosophies and management strategies employed by the directors of prison systems in California, Michigan, and Texas. The author argues that prisons that are ruled as constitutional governments can be safe and humane, despite overcrowding, budget limitations, and racial problems. DiIulio also provides a thorough discussion of Dr. George Beto's management style and penal philosophy.

B.00158 Staff. (1992, January/February). Dr. George J. Beto, criminal justice legend, dies. *Texas Journal of Corrections 18*(1), 7.

> Chronicled in the article is the life and career of Dr. George J. Beto, an internationally known expert on criminal justice, who was widely known as a minister and educator. It is reported that the Texas Department of Corrections achieved a reputation as the best prison system in the world during Dr. Beto's tenure in the 1960s and early 1970s.

B.00159 Wilson, J. Q. (1989). *Bureaucracy: What government agencies do and why they do it.* New York: HarperCollins Publishers.

> In this book the author presents arguments for deregulation in government as a means for bureaucracies to do their jobs in a more effective and responsible manner. According to Wilson, all government agencies create their own organizational culture based on the agency's critical tasks. He suggests that deregulation in government can do for government what deregulation in business has done for business.

BOOT CAMPS

B.00160 MacKenzie, D. L. (1990). Boot camp prisons: Components, evaluations, and empirical issues. *Federal Probation 54*, 48–52.

> This article stems from an evaluation of shock incarceration programs. The researcher provides a description of the components of shock incarceration, evaluates the degree to which shock incarceration meets its stated goals, and identifies which components of the program contribute to its success or failure.

B.00161 MacKenzie, D. L. & Parent, D. G. (1992). Boot camp prisons for young offenders. In J. M. Byrne, A. J. Lurigio and J. Petersilia (eds.), *Smart sentencing: The emergence of intermediate sanctions.* Newbury Park, CA:

Sage Publications.

Provided in this edited book chapter are findings about the recent growth and effectiveness of shock incarceration programs for young offenders.

B.00162 MacKenzie, D. L. & Piquero, A. (1994). The impact of shock incarceration programs in prison crowding. *Crime and Delinquency 40*(2), 222-249.

In this research article, the researchers explain the impact that shock incarceration has had on prison overcrowding. The researchers also discuss the impact such programs have on the overall prison population.

B.00163 MacKenzie, D. L. & Souryal, C. (1991). Boot camp survey: Rehabilitation, recidivism reduction outrank as main goals. *Corrections Today,* 53(6), 90–96.

The author provides a summarization of a survey of boot-camp administrators conducted by the University of Maryland. The administrators reported that rehabilitation and recidivism reduction were the main goals of their programs.

B.00164 McConnell, E. H. (1996). Boot camps for female offenders: A critical perspective, paper presented to the American Society of Criminology, Chicago, IL, November 16.

This research paper is based on data collected in a survey of the 50 state and federal departments of corrections. Presented is an overview of boot camp programming for female offenders, an assessment of current programs, and a discussion of the equity issues associated with differential treatment of female and male offenders.

ZEBULON BROCKWAY

B.00165 Bates, S. (1936). *Prisons and beyond.* New York: Books for Libraries Press. (Reprinted 1938, 1971, New York: Macmillan).

Bates, the first director of the Federal Bureau of Prison, presents a thorough discussion of the following: the structure and administration of the Federal Penal System, the administration of county prisons, ways to improve the prison system, how the Federal system recognizing its deficiencies used science to build a model system, practical problems of administration, what prisoners think about prison, an examination of the parole system, the function of prisons, the price of good prisons, the model for future prisons, and the role of the community in crime prevention. The author's intent is to prove that a prison system utilizing rehabilitation provides the best protection to society. Bates also acknowledges Zebulon Brockway's contributions to penology.

B.00166 Clear, T. R. & Cole, G. F. (1994). *American corrections* (3rd ed.). Belmont, CA: Wadsworth.

Provided in this textbook is a review of historic problems in corrections, how the system evolved to its present state, and current issues in corrections, for example, incarceration trends, capital punishment, and surveillance of inmates in the community. Also included is a discussion of Zebulon Brockway's contributions to corrections.

B.00167 McKelvey, B. (1936). *American prisons: A history of good intentions*. Chicago, IL: University of Chicago Press. (Reprinted Montclair, NJ: Patterson Smith, 1968, 1977).

The author provides a thorough historical analysis of the American prison system from 1835 to 1977. Specifically addressed are changing standards, reform movements, criminological theories, and confrontations in American penology. Also noted are the many contributions to corrections made by Zebulon Brockway.

BUILDING TENDERS

B.00168 Carleton, M. T. (1971). *Politics and punishment: The history of the Louisiana State Penal System*. Baton Rouge, LA: Louisiana State University Press.

Contained in this book is a historical analysis of the development of the Louisiana State Penal System. The author addresses the impact of state and local politics on the development of the penal system as well as commonly held perspectives on punishment. Also discussed is the penal system's use of inmates in the supervision of other inmates.

B.00169 Crouch, B. M. & Marquart, J. W. (1989). *An appeal to justice:Litigated reform of Texas prisons*. Austin, TX: University of Texas Press.

Provided in this book is a description of how the Texas Department of Corrections (TDC) was transformed by the decision in *Ruiz v. Estelle*, one of the most sweeping class–action suits in correctional law. Data for the study were collected using archival resources and personal interviews with hundreds of prisoners, administrators, and correctional staff. One of the many issues litigated was the TDC's use of inmates as building tenders (inmate guards) to police inmate housing facilities.

B.00170 DiIulio, J. J., III. (1987). *Governing prisons: A comparative study of correctional management.* New York: Free Press.

Contained in this book is a comparative analysis of the differing philosophies and management strategies in use in prison systems in California, Michigan, and Texas. The author argues that prisons that are ruled as constitutional governments can be safe and humane, despite over-crowding, budget limitations, and racial problems. The author also provides a brief discussion of building tenders as a management strategy employed by the Texas Department of Corrections.

B.00171 Martin, S. J. & Ekland–Olson, S. (1987). *Texas prisons: The walls came tumbling down.* Austin, TX: Texas Monthly Press.

In this book the authors analyze the personalities and events that were involved in the reform of the Texas prison system, from 1967 through 1987. Particular attention is paid to the use of building tenders (inmate guards) to supervise areas of the institution. Also discussed are the changes brought about by *Ruiz v. Estelle.*

Cases

B.00172 *Ruiz v. Estelle,* 503 F Supp. 1265 (1980)

This case, brought by inmate Ruiz, became the most comprehensive civil action in the realm of correctional law. The plaintiff alleged that the Texas Department of Corrections had unconstitutionally exposed prisoners to physically deteriorated, dangerous, and overcrowded conditions. One of the issues litigated was the use of 'building tenders' (inmate guards), to provide information, unlock cell doors, tend to the physical upkeep of the building and watch officers' backs.

C

CHAIN GANGS

C.00173 Barnes, H. E., & Teeters, N. K. (1943). *New horizons in criminology.* New York: Prentice-Hall, Inc.

Contained in this book is a comprehensive discussion of crime, criminals, punishment, and prisons. The authors also offer suggestions for future reforms in the repression of crime and the treatment of criminals. They document the evolution in the architectural design of prisons and discuss the use of chain gangs by many southern penal systems.

C.00174 Burns, R. E. (1932). *I am a fugitive from a Georgia chain gang!* New York: Vanguard.

Presented in this book is the personal story of a disturbed World War I veteran that was sentenced to a chain gang in Georgia for stealing $5.80. He escaped not once but twice. The first time he escaped, he was captured seven years later. Since his second escape, he has not been recaptured. Although this is the story of Burns' incarceration, it is also an indictment of a savage and brutal system characterized by dehumanizing chain gangs.

C.00175 Sellin, J. T. (1976). *Slavery and the penal system.* New York: Elsevier.

Depicted in this book is the influence of slavery on the evolution of penal systems and practices in Europe and the United States. The relationship between slavery and forced inmate labor is discussed.

C.00176 Steiner, J. F. & Brown, R. M. (1927). *The North Carolina chain gang: A study of county convict road work.* Chapel Hill, NC: The University of North Carolina Press. (Reprinted, Montclair, NJ: Patterson Smith, 1969).

This book is the end product of an investigation of African American crime in North Carolina and other southern states. Included are descriptions of how the early chain gangs began, statistical studies of the convict camp populations, and case histories of typical African American convicts.

C.00177 Wilson, W. (1933). *Forced labor in the United States.* New York: International Publishers.

The author wrote this book as a reply to American businessmen's objections to the sale of goods, which were produced by forced labor, in the free world. The history of forced labor in the colonies and ultimately the United States is reviewed and the author defines 'forced labor' and discusses convict labor, chain gangs, and peonage.

CHAPLAINS

C.00178 Acorn, L. R. (1990). Challenges of ministering to a captive audience. *Corrections Today 52*(7), 96–107.

The Clinical Pastoral Education Program offers much insight in dealing with inmate problems such as suicides, depression, psychosis, and behavioral and emotional problems.

C.00179 Acorn, L. R. (1991). Jacob Hoenig: New York chaplain serves all faiths. *Corrections Today 53*(6), 24–25.

The Salvation Army presented Jacob Hoenig with its 1991 Chaplain of the Year award for his ministering to the different faiths of prisoners. Hoenig is the senior chaplain at the Federal Bureau of Prisons' Metropolitan Correctional Center in New York City. Hoenig, a rabbi, is the first non-Christian to win the award.

C.00180 Johnson, H. (1988). *History of criminal justice.* Cincinnati: Anderson Publishing Co.

Through a historical chronology of criminal justice, the author provides the reader with an understanding of the development of criminal justice, including the impact of religion on punishment. Included is a thorough discussion of philosophies and trends leading to the current system, and the role of religion in penology.

C.00181 Scholoegel, J. M. J. & Kinast, R. L. (1988). *From cell to society.* Grand Rapids, MI: W.B. Eerdmans Publishing Co.

Provided in this book is an overview of the Liberation of Ex-Offenders Through Employment Opportunities (LEEO) Program. This program stems from an integration of religious and secular values, systems, and resources. The purpose of the Washington, D.C. based program is to facilitate the reintegration of ex-offenders into society.

C.00182 Schrink, J. (1992). Understanding the correctional counselor. In D. Lester, M. Braswell and P. Van Voorhis (eds.), *Correctional Counseling,* 2nd ed., Cincinnati: Anderson.

This book chapter contains an overview of correctional counseling. For example, the authors address hiring standards, correctional counselor work, counseling as part of a team, duties and responsibilities, and special problems and challenges.

CHILDREN OF PRISONERS

I. Mothers' Issues

C.00183 American Correctional Association. (1990). *The female offender: What does the future hold?* Washington, DC: St. Mary's Press.

The American Correctional Association report the results their Task Force Study of the female offender. The group studied the policy implications of the rapid growth in the number of female offenders and correctional needs of the female inmate population and in this report offer their findings.

C.00184 Austin, J., Bloom, B. & Donahue, T. (1992). *Female offenders in the community: An analysis of innovative strategies and programs.* Washington, DC: National Institute of Corrections.

Provided in this report is a descriptive analysis of the researchers' evaluation of strategies and programs that appear to provide effective supervision and/or treatment of female offenders in community settings. The researchers provide the findings from their evaluation.

C.00185 Baunach, P. J. (1985). *Mothers in prison*. New Brunswick, NJ: Transaction Press.

Contained in this book are the results of two program evaluations. The programs were designed to help inmate mothers maintain ties with their children during incarceration and to explore inmate mothers' perceptions of the effects of separation on themselves, their children, and the mother-child relationship.

C.00186 Bloom, B. & Steinhart, D. (1993). *Why punish the children? A reappraisal of the children of incarcerated mothers in America*. San Francisco: National Council on Crime and Delinquency.

This book, based on recent research findings, indicates that the number of women in jails and prisons has tripled in the past decade and that 75% of the women are mothers. An agenda of reform is also presented.

C.00187 Fishman, S. H. (1982). The impact of incarceration on children of offenders. *Journal of Children in Contemporary Society 15*, 89–99.

The author discusses the problems encountered by children of incarcerated parents as well as other family members. Described is the impact of incarceration on both the children of male and female offenders as well as other members of the family unit.

C.00188 McGowan, B. G. & Blumenthal, K. L. (1978). *Why punish the children? A study of children of women prisoners*. Hackensack, NJ: National Council on Crime and Delinquency.

This publication stems from a study of children whose mothers are incarcerated. The researchers investigated the children's situation and made recommendations for meeting the children's needs.

C.00189 Sack, W. H., Seidler, J. & Thomas, S. (1976). The children of imprisoned parents: A psychosocial explanation. *American Journal of Orthopsychiatry 46*, 618–628.

The article is based on research which was conducted to measure the reactions of children to the imprisonment of a parent. The authors identify temporary behavioral symptoms that are commonly associated with the incarceration of a parent, as well as antisocial behaviors that are manifested by some pubertal children.

C.00190 Sametz, L. (1980). Children of incarcerated women. *Social Work 25*,

298–303.

Contained in this article is a discussion of the reasons why prison reforms need to preserve the relationship between incarcerated mothers and their children. The researcher reports several negative behavioral symptoms of children who are separated from their parents.

C.00191 Stanton, A.M. (1980). *When mothers go to jail.* Lexington, MA: Lexington Books.

Discussed are the problems and circumstances experienced by incarcerated mothers and their children. The purpose of the book is to inform the reader about the consequences of separations that stem from incarceration of mothers.

II. Fathers' Issues

C.00192 Hairston, C. F. (1989). Men in prison: Family characteristics and parenting views. *Journal of Offender Counseling, Services, and Rehabilitation 14*, 23–30.

Reported in this research article are the results of a study of the family characteristics and parenting experiences of long-term male prisoners. Discussed are some of the family problems that result from incarceration of fathers.

C.00193 Hairston, C. F. & Lockett, P. (1985). Parents in prison: A child abuse and neglect prevention strategy. *Child Abuse and Neglect 9*, 471–477.

Parents in Prison, an innovative family support program for male inmates at the Tennessee State Prison is the basis for this article. It was developed in response to inmates's recognition of a need for child abuse and neglect prevention information.

C.00194 Lanier, C. S. (1991). Dimensions of father-child interaction in a New York state prison population. *Journal of Offender Rehabilitation 16*(3/4), 27–42.

The author studied both proximal and distal types of father-child interactions in a New York State maximum security male prison. The results indicate that a significant number of inmates do not take advantage of their visitation rights and that visitation is related to the fathers' pre-prison residential status.

C.00195 Lanier, C. S. (1993). Affective states of fathers in prison. *Justice Quarterly 10*, 51–68.

Studied in this article is the relationship between incarcerated fathers and their children. The researchers analyzed whether somatic and emotional difficulties were present in the relationships. Data were derived from interviews with 302 maximum security inmates housed at the Eastern New York Correctional Facility.

C.00196 Lanier, C. S. & Fisher, G. (1990). A Prisoner's Parenting Center (PPC): A promising resource strategy for incarcerated fathers. *Journal of Correctional Education 41(4)*, 158–165.

Analyzed by these researcher are the proximal and distal types of father-child interactions. Data were derived from interviews with 302 maximum security inmates housed at the Eastern New York Correctional Facility. The researchers discussed the types of contact between incarcerated fathers and their children, the frequency of interactions, and the reasons for infrequent or absence of interactions.

C.00197 Morris, P. (1967). Fathers in prison. *British Journal of Criminology 7*, 424–430.

Contained in this article is a discussion about incarcerated fathers and some of their more important concerns, for example, visitation for children, parental rights, and children's well-being.

THE CIVIL RIGHTS OF INSTITUTIONALIZED PERSONS ACT

C.00198 Cory, B. (1982). Politics and the Institutionalized Persons Act. *Corrections Magazine*, 8(5), 25.

This article consists of a one page summary of the Institutionalized Persons Act passed by Congress in 1977.

C.00199 Cory, B. (1982). Progress and politics in resolving inmate grievances. *Corrections Magazine*, 8(5), 20–24 ff.

According to the author, the 50 states have inmate grievance resolution systems, however, there is considerable variation in specific procedures for dealing with inmate problems.

C.00200 Lay, D. (1986). Exhaustion of grievance procedures for state prisoners under Section 1997 (e) of the Civil Rights Act. *Iowa Law Review 71*, 935–974.

Contained in this article is a description of states' compliance with 42 USC Section 1997e. This requires that a 90-day continuance of section 1983 inmate actions filed in Federal district court be granted, while the inmate exhausts remedies provided by the state's federally certified prison grievance machinery.

C.00201 Harvard Law Review (1991). Resolving prisoners' grievances out of court: 42 U.S.C. 1997e. *Harvard Law Review 104*, 1309–1329.

Provided in this article is information about the processes that prisoners can use to resolve grievances rather than litigating the grievances. Specifically addressed are insitutitional grievance procedures.

C.00202 Turk, J. C. (1983). The Nation's first application of the exhaustion requirement of 42 U.S.C. 1997e: The Virginia experience. *American Journal of Trial Advocacy 7*, 1–18.

This article contains a discussion of 42 U.S.C. 1997e, which was passed by Congress to avoid prisoner lawsuits, thus alleviating some of the burden placed on the federal court. The author focuses on how the Western District of Virginia Federal Court, recognized as one of the busiest courts in the federal system, has been impacted by the passage of section 1997e.

Cases

C.00203 *McCarthy v. Madigan*, 503 U.S. ___, 112 S.Ct. 1081, 117 L.Ed.2d 291 (1992)

The legal principle supported by this case is that an inmate must be allowed to file court action. It is deemed a "fundamental" right because it is a way of preserving all other intended rights.

C.00204 *Mann v Adams*, 846 F.2d 589 (9th Cir. 1988)

The legal issue challenged in this case is the right to privacy. The court determined that inmate mail can be checked by prison officials when security issues so warrant. The court concluded that security of all inmates is a greater concern than the individual inmate's right to privacy.

C.00205 *Martin v. Catalanotto*, 895 F.2d 1040 (5th Cir. 1990)

An inmate at the Angola prison in Louisiana filed suit against three correctional officers. He alleged that he requested protection from his enemy who beat him while he was shackled and handcuffed and that a prison correctional lieutenant beat him as well. He claimed the guards denied him medical treatment after the assault. The District Court denied Martin's civil rights suit stating that the inmate had not exhausted the prison grievance procedure. On appeal, the Court affirmed the lower court's decision.

C.00206 *Owin v. Kimmel*, 693 F.2d 711 (7th Cir. 1982)

A prisoner alleged that prison officials illegally confiscated a piece of furniture during a shakedown search of inmate cells. The District Court granted the plaintiff's motion for summary judgement and dismissed the plaintiff's Section 1983 suit. The appellant court reversed and remanded.

C.00207 *Patsy v. Florida Board of Regents*, 457 U.S. 495, 102 S.Ct. 2557, 73 L.Ed.2d 172 (1981)

The petitioner filed an action alleging her employer had denied her employment solely on the basis of her gender and race. The issue involved whether state remedies needed to be exhausted before a case could be brought to the Federal level. The Court held that exhaustion of state administrative remedies is not a prerequisite to an action under section 1983 of the Civil Rights Act.

C.00208 *Rocky v. Vittorie*, 813 F.2d 734 (5th Cir. 1987)

Rocky, an inmate at Angola prison in Louisiana, filed suit alleging that various prison officers violated his civil rights. He said he was falsely accused of possessing contraband, a knife. He said he was falsely accused because of his active involvement with a prisoners' rights group. The District Court ordered the civil suit be continued requiring the inmate to exhaust all administrative remedies. The prison claimed the inmate did not exhaust all administrative remedies in a timely manner, as a result the District Court ordered that the inmate's case be "dismissed with prejudice." On appeal, the court reversed this decision.

CLASSIFICATION SYSTEMS

C.00209 Alexander, J. A. (1986). Classification objectives and practices. *Crime and Delinquency 32*, 323–338.

Provided in this article is a thorough discussion of the inherent limitations to the predictive ability of inmate classification instruments. The author also addresses four other objectives of classification instruments.

C.00210 Alexander, J. A. & Austin, J. (1992). *Handbook for evaluating objective prison classification Systems.* Washington, DC: National Institute of Corrections.

Based on an evaluation of current classification systems, the authors recommend standards and components for an ethical and objective classification system.

C.00211 American Correctional Association. (1993). *Classification: A tool for managing today's offenders.* Laurel, MD: American Correctional Association.

This publication contains a collection of ten previously unpublished articles in which are described effective classification programs in corrections.

C.00212 Andrews, D. A., Bonta, J. & Hoge, R. D. (1990). Classification for effective rehabilitation: Rediscovering psychology. *Criminal Justice and Behavior 17*, 19–52.

Contained in this research article is a discussion of the four principles of rehabilitation: risk of recidivism, criminogenic need, the responsivity of offenders to different service options, and professional override or the responsibility of professionals to intervene when the situation warrants.

C.00213 Bonta, J. & Motiuk, L. L. (1992). Inmate classification. *Journal of Criminal Justice 20*, 343–353.

In this research project the researcher explores the extent to which an objective risk instrument developed for community-based offenders can be generalized to an institutional setting. The research subjects consisted of 580 male Canadian inmates who were administered the Level of Supervision Inventory (LSI). The scores and prison disciplinary data were used as the basis for developing a classification model to predict security needs of individual inmates.

C.00214 Brennan, T. (1987). Classification: An overview of selected methodological issues. In D. M. Gottfredson and M. Tonry, (eds.) *Prediction and classification: Criminal justice decision making. Crime and justice: A review of research 9,* (pp. 201–248). Chicago: University of Chicago Press.

Presented in this reading are the results of an analysis of classification methods. The author discusses its historical development, the key ingredients of classification, methods used by criminologists, and strategies for future research.

C.00215 Brennan, T. (1987). Classification for control in jails and prisons. In D. M. Gottfredson and M. Tonry, (eds.) *Prediction and classification: Criminal justice decision making. Crime and justice: A review of research 9.* Chicago: University of Chicago Press.

Presented in this book chapter is an examination of the shift in prison and jail classification from a judgmental approach to a more objective data-based one.

C.00216 Buchanan, R. A. & Whitlow, K. L. (1987). *Guidelines for developing, implementing, and revising an objective prison classification system.* Rockville, MD: National Institute of Justice/National Criminal Justice Reference Service.

Using the results of a national survey of objective prison classification systems, the authors evaluate the effectiveness of classification systems and develop guidelines for agencies wanting to implement a new classification system or revise an old one.

C.00217 Buchanan, R. A., Whitlow, K. L. & Austin, J. (1986). National evaluation of objective prison classification systems: The current state of the art. *Crime and Delinquency 32,* 272–290.

Intended to assist correctional administrators in addressing prison overcrowding, this study was conducted to assess the effectiveness of objecttive prison classification systems. Survey data were collected from 33 of the 39 U.S. jurisdictions which use objective classification systems. During data collection, the researchers made site visits in California, Illinois, and Wisconsin where they conducted in-depth assessments.

C.00218 Burke, P. & Adams, L. (1991). *Classification of women offenders in state correctional facilities: A handbook for practitioners.* Washington, DC: National Institute of Corrections.

This document was developed to assist practitioners in the classification of female offenders in state correctional facilities. It is based on data collected in four states, Georgia, Wyoming, Illinois, and New York. The data were collected through a telephone survey of representatives of 48 state institutions and from agency documents.

C.00219 Craddock, A. (1992). Formal social control in prisons: An exploratory examination of the custody classification process. *American Journal of Criminal Justice 17*, 63–87.

Contained in this article are the findings from a study of the role of classification in the formal social control of the prison population. The researcher used data that were derived from the computerized administrative records of a cohort of 4,622 male felons admitted to the North Carolina Division of Prisons in 1980. During the study period, North Carolina used a traditional, clinically oriented classification process to assign inmates to programs and to one of four custody levels.

C.00220 Kane, T. (1986). The validity of prison classification: An introduction to practical considerations and research issues. *Crime and Delinquency 32*, 367–390.

Contained in this article is a thorough discussion of the major validity issues regarding prison classification instruments. The author reviews research designs and methods relevant to prison classification systems.

C.00221 National Institute of Corrections. (1982). *Prison classification: A model systems approach*. Washington, DC: National Institute of Corrections.

Contained in this document is a model classification system for prison classification. Stengths and weakness are discussed.

C.00222 Rans, L. L. (1984). The validity of models to predict violence in community and prison settings. *Corrections Today 46*(3), 50-51, 62–63.

In this article, the author summarizes papers presented at the Bellevue Forensic Psychiatric Symposium on Psychiatric and Psychological Services in Prisons and Jails. Presented is an overview of classification systems, too include prison classification and community release classification. Security designation, security designation with violent risk, and custody classification are three of the prison classification models discussed. Violence risk assessment, violence and recidivism risk assessment, and recidivism risk assessment are three of the community release classification models discussed.

Cases

C.00223 *Glover v. Johnson*, 659 F.Supp. 621 (E.D. Mich. 1987)

> This case consists of a class action suit challenging the disparities of Michigan's programs for female inmates. The court described in some detail what is required to meet the demands of the Equal Protection Clause. Women have a constitutional right to "parity of treatment" which means that treatments available to men must be made available to women.

C.00224 *Holt v. Sarver*, 300 F. Supp. 825 (E.D. Ark. 1969); 309 F. Supp. 362 (E.D. Ark. 1970) *affd.* 442 F.2d 304 (8th Cir. 1971)

> In this case Arkansas prisoners alleged savage treatment and inhumane conditions. The Federal Court declared the entire Arkansas State Prison system to be in violation of the Eighth Amendment.

C.00225 *Jackson v. Cain*, 864 F.2d 1235 (5th Cir. 1989)

> An inmate filed a suit alleging that the employees of the Louisiana Department of Corrections violated his civil rights. The District Court granted summary judgement on all issues. The Appellate Court upheld the summary judgements on the issues of handcuffing, mail tampering and medical treatment. However, the other summary judgements, i.e., cruel and unusual punishment, retaliation claims, failure to follow punishment limitations, and procedural due process claims were in error. The Appellate Court remanded the case to the District Court for discovery and trial on these issues.

C.00226 *Laaman v. Helgemoe*, 437 F.Supp. 269 (D.N.H. 1977)

> According to this case, effective diagnostic and classification systems permit the separation and proper handling of prisoners who could benefit from the programs the institution has to offer. Failure to identify and diagnose medical needs during classification is unconstitutional.

C.00227 *Lanier v. Fair*, 876 F.2d 243 (1st Cir. 1989)

> The plaintiff alleged his 14th Amendment due process rights were violated when he was removed from a halfway house program and by the reinstatement of his parole date. The District Court found in favor of the defendant. The Court of Appeals affirmed the decision of the District Court.

C.00228 *Morris v. Travisono*, 310 F.Supp. 857 (D.R.I. 1970)

Morris filed a class action suit on behalf of the inmates at the Adult Correctional Institution in Rhode Island. The prisoners alleged violations of their civil rights because of the practices, rules and conditions of life at the Institution. Specific issues focused on medical treatment, discipline, and classification. The Court ultimately specified the rules and regulations for the prison to follow when disciplining and classifying inmates.

C.00229 *Palmigiano v. Garrahy*, 443 F.Supp. 956 (D.R.I. 1977)

A class action suit representing prisoners and pretrial detainees alleging that confinement conditions in the Rhode Island prison system violated the Eighth and Fourteenth Amendments. The Court concluded that the "totality of conditions of confinement . . . do not provide the tolerable living environment."

C.00230 *Pugh v. Locke*, 406 F.Supp. 318 (M.D.Ala. 1976)

According to the Court, classification systems should be used to protect inmates from assaults by other inmates. Specifically, unchecked assaultive homosexual behavior might violate inmates' rights to be free from assaults. As a result, behaviors such as this need to be considered in the classification process.

C.00231 *Stephany v. Wagner*, 835 F.2d 497 (3rd Cir. 1986)

Reclassification of prisoners is at the discretion of the institution and is non binding. This means prisoners have no inherent right, constitutional or otherwise, to be given a particular classification.

C.00232 *Wallace v. Robinson*, 940 F.2d 243 (7th Cir. 1991)

In this case the Court found that the state does not guarantee inmates any job, much less the job the inmate prefers, and prison regulations do not create a liberty or property interest in a particular job placement.

C.00233 *Wilson v. Canterinson*, 546 F.Supp. 174 (W.D. Ky. 1982)

The plaintiffs are female inmates at the Kentucky Correctional Institution who seek a broad range of relief concerning the conditions of their confinement, disparate treatment of men and women inmates in the Kentucky prison system, and the denial of opportunities for education and vocational training. The court ruled that substantial changes must take place at the Kentucky Correctional Institution.

C.00234 *Withers v. Levine*, 615 F.2d 158 (4th Cir. 1980)

In this case the Court determined that classification systems should be used to control or avoid sexual assault among inmates.

C.00235 *Woodhouse v. Commonwealth (Virginia)*, 487 F.2d 889 (4th Cir. 1973)

The Court determined in this case that there is no requirement for a prisoner to wait until he/she is actually assaulted before trying to obtain relief through reclassification.

COED CORRECTIONAL FACILITIES

C.00236 American Correctional Association. (1990). *The female offender: What does the future hold?* Laurel, MD: American Correctional Association; Rockville, MD: National Institute of Justice/National Criminal Justice Reference Service.

Because of the rapid growth in the number of female offenders, the American Correctional Association's Task Force on Female Offenders studied policy implications and the correctional needs of female inmates. This document contains policy recommendations that address current issues regarding female inmates as well predictions about what to expect in the future.

C.00237 Chesney–Lind, M. & Rodrigues, N. (1983). Women under lock and key: A view from the inside. *The Prison Journal 63,*47-65.

The data for the present study were collected through interviews with 16 sentenced female felons, held at the Oahu Community Correctional Center, Hawaii. The researchers   focused on the socioeconomic back-grounds and criminal careers of the inmates. One of the more common characteristics of the subjects were their histories of repeated and long-term physical and sexual abuse as children.

C.00238 Hunzeker, D. (1986). Coed prison's survey finds 35 prisons house both men and women. *Corrections Compendium 10*(12), 7, 14–15.

In this national survey of correctional institutions it was revealed that 35 institutions in 23 correctional systems are co-correctional facilities. The inmate populations in these institutions consist of females and males.

C.00239 Mahan, S. (1986). Co-corrections: Doing time together. *Corrections Today 48*(6), 134, 136, 138, 140, 164–165.

This research was conducted to determine the advantages and disadvantages of co-correctional penal facilities. Using interviews and seminars, the researchers collected data from inmates at the federal co-correctional facility at Forth Worth, Texas.

C.00240 Mahan, S., Mabli, J., Johnston, B., Trask, B. & Hilek, J. (1989). Sexually integrated prisons: Advantages, disadvantages and some recommendations. *Criminal Justice Policy Review 3*(2), 149–158.

Compared in this research article are the opinions of inmates and staff about coed correctional facilities. Using data collected through questionnaires the researchers evaluated the co-correctional process at FCI-Ft. Worth, the Federal institution with the longest history of sexual integration.

C.00241 Rafter, N.H. (1990). *Partial justice: Women, prisons, and social control.* New Brunswick, NJ: Transaction Publishers.

Contained in this book are the results of an examination of women's prisons in the United States from the late 1800s until 1935. The data were derived from a national survey of all institutions that housed only female populations during the period under study. Prison reports, legislative and archival documents, as well as prison registries in three states were analyzed for demographic and offense data on 4,600 inmates.

C.00242 Schweber, C. (1984). Beauty marks and blemishes: The coed prison as a microcosm of integrated society. *Prison Journal 64*(1), 3–14.

The author determined that although female inmates in co-correctional institutions have access to more rehabilitative programs than in a segregated institution, female inmates' roles and interests remain subordinate to those of male inmates. The author presents an alternative model to the segregated or integrated model in a effort to minimize the liabilities of either.

C.00243 Smykla, J. O. (1980). *Coed prison.* New York: Human Sciences Press.

This book contains an examination of the major issues related to coed prisons. In particular, the author addresses administrative, interpersonal, and research issues that are characteristic of penal facilities where women and men have been incarcerated together.

COMMISSARIES

C.00244 Bates, S. (1936). *Prisons and beyond.* New York: Books for Libraries Press. (Reprinted, New York: Macmillan, 1971).

Bates, the first director of the Federal Bureau of Prison, presents a thorough discussion of the following: the structure and administration of the Federal Penal System, the administration of county prisons, what is wrong with the prison system, how the Federal system recognizing its deficiencies used science to build a model system, practical problems of administration, what prisoners think about the prison system, an examination of the parole system, the function of prisons, the price of good prisons, the prison model of the future, and the fundamental importance of community efforts at crime prevention. The author's intent is to prove that a prison system utilizing rehabilitation provides the best protection to society. Bates also acknowledges the role of commissaries in prisons.

C.00245 Bureau of Prisons. (1979). *The development of the Federal Prison System.* Washington, DC: Bureau of Prisons.

Provided in this publication is information about the history and development of the federal prison system. A discussion of commissaries and their changing role in federal prisons is presented.

C.00246 Fleisher, M. S. (1989). *Warehousing violence: Frontiers of anthropology, Vol. 3.* Newbury Park, CA: Sage Publications, Inc.

This article was based on research that was conducted to determine a more cost effective method for management of violent offenders. Data were collected through long-term participant observation in a maximum security institution and open-ended interviews.

COMMUNITY RELATIONS

C.00247 Carlson, K. A. (1992). Doing good and looking bad: A case study of prison/community relations. *Crime and Delinquency 38,* 56–69.

Analyzed in this research article are data from a case study of the relations between prisons and their surrounding community. The researchers concluded that the objective effects of a prison on its host community was generally favorable. This however was not reflected in the attitudes of the community residents, they generally held unfavorable attitudes toward prisons.

C.00248 Cohen, N. P. (1976). The English board of visitors: Lay outsiders as inspectors and decision makers in prisons. *Federal Probation 40*, 24–27.

Contained in this article is an overview of the advantages and disadvantages of the English Board of Visitors, an external body that was established to enhance relations between the community and the prison. The rationale for including external groups is that they offer a means for engaging the community in the operation of the prison. The author's conclusions were somewhat mixed. It was pointed out that even though members of the board are not generally representative of the community at large, community relations is still enhanced due to the perception that community control has increased.

C.00249 Jacobs, J. B. (1976). The politics of corrections: Town/prison relations as a determinant of reform. *Social Service Review 50*, 623–631.

The focus of this article is on the merits of establishing small, flexible, experimental, and humane prison facilities in rural communities. Historically, criminologists have had a bias against placement of prison facilities in rural communities. Jacobs supports the new approach by describing the imaginative and successful minimum-security prison which was established and is functioning in rural southern Illinois. One of the major issues addressed by Jacobs is the pivotal role of the community.

C.00250 Krause, J. D. (1992). The effects of prison siting practices on community status arrangements: A framework applied to the siting of California state prisons. *Crime and Delinquency 38*, 27–35.

The researcher conducted the present research to determine the merits of positive community relations between penal facilities and their host communities. It was determined that positive relations between prison facilities and communities are important and far reaching. For example, positive relations enhance the overall quality of life experienced by correctional staff, inmates who are being reintegrated, and non-correctional community members.

C.00251 Lombardo, L. X. (1981). *Guards imprisoned: Correctional officers at work.* New York: Elsevier North-Holland.

This book is based on research in which the work, motivations, and experiences of correctional officers were assessed. The research stems from extensive interviews with correctional officers and six years as a participant observer at the Auburn Correctional Facility in New York.

C.00252 National Advisory Commission on Criminal Justice Standards and Goals. (1973). *Corrections.* Washington, DC: U.S. GPO.

Contained in this publication are the standards and recommendations for corrections by the National Advisory Commission on Criminal Justice Standards and Goals (NACCJS). The NACCJS presents the standards and recommendations in an effort to influence reform of the criminal justice system in the United States. One of the more important issues addressed in the recommendations is the need for correctional managers to maintain positive community relations.

C.00253 Schwartz, J. A. (1989). Promoting a good public image. *Corrections Today 51,* 38, 40, 42.

In this article, the author focuses on public perceptions about correctional facilities. The author suggests that many believe that the media is responsible for the negative public image of corrections in the United States. It is recognized that the media plays a role in shaping the public's image of corrections, however, it is argued that those who work in corrections are, in the end, responsible for those images.

C.00254 Shichor, D. (1992). Myths and realities in prison siting. *Crime and Delinquency 38*(1), 70–87.

Debunked in this article are many of the myths associated with prison site selection. The author offers the reader many insights into the real issues of site selection. Presented is a review of the positive and negative site selection arguments. Particular emphasis is given to the importance of positive community relations in site selection decisions.

C.00255 Zaner, L. O. (1989). The screen test: Has Hollywood hurt corrections' image? *Corrections Today 51,* 64–66, 94–95, 98.

Examined in this article is the impact of movies on the public's perception of corrections. The author acknowledges that although many reforms have been made in corrections in the past two decades, the movie industry seems to ignore the reforms and accentuate the negative.

CONJUGAL VISITS

C.00256 Balogh, J. K. (1964). Conjugal visitations in prisons: A sociological perspective. *Federal Probation 28*(3), 52–58.

This article is based on a study which was conducted to evaluate the attitudes of prison administrators with regard to conjugal visitations. The researcher's primary objective was to measure changes in the administrators'attitudes toward conjugal visitation.

C.00257 Bates, T. M. (1989). Rethinking conjugal visitation in light of the "AIDS" crisis. *New England Journal on Criminal and Civil Confinement 15*(1), 121–145.

The Federal Bureau of Prisons estimate that 30 percent of inmates engage in homosexual activities. The author argues that since AIDS is transmitted through either blood or semen, conjugal visits should cut down on the amount of homosexual activity hence a reduction in the transmission of AIDS in prisons.

C.00258 Carlson, B. E. & Cervera, N. J. (1992). *Inmates and their wives: Incarceration and family life.* Westport, CT: Greenwood Press.

This book is based on a study of the New York Family Reunion Program for inmates. The authors provide an overview of inmate family relations, highlight the positive points of the Family Reunion Program, and suggest policies and programs that could help correctional officials inaugurate similar programs.

C.00259 Goetting, A. (1982). Conjugal association in prison: Issues and perspectives. *Crime and Delinquency 28*(1), 52–71.

The author presents an overview of the conjugal visitation programs now operating in U.S. prisons. Drawing on the research literature, the merits of conjugal visitation programs are discussed.

C.00260 Goldstein, S. (1990). Prisoners with AIDS: Constitutionality and statutory rights implicated in family visitation programs. *Boston College Law Review 31*(4), 967–1025.

In this law review article, the author examines the constitutional and statutory issues relating to conjugal visitation of AIDS infected inmates.

In particular, differing family visitation processes accorded to inmates with AIDS and their families are examined.

C.00261 Hopper, C. B. (1989). Evolution of conjugal visiting in Mississippi. *Prison Journal 69*(1), 103–109.

The author presents a historical analysis of the conjugal visitation program at Mississippi State Prison at Parchman. According to the author, inmates and staff support the conjugal visitation program which unofficially began as early as 1900.

C.00262 Howser, J. F., Grossman, J. and MacDonald, D. (1983). Impact of family reunion program on institutional discipline. *Journal of Offender Counseling, Services and Rehabilitation 8*(1–2), 27–36.

The primary focus of this article is how family reunion programs are used for the social control of inmates. The authors recognize that although it is generally accepted that the primary purpose of prison programs is to assist offenders in preparing them for their return to society, correctional administrators frequently use programs to control inmate behavior in the institution. For example, if one does not behave, then one could lose the privilege of visiting with one's family.

C.00263 Howser, J. F. & MacDonald, D. (1982). Maintaining family ties. *Corrections Today 44*, 96–98.

Contained in this article is an overview of the two major family programs operated by the New York State Department of Correctional Services. The two family programs are a pilot visiting program established, in 1974, to provide bus transportation for prison visits for indigent family members and a Family Reunion Program which assists inmates in maintaining family ties through contact visits in prison.

C.00264 McConnell, E. H. (1998). Debate 2, Are Conjugal and Familial Visitation Effective Rehabilitative Concepts? NO. In C.B. Field's *Controversial Issues in Corrections*, Allyn and Bacon, forthcoming 1998.

Based on a review of the research literature, the author discusses the arguments against conjugal visits. Some of the more paramount issues are, its exclusive nature, health concerns about pregnancy and AIDS, and does it work? In the same chapter are arguments supporting its rehabilitative effectiveness.

CONTACT VISITS

C.00265 Carlson, B. E. & Cervera, N. J. (1991). Incarceration, coping, and support. *Social Work 36*, 279–285.

Addressed in this research article is the stress which inmates experience as result of incarceration. The authors recognize that visitation by family and friends can aid in alleviating stress, thus visitation should be encouraged by the prison administration. Reducing inmate stress levels is advantageous for both inmates and staff.

C.00266 Hairston, C. F. (1988). Family ties during imprisonment: Do they influence future criminal activity? *Federal Probation 52(1)*, 48–52.

In this article the author presents the conclusions from five empirical studies of the relationship between inmate-family ties during incarceration and post-release success. Indicated in the studies, conducted since 1970, is that maintenance of family and community ties is positively related to better parole outcomes, fewer disciplinary infractions, and lower recidivism rates.

C.00267 Schafer, N. E. (1989). Prison visiting: Is it time to review the rules? *Federal Probation 53(4)*, 25–30.

The author evaluates the status of visitation in American prisons by analyzing prison visitation procedures. The overall conclusions indicate that prison visits are the most important method of preserving family relationships of offenders. The author also notes that strong family relationships play an integral role in inmates' successful reintegration to the community.

C.00268 Schafer, N. E. (1991). Prison visiting policies and practices. *International Journal of Offender Therapy and Comparative Criminology 35(3)*, 263–275.

Contained in this article are the results of a study which was conducted to assess changes in prison visitation procedures. In particular, the research measured the extent to which prison officials changed visiting policies in light of empirical research which indicates that visiting is significantly related to parole success. The researcher collected data on visitation procedures from 213 adult, long-term correctional facilities in 45 states. Change was measured by comparing the present data with data collected in 1978 and 1954.

WILLIAM CONTE

C.00269 Camp, C. G. & Camp G. M. (1988). *Management strategies for combating prison gang violence, Part II, Combating violent inmate organizations at the Washington State Penitentiary at Walla Walla: A case study*. Washington, DC: National Institute of Justice.

In this article the authors address issues that stem from prison gang violence, discuss choices for resolving prison gang violence that are available to prison administrators, and point out consequences of the various choices. The authors' conclusions are based on data collected in five correctional institutions in Washington and Illinois.

C.00270 Cardozo–Freeman, I. and Delorme, E. P. (1984). *The Joint: Language and culture in a maximum security prison*. Springfield, IL: Charles C. Thomas.

This book is based on research conducted at Washington State Penitentiary at Walla Walla. The researchers collected data, through taped interviews, with inmates to test the hypothesis that language shapes and is shaped by culture.

C.00271 Conte, W.R. (1990). *Is prison reform possible? The Washington State experience in the sixties*. Tacoma, WA: Unique Press.

The author describes and discusses the history of penal problems and reform and the approach used briefly in Washington state in the 1960s. Conte advocates a rehabilitation approach that focuses on understanding human behavior and treating inmates with dignity.

C.00272 Stastny, C. & Tyrnauer, G. (1982). *Who rules the joint? The changing political culture of maximum security prisons in America*. Lexington, MA: Lexington Books, D.C. Heath and Co.

Contained in this book are the results of an extensive study of the struggle for power at Washington State Penitentiary at Walla Walla. The researchers conducted a historical examination of the struggle for power among the following conflicting groups: prisoners, guards, wardens, governors and legislators, judges, outside community influences, and professionals.

C.00273 Tyrnauer, G. (1981). What went wrong at Walla Walla? *Corrections Magazine 7*(3), 37–41.

In this article the researcher offers insight about the inmate self-govern ment experiment at Washington State Penitentiary at Walla Walla. Described is the process of inmate self-government and with some suggestions about possible causes of its failure.

CONTRABAND

C.00274 Hill, M. O. (1984). Permanent confiscation of prison contraband: The Fifth Amendment behind bars. *Yale Law Journal 93*, 901–917.

The author of this article reports that the courts have generally failed to recognize that a prisoner has a property interest in prison contraband. As a result prison officials can permanently confiscate prison contraband as well as subject offending prisoners to traditional means of discipline, such as loss of privileges or good-time credit. The author argues that although prisoners do not retain possessory rights in prison contraband, they do retain ownership rights, and thus a property interest, in items that were legally possessed before being smuggled into prison.

C.00275 Kalinich, D. B. (1980). *The inmate economy.* Lexington, MA: Lexington Books.

Presented in this book is an overview of contraband in prisons. Empirical data on prison contraband is offered to support the author's discussion. Specifically, the researcher analyzed the legitimate and illegitimate market subcultures in a maximum security prison in Michigan where the data on contraband were collected.

C.00276 Sexton, P. S. (1985). Contraband control and the use of x-rays in the prison environment. *Pacific Law Journal 16*(2), 409–430.

Contained in this law review article is a summary of legal issues associated with the use of low-level radiation as a method for detecting contraband on inmate visitors. The author cites the court cases which are germane to the discussion.

CORPORAL PUNISHMENT

C.00277 Barnes, H. E. (1930). *The story of punishment: A record of man's inhumanity to man..* Boston: Stratford. (2nd Edition, Montclair, NJ: Patterson Smith, 1972).

The author discusses the various methods of punishment used by modern man to punish criminals. The author proposes that punishment should be discarded since there is no empirical evidence that punishment produces non criminal behavior. Instead, Barnes suggests that psychiatry is the more appropriate method for the treatment of criminals.

C.00278 Bowker, L. H. (1980). *Prison victimization.* New York: Elsevier North–Holland.

Provided in this book is a thorough discussion of the many facets of prison victimization. In particular, the author reviews the physical, economic, psychological, and social harm experienced by staff and inmates in prison. The author also discusses the way corporal punishment victimizes those that punish and those who are punished.

C.00279 Caldwell, R. G. (1947). *Red Hannah: Delaware's whipping post.* Philadelphia: University of Pennsylvania Press.

This book contains a historical analysis of the criminal law and codes of Delaware from 1638 to the present time. The central theme of the book is whether corporal punishment, specifically the use of the whipping post, was an effective deterrent to crime.

C.00280 Hirsch, A. J. (1992). *The rise of the penitentiary: Prisons and punishment in early America.* New Haven, CT: Yale University Press.

Provided in this book is a historical review of the emergence of penitentiaries in America. The author presents a comprehensive discussion of the origins and development of American penitentiaries, including the role of corporal punishment.

C.00281 Keve, P. W. (1986). *The history of corrections in Virginia.* Charlottesville, VA: University Press of Virginia.

This book contains a history of corrections in Virginia from colonial times into the 1980s. The author includes a discussion of the political and social influences that shaped the development of corrections in Virginia and the use of corporal punishment.

C.00282 Murton, T. & Hyams, J. (1969). *Accomplices to the crime: The Arkansas prison scandal.* New York: Grove Press.

Arguments for reforming and modernizing the Arkansas penal system are presented in this book It is based on the personal experiences of

Superintendent Murton at the Arkansas Prison Farm. Particular attention is directed at the various types of corporal punishment that were practiced in the Arkansas penal system.

C.00283 Newman, G. (1983). *Just and painful: A case for the corporal punishment of criminals*. Riverside, NJ: Macmillan Publishing Co.

The author of this book suggests that only the worst of repeat or truly violent offenders should be sentenced to prison. It is recommended that offenders who commit less serious acts should be subjected to corporal punishment. For example, they should be punished in public via the administration of temporary physical pain, such as electric shock, or a whipping. The author discusses the merits of both physical pain and the emotional pain associated with public humiliation.

C.00284 Rothman, D. J. (1971). *The discovery of the asylum: Social order and disorder in the New Republic*. Boston: Little, Brown and Co.

Contained in this book is a functionalist perspective on asylums and the social structure. Rothman proposes that society's institutions, whether social, political, or economic, cannot be understood apart from the society in which they exist. The author argues that asylums and society are interdependent, each supporting the other. The author discusses the relationship between punishment and asylums.

Cases

C.00285 *Jackson v. Bishop*, 268 F.Supp. 804 (E.D. Ark. 1967), 404 F.2d 571, (8th Cir. 1968)

In this case the defendant challenged the constitutionality of corporal punishment, specifically whipping. The court decided that whipping as means of enforcing prison discipline violates the Eighth and Fourteenth Amendments.

C.00286 *Talley v. Stephens*, 247 F.Supp 683 (E.D. Arkansas 1965)

The defendant challenged the constitutionality of whipping. The court refused to declare whipping unconstitutional as such, but did stipulate that it must not be excessive and must be inflicted as dispassionately as possible.

CORRECTIONAL OFFICERS

I. History

C.00287 Barnes, H. E., & Teeters, N. K. (1943). *New horizons in criminology.* New York: Prentice-Hall, Inc.

This book contains a comprehensive discussion of crime, criminals, punishment, and prisons. The authors also offer suggestions for future reforms in the repression crime and the treatment of criminals. They provide information on the evolution of correctional officers.

C.00288 Dix, D. L. (1845). *Remarks on prison and prison discipline in the United States.* (Reprinted, Montclair, NJ: Patterson Smith, 1967).

Contained in this book are the results of a four year investigation of all the prisons in the New England and Middle Atlantic states. The author found these prisons characterized by cruelty, injustice, and laxity of punishment. She concluded that although the Pennsylvania System was not perfect, it was the most perfect system that had been devised. She also discusses the evolving role of correctional officers.

C.00289 O'Hare, K. (1923). *In prison.* New York: Alfred Knopf.

Presented in this book are the personal experiences of an inmate in the state penitentiary in Jefferson City, Missouri. An appalling picture of the prison system is presented as well as day-to-day life within the prison. The author addresses how correctional officers impact the lives of inmates.

C.00290 Schade, T. (1986). Prison officer training in the United States: The legacy of Jessie O. Stutsman. *Federal Probation 50*(4), 40–46.

Contained in this article is a historical review of the prison officer training program developed by Jessie O. Stutsman. The author acknowledges that Stutsman opened the first training school for Federal prison officers on January 2, 1930.

II. Selection and Training

C.00291 Benton, N. (1988). Personnel management: Strategies for staff development. *Corrections Today 50*(5), 102, 108.

The author of this article highlights the survey results of a project in which management practices were examined. Issues addressed are employee attrition, personnel directors, unions, hiring policies and practices, task analysis, psychological testing, applicant screening, supervisory training, motivational programs, polygraph tests, disciplinary practices, educational assistance, and equal opportunity employment.

C.00292 Brown, P. W. (1987). Probation officer burnout: an organizational disease/an organizational cure, Part II. *Federal Probation 51*(3), 17–21.

Included in this article is a review of specific management approaches for reducing organizationally induced burnout and stress in probation officers. The authors identify causes of probation officer burnout and stress and suggest that managers and supervisors can play a pivotal role in alleviating the problem.

C.00293 Carter, D. (1991). Status of education and training in corrections. *Federal Probation 55*(2), 17–23.

Discussed in this article is the status of education and training in corrections. The author specifically addresses correctional managers' participation in training, educational programs, a comparison of training in private industry to correctional training, correctional training standards and requirements, and state and local correctional training requirements.

C.00294 Cherniss, C. & Kane, J. S. (1987). Public sector professionals: job characteristics, satisfactions, and aspirations for intrinsic fulfillment through work. *Human Relations 40*, 125–136.

This article contains the results of work-experience research which was conducted by collecting data from public sector professionals and blue–collar workers employed by a state government. Work experiences were evaluated on the basis of characteristics, satisfaction, and fulfillment of one's job. Correctional positions were among those evaluated.

C.00295 Lawrence, R. (1984). Professionals or judicial civil servants? An examination of the probation officer's role. *Federal Probation 48*(4), 14–21.

The results of a research study, conducted to assess probation officer's perceptions about their jobs, are presented in this article. The author surveyed 139 adult probation officers in a Southwestern State to determine their perceived roles and functions.

C.00296 Lombardo, L. X. (1981). *Guards imprisoned: Correctional officers at work*. New York: Elsevier North-Holland.

This book is based on research in which the work, motivations, and experiences of correctional officers were assessed. The research stems from extensive interviews with correctional officers and six years as a participant observer at the Auburn Correctional Facility in New York.

C.00297 Lundberg, D. E. (1947). Methods of selecting prison personnel. *Journal of Criminal Law and Criminology 38*, 14–39.

Suggested in this article are general psychological principles and techniques which can be adapted to the problems of correctional administration. The author addresses such things as prison guard selection and recruitment. He acknowledges that "good" is defined differently by the warden, the educational director, and the industrial director.

C.00298 Morton, J. B. (Ed.) (1991). *Public policy for corrections* (2d ed.). Laurel, MD: American Correctional Association; Rockville, MD: National Institute of Justice/National Criminal Justice Research Service.

Contained in this book are the American Correctional Association's (ACA) policies for corrections. The author suggests that correctional professionals who have experience and expertise should be a part of the policy development process.

C.00299 Sanchez, C. M. (1989). Attracting and selecting a top-notch staff: The California experience. *Corrections Today 51*(7), 58–59, 72, 166.

Presented in the article are the results of the California Department of Corrections' centralized hiring process. The process was begun during a major prison system expansion, it was implemented in an effort to bring about professional and effective recruitment.

C.00300 Sechrest, D. K. & Reimer, E. G. (1982). Adopting national standards for correctional reform. *Federal Probation 46*(2), 18–25.

The researchers present arguments for the support of national standards for correctional reform. In particular, they suggest that the standards should include sound administration and fiscal controls, an adequate physical plant, adherence to legal criteria, and the provision of basic services.

C.00301 Toch, H. (1978). Is a 'correctional officer,' by any other name, a 'screw.' *Criminal Justice Review 3*(2), 19–35.

Using the interview method, the author determined that the correctional officer, through the use of discretion, provides support to vulnerable inmates, thus expanding the correctional officer's role beyond custodial care.

C.00302 Wahler, C. & Gendreau, P. (1985). Assessing correctional officers. *Federal Probation 49*(1), 70–74.

The authors propose that administrators use a correctional officer selection model that takes into consideration the behavioral skills that are directly related to the job. They based their support for this model after critiquing the traditional models used for the hiring of correctional officers.

III. Career Opportunities

C.00303 Camp, G. M. & Camp. G. C. (1994). *The corrections yearbook: 1993*. South Salem, NY: Criminal Justice Institute.

This is an official source book that contains annual correctional statistics, including information about correctional personnel.

C.00304 Delucia, R. C. & Doyle, T. J. (1990). *Career planning in criminal justice*. Cincinnati: Anderson Publishing Company.

Presented in this book is information about career planning and education in the criminal justice field. The authors examine a variety of correctional and law enforcement occupations, offering the reader information on responsibilities of the job as well as the qualifications required for each.

C.00305 Kratcoski, P. C. (Ed.). (1994). *Correctional counseling and treatment* (3rd ed.). Prospect Heights, IL: Waveland Press.

This is an edited book in which numerous contributors discuss some of the widely used treatment techniques in American corrections. Some of the treatment issues addressed in the text are validity and value of inmate classification, and factors that affect treatment outcomes such as offender characteristics, correctional officer characteristics, and prison environment.

C.00306 Lombardo, L. X. (1989). *Guards imprisoned: Correctional officers at work* (2nd ed.). Cincinnati: Anderson Publishing Company.

This book contains the update of an earlier study of the working life of prison guards at the Auburn Prison in New York State. The earlier study conducted in 1981 is based on research in which the work, motivations, and experiences of correctional officers were assessed. The research stems from extensive interviews with correctional officers and six years as a participant observer at the Auburn Correctional Facility in New York.

C.00307 Stinchcomb, J. D. (1989). *Opportunities in law enforcement and criminal justice careers*. Lincolnwood, IL: VGM Career Horizons.

Provided in this book is a comprehensive review of the history and scope of law enforcement as well as criminal justice career opportunities at the city, county, state, and federal levels. The author also provides information on salaries, employment conditions, educational require-ments, and related careers in criminal justice and public safety.

C.00308 Williamson, H. E. (1990). *The corrections profession*. Newbury Park, CA: Sage.

Contained in this book is an overview of the profession of corrections. The author provides information about the working environment in corrections, offender behavior, the status of the corrections' professional, career preparation for corrections employment, and tasks of the correct-tions professional. The book was written primarily for undergraduate college students who are considering a career in corrections.

IV. Subculture

C.00309 Athens, L. H. (1975). Differences in the liberal-conservative political attitudes of prison guards and felons. *International Journal of Group Tensions 5*(3), 143–155.

In this research article the author examined attitudes of 84 convicted felons and 50 prison guards. He found that African American inmates tended to have liberal political attitudes, while Caucasian inmates and guards tended to have more conservative political attitudes. He acknow-ledged that differences in liberal and conservative attitudes may cause tension and conflict between African American inmates and Caucasian prison guards.

C.00310 Crouch, B. M. and Marquart, J. W. (1980). On becoming a prison guard. In B. M. Crouch (Ed.), *The keepers: Prison guards and contemporary corrections*. Springfield, IL: Charles C. Thomas.

Presented in this edited book chapter is a discussion of the socialization process experienced by prison guards in the course of their daily work. The authors provide a thorough discussion of the interactions among inmates, correctional officers, and correctional administrators. Special attention is focused on the development and entry into the guard subculture.

C.00311 Cullen, F. T., Lutze, F. E., Link, B. G. & Wolf, N. T. (1989). Correctional orientation of prison guards: Do officers support rehabilitation? *Federal Probation Quarterly 53*(1), 33–42.

This research article is based on an exploration of the nature and sources of prison guards' perspectives on rehabilitation. The researchers assess the degree to which correctional officers support rehabilitation and determine the source of the officer's perspectives on rehabilitation.

C.00312 Johnson, R. (1987). *Hard time: Understanding and reforming the prison*. Pacific Grove, CA: Brooks/Cole Publishing Co.

Presented in this book are the results of an analysis of life in a maximum–security prison for men. The author determined that mature coping is possible in prison, coping can be facilitated by the staff, coping can be facilitated by correctional programs, coping can result in the rehabilitation of offenders.

C.00313 Kaufman, K. (1981). Prison officers' attitudes and perceptions of attitudes: A case of pluralistic ignorance. *Journal of Research in Crime and Delinquency 18*(2), 272–294.

The article stems from research in which the researcher tested the hypothesis that among prison officers, perceived group norms differ substantially and systematically from the views expressed by individuals in the group. Correctional officers' attitudes toward inmates and treatment programs were assessed using data collected from a sample of Connecticut prison officers.

C.00314 Klofas, J. & Toch, H. (1982). The guard subculture myth. *Journal of Research in Crime and Delinquency 19*(2), 238–254.

The authors present a discussion of the prison guard subculture. Based on data collected from correctional officers, the researchers concluded that correctional officers underestimate other officers' professional orientation and overestimate the degree to which fellow officers are cynical.

C.00315 Lombardo, L. X. (1981). *Guards imprisoned: Correctional officers at work.* New York: Elsevier North-Holland.

This book is based on research in which the work, motivations, and experiences of correctional officers were assessed. The research stems from extensive interviews with correctional officers and six years as a participant observer at the Auburn Correctional Facility in New York.

C.00316 Sykes, G.M. (1958). *The society of captives: A study of a maximum security prison.* Princeton, NJ: Princeton University Press.

This book is a classic, it is based on a study of a maximum-security prison from a sociological perspective. The researcher examined the prison's organizational dysfunctions and their consequent effects. One of the consequent effects is the prison subculture and its attendant language norms.

C.00317 Toch, H. (1977). *Living in prison: The ecology of survival.* New York: Free Press.

Documented in this book is how men adapt to the stress of living in prison. The author provides a discussion of the personal impact that loss of security has on individual inmates.

V. Stress

C.00318 Adwell, S. & Miller, L. E. (1985). Occupational burnout. *Corrections Today 47*(7), 70, 72.

In this article the authors discuss stress and burnout in correctional officers. These terms are associated with "occupational burnout." The authors suggest that correctional officers are at greater risk for heart attacks, ulcers, and hypertension than the general population. The authors examine ways to assess burnout and offer suggestions on how to cope with it.

C.00319 Archambeault, W. G. & Wierman, C. L. (1983). Critically assessing the utility of police bureaucracies in the 1980s: Implications of Management

Theory Z. *Journal of Police Science and Administration 11*(4), 420–429.

According to the authors, Management Theory Z, imported from Japan, should be adopted by police managers because it promotes a work climate that responds effectively to police employees that are better educated and more sophisticated that their predecessors.

C.00320 Cheek, F. E. (1984). *Stress management for correctional officers and their families.* Laurel, MD: American Correctional Association.

Provided in this book is an examination of the nature, source, and consequences of stress on correctional officers. Also offered are strategies that correctional officer can use to cope with stress at home and in the workplace.

C.00321 Jurik, N. C. & Winn, R. (1987). Describing correctional-security dropouts and rejects: An individual or organizational profile? *Criminal Justice and Behavior 14*(1), 5–25.

The authors argue that a high turnover rate among correctional staff is a chronic problem in corrections today. Moreover, their research of the problem indicated that very little empirical data on the instability of prison staffs exist.

C.00322 Maslach, C. (1982). *Burnout: The cost of caring.* Englewood Cliffs, NJ: Prentice-Hall.

Contained in this book is an overview on the burnout experienced among human service providers. The author defines burnout, identifies sources of burnout in work, self, and family, explains how it may be monitored and "cured", and discusses ways to prevent it.

C.00323 Philliber, S. (1987). Thy brother's keeper: A review of the literature on correctional officers. *Justice Quarterly 4*(1), 9–35.

This research article is based on a review of the literature of correctional officers. The researcher focuses on characteristics and attitudes of correctional officers. Discussed in the article is the relationship between officers' characteristics and stress.

C.00324 Slate, R.N. (1993). *Stress levels and thoughts of quitting of correctional personnel: Do perceptions of participatory management make a difference?* Ann Arbor, MI: University Microfilms.

This study was designed to examine the relationship between stress levels of corrections employees, their perceptions of participation in decision making in the workplace, and their thoughts about quitting their jobs. Correctional personnel from six public and two private institutions participated.

C.00325 Terry, W.C., III (1983). Police stress as an individual and administrative problem: Some conceptual and theoretical difficulties. *Journal of Police Science and Administration 11*(2), 156–165.

The author recognizes that job related stress is common among police officers. It is suggested that intervention efforts to alleviate job related stress focus on specific job-related and personal problems encountered by police, for example, alcoholism, drug abuse, marital and family problems, difficulties stemming from shift work, and lack of participation in departmental decision making.

C.00326 Weiner, R.I. (1982). Management strategies to reduce stress in prison: Humanizing correctional environments. In R. Johnson and H. Toch (eds.), *Pains of imprisonment* (pp. 299–309). Newbury Park, CA: Sage Publications, Inc.

Managers in a correctional facility must minimize stress felt by inmates and guards. This can be done by humanizing the work environment, introducing alternative institutional structures, and implementing programs to handle job stress.

C.00327 Whitehead, J. T. & Lindquist, C. A. (1986). Correctional officer job burnout: A path model. *Journal of Research in Crime and Delinquency 23*(1), 23–42.

The article stems from research which was conducted to measure correctional officer burnout. The researchers employed a path model to explain job burnout among correctional officers employed in a Southern state.

VI. Turnover

C.00328 Benton, F. W., Rosen, E. D. & Peters, J. L. (1982). *National survey of correctional institution employee attrition.* New York: Center for Public Productivity.

The authors surveyed over 600 institutions representing all adult post-trial felony correctional institutions in the United States. It was determined that a high attrition rate among correctional employees was related to the general areas of benefits and perceived benefits, supervisory style, management practices, job content, and unionization. To reduce the attrition rate, the researchers suggest implementation of strategies that take into consideration these general areas of concern.

C.00329 McShane, M. D., Williams, F. P. III, McClain, K. L. & Shichor, J. D. (1991). Examining employee turnover. *Corrections Today 53*(5), 220, 222, 224–225.

This article was based on research which was conducted to determine why prison employees resign from their jobs. In particular, the researchers surveyed correctional wardens and superintendents, soliciting their opinions as to why prison employees quit their jobs.

C.00330 Wright, T. A. (1993). Correctional employee turnover: A longitudinal study. *Journal of Criminal Justice 21*(2), 131–142.
A questionnaire was administered to 97 criminal justice supervisory staff personnel in a short-term detention center for juveniles in a large metropolitan area on the West Coast to determine their job satisfaction, work performance, growth orientation, and tenure. The sample was primarily male, had completed at least two years of college, was racially representative, and the mean job tenure was over 12 years.

C.00331 Wright, T. A. and Bonett, D. G. (1991). Growth coping, work satisfaction and turnover: A longitudinal study. *Journal of Business and Psychology 6*(1), 133–145.

In this field study the authors examined work satisfaction and employee growth coping as joint predictors of job turnover. They tested the Person-Environment Fit Theory which indicates that an incongruent relationship between individual and organizational demands leads initially to job stress and subsequently to potentially maladaptive outcomes such as work dissatisfaction, decreases in work performance, and increases in absenteeism and turnover. The data were collected over a two year period from 113 criminal justice supervisory staff personnel.

C.00332 Wright, T. A. & Sweeney, D. (1990). Correctional institution workers' coping strategies and their effect on diastolic blood pressure. *Journal of Criminal Justice 18*(2), 161–169.

The authors examined 95 youth counselors and juvenile probation officers to determine how these individuals coped with the stressful events of their daily lives. Lazarus's cognitive-phenomenological analysis of psychological stress provided the theoretical framework for this study.

CROWDING

I. Introduction

C.00333 Cory, B. & Gettinger, S. (1984). *A time to build? The realities of prison construction.* New York: Edna McConnell Clark Foundation.

This publication focuses the reader's attention to problems associated with prison and jail overcrowding. Some of the more timely issues discussed are what are the costs and benefits of building new and more jails and prisons and can jails and prisons be managed more efficiently to reduce the prison population?

C.00334 Cox, V. C., Paulus, P. B. & McCain, G. (1984). Prison crowding research: The relevance for prison housing standards and a general approach regarding crowding phenomena. *American Psychologist 39*(10), 1148–1160.

This article contains a summary of research on prison crowding. The researchers offer suggestions to be considered by administrators in their development of prison housing standards.

C.00335 Gaes, G. G. (1985). Effects of overcrowding in prison. In M. Tonry and N. Morris (eds.), *Crime and justice: An annual review of research* (Vol. 6) (pp. 95–146). Chicago: University of Chicago Press.

This chapter, in an edited volume, is the results of research in which the effects of prison crowding on inmate health, recidivism and violence were examined.

C.00336 Klofas, J. M., Stojkovic, S. & Kalinich, D. A. (1992). Meaning of correctional crowding: Steps toward an index of severity. *Crime and Delinquency 38*(2), 171–188.

This article is based on the work of a group of corrections administrators who met at the annual meeting of the American Jail Association. The purpose of their meeting was to develop a model of jail crowding in hopes that it would provide a foundation for assessing crowding levels and to assess conditions in penal institutions.

C.00337 Leger, R. G. (1988). Perception of crowding, racial antagonism, and aggression in a custodial prison. *Journal of Criminal Justice 16*(3), 167–181.

This article is based on research conducted to measure the interrelationship between the perception of crowding, racial antagonism, and aggression. The research site was a custodial prison.

C.00338 McCain, G., Cox, V. C. & Paulus, P. B. (1976). Relationship between illness complaints and degree of crowding in a prison environment. *Environment and Behavior 8*(1), 283–290.

Contained in this article are the results of a correlation study of the relationship between stress manifested in illness and degree of crowdedness. Data consisted of detailed housing and medical histories of samples of inmates at a prison and a county jail.

C.00339 Paulus, P. B. (1988). *Prison crowding: A psychological perspective.* New York: Springer–Verlag.

The author provides the results of a 15 year research project designed to identify the effects of prison crowding and their relationship to the broader field of crowding theories.

C.00340 Ruback, R. B. & Carr, T. S. (1993). Prison crowding over time: The relationship of density and changes in density to infraction rates. *Criminal Justice and Behavior 20*(2), 130–148.

The authors examined 65 Georgia correctional institutions (25 State prisons, 33 county prisons, and 7 transitional centers) each month over a ten year period to determine the relationship between institutions density (population divided by capacity) and institutional infractions (both violent and nonviolent).

C.00341 Vaughn, M. S. (1993). Listening to the experts: A national study of correctional administrators' responses to prison overcrowding. *Criminal Justice Review 18*(1), 12–25.

The author examined administrator responses in adult correctional facilities to overcrowding to identify factors that administrators felt contributed to overcrowding.

II. Court Rulings

C.00342 Call, J. E. (1988). Lower court treatment of jail and prison over-crowding cases: A second look. *Federal Probation, 52(2)*, 34–41.

This article is based on a review of case law on prison overcrowding. The author reviewed all of the published court opinions on prison and jail overcrowding cases which were decided after *Wolfish*. It was concluded that officials who allow jail and prison overcrowding to undermine the quality of inmate living conditions are at considerable risk of being successfully sued.

C.00343 Cole, R. B. & Call, J. E. (1992). When courts find jail and prison overcrowding unconstitutional. *Federal Probation*, 56(1), 29–39.

The authors indicate that there have been two United State Supreme Court cases that dealt with overcrowding, *Wolfish* and *Chapman*. The authors review the remedies the Court has used in the 49 reported jail and prison overcrowding cases since *Chapman*.

C.00344 Rosenblatt, P. M. (1991). The dilemma of overcrowding in the nation's prisons: What are constitutional conditions and what can be done? *New York Law School Journal of Human Rights 8*, 489–520.

Contained in this law review article is a discussion of the constitutional issues surrounding prison overcrowding. The author suggests strategies for alleviating overcrowding, strategies that would bring institutions within constitutional guidelines.

C.00345 Thornberry, T. P. & Call, J. E. (1983). Constitutional challenges to prison overcrowding: The scientific evidence of harmful effects. *Hastings Law Journal 35*, 313–351.

In this law review article the author presents an overview of constitutional challenges to prison overcrowding. The primary focus of the discussion stems from the scientific evidence of the harmful effects of overcrowded jail conditions.

Cases

C.00346 *Bell v. Wolfish*, 441 U.S. 520, 99 S.Ct. 1861, 60 L.Ed.2d 447 (1979)

This case was litigated when inmates of a short-term facility challenged the facility's double-celling procedure. The facility, designed to house pre-trial defendants, placed two inmates in a room that was designed to house one occupant.

C.00347 *Rhodes v. Chapman*, 452 U.S. 337, 101 S.Ct. 2392, 69 L.Ed.2d 59 (1981)

The United States Supreme Court ruled that double-celling in and of itself is not unconstitutional.

C.00348 *Wilson v. Seiter*, 501 U.S. 294, 111 S.Ct. 2321, 115 L.Ed2d 1 (1991)

An Ohio prison inmate, Wilson, filed suit alleging certain conditions of his confinement constituted cruel and unusual punishment in violation of the 8th Amendment. He claimed that the prison officials, once notified of the problems, refused to take remedial action. The District Court granted summary judgement, and the Court of Appeals affirmed. The Supreme Court vacated and remanded because the Court of Appeals erred in failing to consider Wilson's claims under the deliberate indifference standard.

D

KATHERINE BEMENT DAVIS

D.00349 Gillin, J. L. (1926). *Criminology and penology*. New York: The Century Co.

This, most comprehensive textbook on criminology and penology of its time, provides information about Katherine Davis' influence on the evolution of corrections.

D.00350 Harris, J. (1988). *'They always call us ladies': Stories from prison*. New York: Charles Scribner's Sons.

Written from an inmate's perspective, this book is based on personal experiences of an inmate. The author writes about the history and current conditions of the Bedford Hills Correctional Facility in New York. She also acknowledges Katherine Davis's contribution to corrections.

D.00351 McKelvey, B. (1936). *American Prisons: A study in American social history prior to 1915*. Chicago: University of Chicago Press (reprinted, Montclair, NJ: Patterson Smith, 1968, 1977).

Contained in this book is a thorough historical analysis of the American prison system from 1835 to 1977. The author specifically addresses changing standards, reform movements, criminological theories, and confrontations in American penology. Also discussed is the contribution to corrections made by Katherine Davis.

D.00352 Morton, J. B. (1992). Looking back on 200 years of valuable contributions. *Corrections Today 54*(6), 76–78, 80, 82, 84–87.

The article contains an overview of people who have made significant contributions to corrections. The author indicated that women have always been active in the full spectrum of adult and juvenile corrections, probation and parole, and correctional institutions throughout the 200 year history of prisons in the United States. The author recognized the contributions made by Katherine Davis to the development of corrections.

DEATH ROW

D.00353 American Correctional Association. (1989). *Managing death-sentenced inmates: A survey of practices.* Washington, DC: St.Mary's.

This publication contains the results of a survey conducted by the American Corrections Association to assess the management of death row inmates. Correctional staff who manage death row provided data about the day-to-day operations in the housing units for death row inmates as well as demographic characteristics of the personnel who work in the units. The goal of the research was to improve the management of death row inmates.

D.00354 Flack, K. (1993). Managing death row in Florida: A look at day-to-day death row operations. *Corrections Today 55*(4), 74-76, 78.

In this article the author reports that 326 men and five women are currently sentenced to death in Florida. The men are housed at Florida State Prison in Starke and the women are housed in the Broward Correctional Institution located in Pembroke Pines. The average stay on death row in Florida is nine years. The author discusses staffing issues such as training in suicide prevention, medical emergency preparedness and adherence to policy and procedure. The author also discusses the execution protocol.

D.00355 Greenfeld, L. A. & Stephan, J. J. (1993). *Capital punishment, 1992.* Washington, DC: Bureau of Justice Statistics.

In this Bureau of Justice Statistics bulletin the authors present descriptive data on offenders sentenced to death in the United States. They report that 31 prisoners were executed in 13 states in 1992. The executed prisoners served an average of nine years and six months prior to execution. For those prisoners on death row whose criminal history was known, seven in ten had a prior felony conviction.

D.00356 Jackson, B. & Christian, D. (1980). *Death row.* Boston: Beacon Press.

Contained in this book are the results of interviews with 26 men on death row in Texas, as well as prison personnel assigned to the death row unit. The authors describe what a day in the life of death row inmate is like. Also discussed are the legal ramifications of being a death row inmate, family adjustments, psychological adjustments, the boredom, and feelings about the death penalty.

D.00357 Johnson, R. (1989). *Condemned to die: Life under sentence of death.* Prospect Heights, IL: Waveland Press.

This book consist of a descriptive analysis of what it means to live on death row. The data for the book was obtained through 35 interviews of the 37 men confined to Alabama's death row during September 1978. Explored in the study are inmates' perceptions and experiences on death row with recommendations for reform.

D.00358 Johnson, R. (1990). *Death work.* Pacific Grove, CA: Brooks/Cole Publishing Co.

This book, based on several decades of researching capital punishment, is a comprehensive approach to the subject. The author describes the execution process as a form of torture, one in which the condemned are psychologically tormented by their powerlessness and isolation. The author discusses the constant problem of suicide as well as the negative impact that death work has on the personnel who do the work, for example, stress reactions, including anxiety and dehumanized personal identities.

D.00359 Radelet, M. L., Vandiver, M. & Berardo F. (1983). Families, prisons and men with death sentences: The human impact of structured uncertainty. *Journal of Family Issues 4*(4), 595–596.

The authors researched the families of 157 men who were sentenced to death in Florida. About 500 hours were spent collecting data through visits with men sentenced to death. The authors compared the impact of institutionalization on families who had family members on death row and in nursing homes.

DETAINERS

D.00360 Abramson, L. W. (1979). *Criminal detainers.* Cambridge, MA: Ballinger Publishing Co.

Contained in this book is an overview of criminal detainers. The author describes the process by which additional charges or revocation charges are brought against inmates. Inmates' rights and other legal issues are also examined by the author.

D.00361 Clark, T. R. (1986). The effect of violations of the interstate agreement of detainers on subject matter jurisdiction. *Fordham Law Review 54*, 1209–1230.

The author describes the Interstate Agreement on Detainers (IAD) as an interstate compact that provides a procedure by which a prisoner currently incarcerated in one state can be transferred to another state. Issues discussed are, operation of the IAD, language and legislative history, congressional understanding, policy concerns, and the *U.S. v. Mauro* decision.

D.00362 Dauber, E. (1971). Reforming the detainer system: A case study. *Criminal Law Bulletin 7*(8), 669–717.

This article, based on a case study of detainers, contains an overview of detainers. The author describes the nature and scope of the detainer process and provides recommendations for improvement.

D.00363 Gobert, J. J. & Cohen, N. P. (1981). *Rights of prisoners*. Colorado Springs,CO: Shepard's/McGraw Hill.

Provided in this book is an analysis of Supreme Court cases regarding prisoners' rights through 1980. Included in the book are those cases which define inmates' due process with regard to criminal detainers.

D.00364 Necessary, J. R. (1978). Interstate agreement on detainers: Defining the federal role. *Vanderbilt Law Review 31*(4), 1017–1054.

This law review article contains the findings of a study which was conducted to determine federal responsibility in Interstate Agreements on Detainers (IAD). The author provides various Federal interpretations of the process, including guidelines for prisoners and prosecutors.

D.00365 Wexler, D. B. (1973). *The Law of Detainers*. Washington, DC: Superintendent of Documents GPO; Rockville, MD: National Institute of Justice/National Criminal Justice Research Service.

Provided in this publication is an overview of the detainer law. It is acknowledged that many state and federal prison inmates face outstanding charges in other jurisdictions. Typically the other jurisdictions file detainers against inmates so that once the inmates' institutional time is served, the institution will hold an inmate until the other jurisdiction can take possession of the inmate. The author provides a general discussion of laws that pertain to the detainer process.

D.00366 Wexler, D. B. & Hershey, N. (1971). Criminal detainers in a nutshell. *Criminal Law Bulletin 7*, 753–776.

Provided in this article is information about detainers that would be of interest to those who are the subjects of detainers and their lawyers. It is a comprehensive and practical article about the law and practice of detainers. The authors review the precedent setting cases regarding detainers, for example, *Smith v. Hooey, Walsh v. State ex rel Eyman, Kane v. Virginia* and *Ahrens v. Clark*.

Cases

D.00367 *Birdwell v. Skeen*, 983 F.2d 1332 (5th Cir. 1993)

A violation of the Interstate Agreement on Detainers Act (IADA) is not cognizable in a *habeas corpus* proceeding. *Habeas corpus* was granted because time limits were not met by the state courts. [A writ of *habeas corpus* is an order commanding production of a prisoner promptly or by a specific date – A detainer is merely a notice that a prisoner is wanted to face pending criminal charges.]

D.00368 *Burrus v. Turnbo*, 743 F.2d 693 (9th Cir. 1984)

The premise of this case is that the majority of detainers are filed to harass inmates.

D.00369 *Carchman v. Nash*, 473 U.S. 716, 105 S.Ct. 3401 (1985)

Interstate Agreement on Detainers Act (IADA) is not applicable to probationers and probation proceedings

D.00370 *Fex v. Michigan*, 122 L.Ed.2d 406 (1994)

Fex was brought from Indiana to Michigan 196 days after he requested to be extradited even though the transfer occurred 177 days after the prosecutor received the request. Fex alleged that the Interstate Agreement of Detainers Act, which states that 180 days is the limit for transfer, was violated. The Court decided that the time did not start until the Michigan prosecutor received the request. As a result, the 177 days did not exceed the 180 day limit.

D.00371 *Flick v. Blevins*, 887 F.2d 778 (7th Cir. 1989)

A *habeas corpus* writ is not considered to be a detainer under the InterstateAgreement on Detainers Act (IADA). [A writ of *habeas corpus* is an order commanding production of a prisoner promptly or by a specific date – A detainer is merely a notice that a prisoner is wanted to face pending criminal charges.]

D.00372 *United States v. Currier*, 836 F.2d 11 (1st Cir. 1987)

Interstate Agreement on Detainers Act (IADA) does not apply to pretrial detainees who have not yet been tried and convicted.

D.00373 *United States v. Mauro*, 436 U.S. 340, 98 S.Ct. 1834 (1978)

One major purpose of the Interstate Agreement on Detainers Act (IADA) is to avoid disruptions that occur in a prisoner's rehabilitation program by repeated transfers between different jurisdictions.

DETERMINATE SENTENCES

D.00374 Benda, B. B. & Waite, D. (1988). A Proposed determinate sentencing model in Virginia: An empirical evaluation. *Juvenile and Family Court Journal 39*(1),   55–71.

The authors present a brief discussion of the issues that preceded the juvenile justice systems' current disillusionment of indeterminate sentencing practices. The authors then describe a determinate sentencing model that is currently being proposed in Virginia.

D.00375 Griset, P. L. (1991). *Determinate sentencing: The promise and the reality of retributive justice*. Albany, NY: State University of New York Press.

In this book the author evaluates the current status of determinate sentencing by focusing on two questions: what happens when a sentencing model ignores crime control purposes of the criminal sanction and fails to allocate sentencing authority among criminal justice decisions makers, and what happened to the determinate sentencing model.

D.00376 Pillsbury, S. H. (1989). Understanding penal reform: The dynamic of change. *Journal of Criminal Law and Criminology 80*(3), 726–780.

In this review article the author suggests that three major forces shape penal change, idealism, society's need for order, and the efficient operation of penal institutions and staff. The author describes how each influence and guide penal reform.

D.00377 Tonry, M. (1988). Structuring sentencing. In M. Tonry and N. Morris (eds.), *Crime and justice: A review of research, Volume 8* (pp. 267–337). Chicago: University of Chicago Press.

This edited book chapter consists of an overview of the modern sentencing reform movement which began in the mid–1970s. The author informs the reader about what has been learned concerning the effects of efforts to structure sentencing discretion.

D.00378 von Hirsch, A. (1976). *Doing justice: The choice of punishments, Report of the Committee for the Study of Incarceration.* New York: Hill and Wang.

The author discusses the use of imprisonment as a device to give serious criminals what they deserve. The author expresses the viewpoint that lesser criminals, non violent offenders, should not be incarcerated. They should be punished using a less punitive disposition.

DEVELOPMENTALLY DISABLED OFFENDERS

D.00379 Coffey, O. D., Procopiow, N. & Miller, N. (1989). *Programming for mentally retarded and learning disabled inmates: A guide for correctional administrators.* Rockville, MD: National Institute of Justice.

This publication is a guide for correctional administrators and service providers who care for mentally retarded and learning disabled inmates. It provides information that is useful in the planning, development, implementation, and maintenance of academic and vocational training programs and support services.

D.00380 Nelson, C. M., Rutherford, R. B. & Wolford, B. I. (1987). *Special education in the criminal justice system.* Columbus, OH: Charles E. Merrill Publishers.

Contained in this publication is background information and practical advice on the implementation of special education services for mentally challenged offenders.

Cases

D.00381 *Ruiz v. Estelle*, 503 F. Supp. 1265 (S.D. Texas, 1980), Cert. denied, 103 Ct. 1438

This case, brought by inmate Ruiz, became the most comprehensive civil action correctional lawsuit. The plaintiff alleged that the Texas Department of Corrections had unconstitutionally exposed prisoners to physically deteriorated, dangerous, and overcrowded conditions. One of the issues litigated was the placement of mentally ill and mentally retarded inmates in the general population and an absence of programs to meet the special needs of the mentally impaired.

DIAGNOSTIC AND RECEPTION CENTERS

D.00382 Alexander, J. A. (1986). Classification objectives and practices. *Crime and Delinquency 32*(3), 323–338.

Presented in this article is a thorough discussion of the inherent limitations to the predictive ability of inmate classification instruments. The author also addresses specific objectives of classification instruments, as well as their use as a diagnostic tool.

D.00383 American Correctional Association. (1993). *Classification: A tool for managing today's offenders*. Laurel, MD: American Correctional Association.

Discussed in this book are the basics principles of classification systems. The author provides correctional administrators with a model to use in the development of effective classification systems.

D.00384 Buchanan, R. A., Whitlow, K. L. & Austin, J. (1986). National evaluation of objective prison classification systems: The current state of the art. *Crime and Delinquency 32*(3), 272–290.

This article is based on a study which was intended to assist correctional administrators in addressing prison overcrowding. The researchers assessed the effectiveness of objective prison classification systems using survey data collected from 33 of the 39 U.S. jurisdictions which use objective classification systems. During data collection, the researchers made site visits to the agencies and conducted in-depth assessments of the classification systems used in California, Illinois, and Wisconsin. One common feature of all classification systems is that the prison classification process generally begins with admission to diagnostic and reception centers.

D.00385 Clements, C. B. (1984). *Offender needs assessment: Models and approaches.* Rockville, MD: National Institute of Justice.

This manual contains a discussion of how correctional personnel assess the needs of the offender, a process which usually begins in a diagnostic facility or unit. Specifically, the author focuses on needs assessment concepts, various diagnostic models and methods, and principles upon which to build offender needs assessment systems.

D.00386 Clements, C. B. (1986). *Offender needs assessment.* Laurel, MD: American Correctional Association.

Contained in this book is an overview of basic principles for offender needs assessment, various classification systems and classification instruments, and the use of classification instruments by diagnostic facilities.

D.00387 Flynn, E. E. (1975). Problems of reception and diagnostic centers. In L. J. Hippchen (ed.), *Correctional classification and treatment: A reader.* Cincinnati: Anderson Publishing Co.

This edited book chapter contains information about the various types of reception and diagnostic centers. The author provides a critical assessment of the centers and offers suggestions for their future development.

D.00388 Flynn, E. E. (1978). Classification systems. In L. J. Hippchen (ed.), *Handbook on correctional classification: Programming for treatment and reintegration.* Cincinnati: Anderson Publishing Co.; Laurel, MD: American Correctional Association.

Presented in this edited book chapter is an overview of the different dimensions of classification. The author specifically addresses the following: approaches, administration, management, treatment and reintegration, classification procedures, and the initial classification process.

D.00389 Solomon, L. & Baird, S. C. (1982). Classification: Past failures, future potential. In American Correctional Association (ed.), *Classification as a management tool: Theories and models for decision-makers* (pp. 5–9).

College Park, MD: American Correctional Association.

The authors state that classification is a management tool and should be used for setting priorities, to assess the needs and risks for individuals, for program and facility planning, and for the monitoring, evaluating and budgeting of these programs and facilities.

DIET AND FOOD SERVICE

D.00390 American Correctional Association. (1990). *Standards for adult correctional institutions* (3rd ed.). Laurel, MD: American Correctional Association.

These standards for adult correctional institutions were developed by the American Correctional Association and the Commission on Accreditation for Corrections.

D.00391 Ayres, M. B. (1988). *Food service in jails*. Rockville, MD: National Institute of Justice Alexandria, VA: National Sheriffs' Association.

This publication contains the American Correctional Association's standards for food service in jails. Jail administrators and food service managers are provided step-by-step guidelines for food service operations.

D.00392 Boss, D., Schecter, M. & King, P. (1986). Food service behind bars. *Food management* (March), 83–87, 114, 120–136.

This article is based on interviews with four nationally recognized food service managers in U.S. correctional systems. The authors address issues such as inmates right to special diets, basic food service management, accreditation issues concerning equipment and the physical plant, food budgets, and privatemanagement company food services.

D.00393 Boston, B. (1992). Case law report: Highlights of most important cases. *National Prison Project Journal* 7(4), 6–11.

The author provides a review of significant court cases that address the potential consequences for correction officials with regard to the prison tuberculosis epidemic.

DISABLED INMATES

D.00394 *Americans with Disabilities Act* (ADA), 42 USC, Section 12101. Washington, DC: U.S. Government Printing Office.

This Act was designed to protect individuals with disabilities from discrimination. It provides clear, strong, consistent, enforceable standards that address all types of discrimination against those with handicaps. Through it the civil rights of those with disabilities are recognized with guarantees that they receive the same legal rights as everyone else.

D.00395 Bell, R., Conrad, E. H., Gazze, B., Greenwood, S. C., Lutz, J. G. & Suppa, R. J. (1983). *The nature and prevalence of learning deficiencies among adult inmates.* Rockville, MD: National Institute of Justice.

Contained in this publication are the results of a study which was conducted to measure learning deficiencies among adult inmates. The researchers collected data from adult inmates housed in institutions in Louisiana, Pennsylvania, and Washington. The researches provide information on the nature and prevalence of learning deficiencies in the research population.

D.00396 Denkowski, G. C. & Denkowski, K. M. (1985). The mentally retarded offender in the state prison system: Identification, prevalence, adjustment, and rehabilitation. *Criminal Justice and Behavior 12*(1), 55–70.

This article is based on a study of mentally retarded offenders in the state prison systems. The authors provide current national average estimates of the prevalence of mental retardation among state prison inmates, information regarding mentally retarded offenders' adjustment to incarceration, and the level of rehabilitative services provided to mentally retarded offenders.

D.00397 Long, L. M. & Sapp, A. D. (1992). Programs and facilities for physically disabled inmates in state prisons. *Journal of Offender Rehabilitation 18*(½), 191–204.

This article contains the results of a national study of physically disabled inmates. Specifically, the authors evaluated the degree to which prisons and programs are physically accessible to disabled inmates in state correctional systems.

D.00398 Rubin, P. N. (1993). The Americans with Disabilities Act and criminal justice: An overview. *Research in action.* Washington, DC: National

Institute of Justice.

The Americans with Disabilities Act (ADA) may be the most significant piece of legislation to affect law enforcement since the Civil Rights Act more than 30 years ago. The ADA may cause a complete overhaul of hiring practices in most police agencies in the United States. This report provides a framework for agencies to begin assessing the impact of the ADA on their programs.

D.00399 Severson, M. M. (1992). Redefining the boundaries of mental health services: A holistic approach to inmate mental health. *Federal Probation 56*(3), 57–63.

Presented in this article is an evaluation of inmate mental health services. The author suggests that inmate mental health services need redefining such that their boundaries are expanded.

D.00400 Veneziano, L, Veneziano, C. & Tribolet, C. (1987). The special needs of prison inmates with handicaps: An assessment. *Journal of Offender Counseling Service and Rehabilitation 12*(1), 61–72.

Contained in this article is the researchers' assessment of handicap prison inmates for special needs. The authors determined that considerable attention has been focused on special needs of ordinary handicapped citizens, but that little attention has been paid to the problem of handicapped prisoners.

D.00401 Walters, G. D., Mann, M. F., Miller, M. P., Hemphill, L. L. & Chlumsky, M. L. (1988). Emotional disorder among offenders: Inter-and intrasetting comparisons. *Criminal Justice and Behavior 15*(4), 433–453.

Contained in this article are the results of a study of emotional disorders among offenders. The researchers used a structured diagnostic interview to measure the prevalence of serious emotional disorders. The authors found that 7 to 10 percent of the state, federal, and military prison inmates were characterized by serious emotional disorders.

DISCIPLINE

D.00402 American Bar Association. (1974). *Survey of prison disciplinary practices and procedures with an analysis of the impact of Wolff v. McDonnell* (rev.ed.). Washington, DC: American Bar Association.

In 1974 the Supreme Court in *Wolff v McDonnell* held that the Fourteenth

Amendment due process protections, applied to prisoners facing loss of good time or punitive confinement as sanctions of institutional disciplinary proceedings. Contained in the decision in the *Wolff* case are the basic due process rights for inmates' review by institutional disciplinary bodies.

D.00403 Flanagan, T. J. (1982). Discretion in the prison justice system: A study of sentencing in institutional disciplinary proceedings. *Journal of Research in Crime and Delinquency 19*(2), 216–237.

This article stems from a study of institutional disciplinary sentences. The researcher describes how discretion impacts dispositional decisions in disciplinary infraction proceedings in a state prison system.

D.00404 Flanagan, T. J. (1983). Correlates of institutional misconduct among state prisoners: A research note. *Criminology 21*(1), 29–39.

This article is based on a study of institutional disciplinary proceedings. The author found that involvement in rule infractions within prisons is not normally distributed among prisoners in much the same way that participation in illegitimate activities in the larger society is not normally distributed.

D.00405 Harvard Center for Criminal Justice. (1972). Judicial intervention in prison discipline. *Journal of Criminal Law, Criminology and Police Science. 63*(2), 200–228.

Inmate protests, strikes, and rebellions (culminating with Attica) have led to a proliferation of inmate legal actions dealing with internal prison disciplinary matters. This article is the result of a study conducted at the Rhode Island Adult Correctional Institution to determine the impact that *Morris v. Travisono* had on disciplinary problems at the institution.

D.00406 Hewitt, J. D., Poole, E. D. and Regoli, R. M. (1984). Self-reported and observed rule breaking in prison: A look at disciplinary response. *Justice Quarterly 1*, 437–447.

Using the official records of inmate rule breaking, as well as inmate self-reports and guard self-reports of observed inmate rule breaking at a large coed facility, the authors studied rule-breaking and the resulting disciplinary responses. It was found that there were more self-reported rule violations than the official record indicated, the guards observations of rule breaking closely proximated inmate self-reports of rule violations, guards do not report a large percentage of rule violations they observe, and rule breaking has little relationship to the sex or race of the inmates.

D.00407 Johnson, E. H. (1966). Pilot study: Age, race and recidivism as factors in prisoner infractions. *Canadian Journal of Corrections 8*, 268–283.

In this research article the author discusses data collected from 1,063 first time offenders and 1,002 recidivists. He interpreted rule violations from two perspectives, inmates' failure to adjust to prison life and importance of inmate deviations from the perspective of prison administrators. The researcher proposes that manipulation of environment and challenges of control are the two major classes of inmate rule violations.

D.00408 Jones, C. H. & Rhine, E. (1985). Due process and prison disciplinary practices – From *Wolff* to *Hewitt*. *New England Journal on Criminal and Civil Confinement 11*(1), 44–122.

Contained in this article is a review of cases that have established due pocess guidelines for institutional disciplinary proceedings. The authors provide a chronological assessment of the importance of these cases on prison disciplinary due process law.

D.00409 Kassebaum, G., Ward, D. A. & Wilner, D. (1971). *Prison treatment and parole survival: An empirical assessment.* New York: John Wiley and Sons.

The authors report the results of a thirty-six month study carried out at a California Men's Colony-East in Los Padres. It was determined that Group counseling did not alter inmates' existing attitudes and group counseling did not alter the inmates parole performance.

D.00410 McShane, M. D. & Williams, F. P. III (1990). Old and ornery: The disciplinary experiences of elderly prisoners. *International Journal of Offender Therapy and Comparative Criminology 34*(3), 197–212.

In this article the authors report the results of a study in which disciplinary histories of elderly prisoners were assessed. The researchers analyzed data from inmate records in a southwestern prison in the United States. Comparisons of inmate disciplinary histories were provided.

D.00411 Poole, E. D. & Regoli, R. M. (1980). Race, institutional rule breaking, and disciplinary response: A study of discretionary decision making in prison. *Law and Society Review 14*(4), 931–946.

Using self-report questionnaires, the authors tested a discretionary justice model of disciplinary response to inmate rule breaking. The self-report data were supplemented by matching questionnaires with official institutional records for each inmate. It was determined that African American and Caucasian inmates equally engaged in rule-breaking but that African American inmates were more likely to be officially reported for rule violations.

D.00412 Rothman, D. J. (1971). *The discovery of the asylum: Social order and disorder in the New Republic*. Boston: Little, Brown and Co.

Contained in this book is a functionalist perspective on asylums and the social structure. Rothman proposes that society's institutions, whether social, political, or economic, cannot be understood apart from the society in which they exist. The author argues that asylums and society are interdependent, each supporting the other. The author also discusses the relationship between discipline and asylums.

D.00413 Stephan, J. (1989). *Prison rule violators*. Rockville, MD: National Institute of Justice/National Criminal Justice Research Service, Justice Statistics Clearinghouse.

This publication stems from a quasi-replication study of institutional rule infractions by prison inmates. A representative sample of state prison inmates were surveyed in 1986. It was determined that 53 percent had been charged with violating prison rules at least once since entering prison on their current sentence. These results were similar to the those of the last survey which was administered in 1979.

Cases

D.00414 *Wolff v. McDonnell*, 418 US 539, 94 S.Ct. 2963, 41 L.Ed.2d 935 (1974)

In this 6-to-3 decision, the Court held that the due process clause of the 14 Amendment provides inmates with procedural protection, if they are facing a loss of good time or confinement, because of an institutional disciplinary action. Some of the specific procedural requirements are advance written notice of charges, written statement explaining the findings, and opportunity to call witness and present case.

DOROTHEA LYNDE DIX

D.00415 Dix, D. L. (1845). *Remarks on prisons and prison discipline in the United States* (Reprinted, Montclair, NJ: Patterson Smith, 1967).

Contained in this book is the results of a four year investigation conducted by Dix of all the prisons in the New England and Middle Atlantic states. The author found these prisons characterized by cruelty, injustice and laxity of punishment. She concluded that although the Pennsylvania System is not perfect, it is the most perfect prison system that man has produced.

D.00416 Marshall, H. E. (1971). Dorothea Lynde Dix. In E. T. James, J. W. James and P. S. Boyer (Eds.),. *Notable American women 1607–1950: A biographical dictionary* (pp. 486–489). Cambridge, MA: The Belknap Press of Harvard University Press.

Provided in this entry is a brief biographical sketch of Dorothea Lynde Dix and her influence on various social reform movements in the 19th century.

D.00417 Marshall, H. E. (1937). *Dorothea Lynde Dix: Forgotten samaritan.* Chapel Hill, NC: University of North Carolina Press.

The book is a biography of Dorothea Dix. The author focuses much attention on Dix's influence on the social reform movements of her period, especially her contributions to corrections.

D.00418 Rothman, D. J. (1971). *The discovery of the asylum: Social order and disorder in the New Republic.* Boston: Little, Brown and Co.

Contained in this book is a functionalist perspective on asylums and the social structure. Rothman proposes that society's institutions, whether social, political, or economic, cannot be understood apart from the society in which they exist. The author argues that asylums and society are interdependent, each supporting the other. Also discussed are Dorothea Dix's efforts to reform asylums.

D.00419 Wilson, D. C. (1975). *Stranger and traveler: The story of Dorothea Dix, American reformer.* Boston: Little, Brown and Co.

In this biography of Dorothea Dix (1802–1887) she is described as a true American heroine. The author discusses how Dix, an educator and philanthropist, worked to improve the care for the mentally ill and other unfortunates.

DOUBLE CELLING

D.00420 Gaes, G. G. (1985). The effects of overcrowding in prison. In N. Morris and M. Tonry (eds.), *Crime and justice: An annual review of research*, Vol. 6. Chicago: University of Chicago Press.

This chapter, in an edited volume, contains the author's thoughts on overcrowding in prison. Prison overcrowding is often identified as the cause of inmate ill health, misconduct, and post-release recidivism. However, the author suggests that there has been no research on prison crowding that supports these conclusions.

D.00421 Innes, C. A. (1986). *Population density in state prisons*. Washington, DC: Department of Justice, Bureau of Justice Statistics.

Contained in this report, published by the Bureau of Justice Statistics, are statistics on the amount, nature, and use of housing space in state prisons. The statistics were derived from the 1984 Prison Census, a project in which 180,000 housing units, at 694 state prisons, participated.

D.00422 Paulus, P. B. (1988). *Prison crowding: A psychological perspective*. New York: Springer–Verlag.

This book is based on a 15 year research effort which was undertaken to determine the effects of prison crowding and their relationship to the broader field of crowding phenomena and theories. A theme throughout the book is the psychological impact of prison overcrowding.

Cases

D.00423 *Rhodes v. Chapman*, 452 U.S. 337, 101 S.Ct. 2392, 69 L.Ed.2d 59 (1981)

In this landmark case the United States Supreme Court ruled that double-celling in and of itself is not unconstitutional. It was further argued that a 'totality of the circumstances' of the institution must be considered in conjunction with the double celling issue.

DRUG AND ALCOHOL USE IN PRISON

D.00424 Collins, J. J., ed. (1991). *Drinking and crime*. New York: Guilford.

The edited book contains chapters in which the relationship between alcohol use and criminal behavior, environmental variables, family violence, cultural norms, age and life cycle variations, and race are discussed.

D.00425 Harlow, C. W. (1992). *Drug enforcement and treatment in prisons, 1990.* Washington, DC: Bureau of Justice Statistics.

This publication is based on data collected in the 1990 Census of state and federal correctional facilities. The author's purpose was to examine control strategies employed by state and federal correctional facilities to halt drug and alcohol trafficking in the respective institutions. Also addressed are the treatment programs established to help inmates with their drug and alcohol dependencies.

D.00426 Inciardi, J. A., ed. (1993). *Drug treatment and criminal justice.* Newbury Park, CA: Sage.

Contained in this edited book is an anthology of eleven previously unpublished articles on drug treatment programs. The programs are regarded as among the most innovative in the field of criminal justice between the late 1980s and early 1990s.

D.00427 Inciardi, J. A., Lockwood, D. & Quinlan, J. A. (1993). Drug use in prisons: Patterns, processes, and implications for treatment. *Journal of Drug Issues 23*, 119–129.

Presented in this article are the results of research which was conducted to develop a better understanding of the nature of drug use in prison. Research data were collected through interviews of two distinct groups of Delaware inmates during 1992.

D.00428 Inciardi, J. A. & Page, J. B. (1991). Drug sharing among intravenous drug users. *AIDS 5*, 772–773.

In this article the authors describe how intravenous drug users share drugs. They describe the processes of "frontloading and backloading" and explain how these processes have the potential to transmit HIV/AIDS as the processes involve the sharing of needles.

D.00429 Leukefeld, C. G. & Tims, F. M., eds. (1992). *Drug abuse treatment in prisons and jails.* Rockville, MD: National Institute on Drug Abuse.

This edited book contains 18 chapters in which drug abuse treatment in prisons and jails, the current status of drug abuse treatment, drug abuse treatment approaches, evaluation of drug abuse programs, special issues in drug abuse treatment, and recommendations for the future are discussed.

D.00430 Thomas, C. C. & Cage, R. J. (1977). Correlates of prison drug use: An evaluation of two conceptual models. *Criminology 15*, 193–209.

Presented in this article are the results of a study in which hypotheses for the deprivation and importation models of inmate drug use were tested. Specifically, the researchers tested the models' predictive ability with regard to whether inmates would engage in illicit drug use and abuse in a correctional setting.

D.00431 Tonry, M. & Wilson, J. Q. ed. (1990). *Drugs and crime, Volume 13.* Chicago: University of Chicago Press.

Contained in this edited volume are articles written by nationally recognized experts on issues relating to drugs and crime. Provided by the articles is a thorough overview of the critical concerns regarding drugs and crime.

D.00432 Vigdal, G. L. & Stadler, D. W. (1989). Controlling inmate drug use: Cut consumption by reducing demand. *Corrections Today 51(3)*, 96–97.

This article stems from an evaluation of Wisconsin's drug testing program for inmates. According to the authors, after Wisconsin began using random urine-analysis of prisoners, the demand for illicit drugs in prison diminished. The authors also believe that the drug testing program contributed to a safer prison environment, one that is more conducive to positive learning and programming.

D.00433 Wish, E. D. (1990). Drug testing and the identification of drug abusing criminals. In J. A. Inciardi (ed.), *Handbook of drug control in the United States* (pp. 229–244). Westport, CT: Greenwood.

Contained in this edited book chapter is a discussion of methods for identifying drug-abusing offenders. The author reports that in order for states to continue to receive federal criminal justice funds, they must initiate drug-testing programs for arrestees, probationers, and parolees.

DRUG TREATMENT

D.00434 Abadinsky, H. (1989). *Drug abuse: An introduction.* Chicago: Nelson-Hall Publications.

Contained in this book are eight chapters in which the author addresses the diverse issues of drug abuse. The author addresses the complexity of drug abuse by describing how it transcends the disciplines of history, law and law enforcement, pharmacology, political science, psychology, and sociology.

D.00435 Anglin, M. D. & Hser, Y. (1990). Treatment of drug abuse. In M. Tonry and J. Q. Wilson (Eds.), *Drugs and Crime, Volume 13* (pp. 393–460). Chicago: University of Chicago Press.

In this edited book chapter, the authors discuss the evaluation of major drug-treatment methods, methadone maintenance programs, therapeutic communities, and outpatient drug-free programs. The authors argue that all the programs proved to be effective when evaluated with effectiveness measures that incorporate outcome criteria.

D.00436 Chaiken, M. R. (1989). *In-prison programs for drug-involved offenders*. Rockville, MD: National Institute of Justice.

This publication is based on data collected in a national survey of current drug treatment programs for prison inmates and a review of evaluations of past and current programs. The author provides a descriptive analysis of past and present in–prison programs.

D.00437 Hamm, M. S. (1990). Addicts helping addicts to help themselves: The Baltimore City Jail Project. In R. Weisheit (ed.), *Drugs, Crime and the Criminal Justice System* (pp. 361–381). Cincinnati: Anderson Publishing.

In this edited book chapter the author reports that there are no official programs for drug abusers in the Baltimore City Jail (Maryland). As a result, the prisoners started their own program which is now viewed by inmates, guards, teachers, and psychologists as a model treatment program.

D.00438 Hamm, M. S. (1993). Implementing prison drug war policy: A biopsy of the wallet. In P. B. Kraska (ed.), *Altered states of mind: Critical observations of the drug war* (pp. 49–86). New York: Garland Publishing.

The author reviews the current state of drug treatment policy in prisons. He concludes that most of the programs in existence are abysmal failures and suggests that legislators and administrators should show compassion and tolerance for addicts.

D.00439 Lyman, M. D. & Potter, G. W. (1991). *Drugs in society: Causes, concepts and control*. Cincinnati: Anderson Publishing.

This book consists of an overview of drug problems in the United States. The authors primarily focus on causes of the drug problem, control of the drug problem, and difficulties that stem from conceptual disagreements.

D.00440 Stewart, S. D. (1994). Community-based drug treatment in the Federal Bureau of Prisons. *Federal Probation 58*(2), 24–28.

The Federal Bureau of Prisons' stance on drug treatment is the belief that inmates are personally responsible for choices they have made, i.e., criminality and drug abuse. Contained in this perspective is the recognition that many factors influence choices and behavior.

D.00441 Wallace, S., Pelissier, B., McCarthy, D. & Murray, D. (1990). Beyond "nothing works": History and current initiatives in BOP drug treatment. *Federal Prison Journal, 1(4)*, 23–26.

In this research article is a brief history and discussion of the current initiatives of the Federal Bureau of Prisons drug treatment programs.

Cases

D.00442 *Robinson v. California*, 370 U.S. 660, 82 S.Ct. 1417, 8 L.Ed.2d 758 (1962)

In this landmark case the Supreme Court ruled that sickness cannot be made a crime nor can sick people be punished for being sick. Moreover, narcotics addiction is considered to be an illness and is not a punishable offense.

DUE PROCESS RIGHTS OF PRISONERS

D.00443 Schafer, N. E. (1986). Discretion, due process, and the prison discipline committee. *Criminal Justice Review 11*(2), 37–46.

In this research article the author presents the results of a case study of the activities of a prison disciplinary committee (PDC) in Indiana. Data were collected from 4,339 PDC reports over a period of 11 months. In-cell restriction was the most common disposition, in fact, it was used twice as often as punitive segregation. The PDC had broad discretion to choose among several disposition alternatives. However, its greatest discretionary power was in its ability to increase or decrease the amount of time inmates serve.

Cases

D.00444 *Coffin v. Richard*, 143 F2d 443 USCA 6th (1944)

In this case the Court decided that inmates retain all the rights of ordinary citizens except those expressly, or by necessity, taken away due to incarceration.

D.00445 *Gagnon v. Scarpelli*, 411 US 778, 93 S.Ct 1756, 36 L.Ed.2d 656 (1973)

In this case the Court decided that probationers and parolees have a constitutionally limited right to counsel in revocation hearings. This case resulted in providing some control over the unlimited discretion, which had been exercised in the past, by probation and parole personnel in revocation proceedings.

D.00446 *Harrison v. Sahm*, 911 F.2d 37 (1990).

The outcome of this case was clarification of the due process right of written notice of charges. The Court determined that inmates are entitled to written notice of charges within 72 hours of being suspected of committing an offense. However, they are entitled only to written notice of the terms of the hearing and are NOT entitled to advance written notice of other matters, such as, the results of drug tests.

D.00447 *Morrissey v. Brewer*, 408 US 471, 92 S.Ct 2593, 33 L.Ed.2d 484 (1972)

As a result of this case, the Court established due process procedures for parole and probation revocation hearings. Some of the specific procedural requirements are probable cause hearing, notification of charges, opportunity to confront witnesses and be heard, written explanation of findings, and a formal revocation hearing.

D.00448 *Patterson v. Coughlin*, 905 F.2d 564 USCA 2 NY (1990)

The state prisoner in this case alleged that he was placed in isolation by state officials in violation of state law and without being afforded a prior hearing, a due process requirement. The Court agreed that a hearing should have been convened before the decision to discipline was final.

D.00449 *Proffitt v. United States*, 758 F.Supp. 342 E.D. VA (1990)

The prisoner in this case alleged that his rights were violated when his disciplinary hearing was heard by one person. The Court found that a disciplinary hearing comprised of only one member does not violate the rights of inmates.

D.00450 *Ruffin v. Commonwealth*, 62 VA 90 (1871)

At the time this case was litigated, correctional systems did not recognize legal rights of prisoners. Moreover, incarceration and every aspect of incarceration was left to the unregulated discretion of the prison administration. In this case the Court continued its "hands-off" approach regarding correctional issues.

D.00451 *Willoghby v. Luster*, 717 F. Supp. 1439 DC Nev (1989)

According to the Court, right to fair and impartial prison disciplinary hearing does not require that members of the committee come from outside the prison. However, prison inmates do have a constitutional right to a committee that does not contain members who investigated or witnessed the alleged disciplinary violation.

D.00452 *Wolff v. McDonnell*, 418 US 539, 94 S.Ct. 2963, 41 L.Ed.2d 935 (1974)

In this 6-to-3 decision, the Court held that the 'due process clause' of the 14th Amendment provides inmates with procedural protection if they are facing a loss of good time or confinement, because of an institutional disciplinary action. Some of the specific procedural requirements provided are advance written notice of charges, written statement explaining the findings, and an opportunity to call witnesses and present ones case.

E

EASTERN STATE PENITENTIARY

E.00453 Atherton, A. (1987). Journal retrospective, 1845–1986: 200 years of Prison Society history as reflected in the *Prison Journal*. *Prison Journal 67*(1), 3–37.

Presented in this article is a historical overview of The Pennsylvania Prison Society, founded over 200 years ago. One of the ways the society has worked to improve prisons and to make life better for inmates is through the publication of its journal, *Prison Journal*, since 1845.

E.00454 Barnes, H. E. (1927). *The evolution of penology in Pennsylvania: A study in American social history.* Indianapolis, IN: The Bobbs-Merrill Co. (Reprinted, Patterson Smith Publishing Co., 1968).

Contained in this book is an excellent review of the Pennsylvania prison system. The author provides a thorough description of the Pennsylvania system and analyzes its impact on the development of penology.

E.00455 Teeters, N. K. (1937). *They were in prison: A history of the Pennsylvania Prison Society 1787–1937.* Chicago: John C. Winston Co.

The book is a chronicle of the Pennsylvania prison system. The author discusses the main differences between the Auburn and Pennsylvania systems. This reference book contains excerpts from prison records.

E.00456 Teeters, N. K. & Shearer, J. (1957). *The prison at Philadelphia, Cherry Hill: The separate and solitary system of penal discipline, 1829–1913.*

New York: Columbia University Press for Temple University Publications.

Reflected in this book is the first full scholarly account of the Cherry Hill Prison in Philadelphia. The authors provide a detailed discussion of the effectiveness of the institution's treatment approach, a stringent work program in solitary confinement.

EDUCATIONAL PROGRAMS

E.00457 Brockway, Z. (1912). *Fifty years of prison service: An autobiography.* Montclair, NJ: Patterson Smith, (Reprinted, Patterson Smith, 1969).

Contained in this autobiographical book is the famous prison Administrator's views on prison reform. The author focuses on his experiences during the 25 years he was superintendent of the New York State Reformatory at Elmira. Of particular note is Brockway's perspectives on indeterminate sentences and education programs as central features of prison reform.

E.00458 Gehring, T. (1980). Correctional education and the United States Department of Education. *Journal of Correctional Education 31*(3), 4–6.

According to the author, the Correctional Education Association has been working diligently to encourage the new Department of Education to establish an office of Correctional Education. Gehring acknowledges that about 562,000 adult inmates and 40,000 juvenile wards are confined in America's federal, state and local institutions and about 5.5 billion dollars is spent annually on corrections. The author recommends that the Secretary of Education coordinate Federal funding programs for correctional education, establish meaningful liaison services, provide technical assistance to the states, and disseminate information about successful programs to correctional and public school systems.

E.00459 Kuhn, T. S. (1970). *The structure of scientific revolutions* (2nd ed.). Chicago: University of Chicago Press.

In this book, the author provides his perspective on the evolution of scientific thought.

E.00460 MacCormick, A. H. (1931). *The education of adult prisoners: A survey and a program.* New York: National Society of Penal Information, (Reprinted, AMS Press, 1976).

Contained in this book are the results of one of the first studies of adult inmate education programs. The author presents findings and recommendations based on data which were collected between November, 1927 and August, 1928.

E.00461 Makarenko, A. S. (1973). *The road to life: An epic in education* (I. Litvinov and T. Litvinov, Trans.). New York: Sentry Press. (Original work published 1951).

During the 1920s the author, a Ukrainian educator, was placed in charge of a facility for wayward youth. He developed a philosophy that espoused authority and discipline, egalitarianism, and the unity of individuals. His approach to corrections fostered the development of integrity and identity for individuals through communal experiences.

E.00462 Ross, R., & Fabiano, E. (1985). *Time to think: A cognitive model of delinquency prevention and offender rehabilitation.* Johnson City, TN: Institute of Social Sciences and Arts.

Contained in this book is a literature review of juvenile offender rehabilitation programs. Special attention is directed towards education programs. The authors discuss why some programs work and others fail.

E.00463 Snedden, D. S. (1907). *Administration and educational work of American juvenile reform Schools.* New York: Teachers College, Columbia University.

The author presents a history of reform schools in the United States and how they have changed over the years. Also addressed are the types of children incarcerated in reform schools, training programs, and probation and parole. The author concludes that public schools could learn from reform schools.

E.00464 Tannenbaum, F. (1933). *Osborne of Sing Sing.* Chapel Hill: The University of North Carolina Press.

Thomas Mott Osborne was appointed warden of Sing Sing Prison in 1914. What he found were conditions that had not changed since the 1850s. He systematically and almost single-handedly began the movement to change these conditions. The author discusses Osborne's philosophy and the problems he encountered in seeking to accomplish his goals.

E.00465 Werner, D. (1990). *Correctional education: Theory and practice.* Danville, IL: Interstate.

Provided in this book is an overview of education programs in correctional settings. The author reviews the theoretical basis for educational programs in corrections and provides an assessment of their effectiveness.

ELDERLY INMATES

E.00466 Aday, R. H. (1994). Aging in prison: A case study of new elderly offenders. *International Journal of Offender Therapy and Comparative Criminology 38*(1), 79–91.

Using a case study approach and data collected through in-depth interviews, the author describes elderly offenders' prison experiences. He determined that the initial reactions, of elderly offenders to incarceration, are characterized by family conflicts, depression, thoughts of suicide, and fears of dying in prison.

E.00467 Camp, G. M. & Camp, C. G. (1993). *The corrections yearbook, 1993.* South Salem, NY: Criminal Justice Institute.

Contained in this official sourcebook are annual national statistics collected from correctional sytems. Included in the statistics are demographic data for elderly offenders.

E.00468 Chaneles, S. & Burnett, C. (eds.). (1989). *Older offenders: Current trends.* New York: Haworth Press.

Covered in this edited book is an overview of issues relating to older offenders. Chapters in the book include discussions of the following dimensions and motivations of crimes by older-offenders, factors in sentencing and treatment and correctional management of older inmates.

E.00469 Hall, M. (1990). *Special needs inmates: A survey of state correctional systems.* Rockville, MD: National Institute of Justice.

To determine the prevalence of inmates with special medical or mental health needs, the 50 state prison systems were surveyed. Thirty-one institutions responded. The results indicated that between 0.8 percent and 8.2 percent of prison inmates are housed in special housing or infirmaries. Also discussed were other inmate populations including those with chronic illnesses, those over the age of 50, terminally-ill inmates, mentally-ill inmates and ambulatory inmates.

E.00470 McCarthy, B. & Langworthy, R. eds. (1988). *Older offenders: Perspectives in criminology and criminal justice.* New York: Praeger.

Presented in this edited book are contributions by twelve researchers and practitioners, each of whom have expertise in the area of older offenders. The contributors examine issues relating to crimes committed by elderly individuals and the criminal justice system's response to this type of offenders.

E.00471 McShane, M. D. & Williams, F. P. III (1990). Old and ornery: The disciplinary experiences of elderly prisoners. *International Journal of Offender Therapy and Comparative Criminology 34*(3), 197–212.

Contained in this article are the results of a study in which disciplinary histories of elderly prisoners were assessed. The researchers analyzed data from inmate records in a southwestern prison in the United States. The researchers compared elderly inmate disciplinary histories with those of younger inmates.

E.00472 Moore, E. O. (1989). Prison environments and their impact on older citizens. *Journal of Offender Counseling, Services and Rehabilitation 13(2),* 175–191.

In this research article, the author presents the results of a study which was conducted to examine the impact of transferring older inmates from a very large institution to a much smaller facility. Specifically, the researcher measured the effect of moving inmates from an open block, age integrated facility to a smaller, age-segregated facility. The research was conducted in Michigan and the sample consisted of 52 male inmates who were more than 50 years old.

E.00473 Morton, J. B. (1992). *An administrative overview of the older inmate.* Rockville, MD: National Institute of Justice.

The author presents an examination of the problems correctional policy makers, administrators, and staff experience when handling older offenders. A review of policy and program issues, relevant to this population, is provided.

E.00474 Morton, J. B. (1993). Training staff to work with elderly and disabled inmates. *Corrections Today 55(1),* 42, 44–47.

In this article, the author provides an overview of training curriculum concerns of the South Carolina Department of Corrections with regard to elderly and disabled inmates. The author addresses the following curriculum issues: planning, implementation, content, and training.

ELMIRA REFORMATORY

E.00475 Beltzer, W. & Spears, E., (eds). (1976). *Elmira: 1876–1976 centennial acknowledgment of its history, programs, and purpose.* Albany, NY: New York State Department of Correctional Services, Office of Public Relations.

In this booklet the authors provide readers with a precise description of what life is like in a correctional facility. Valuable information, about the daily correctional process, is presented through this broad view of daily schedules at Elmira. Booklet sections include history, resident profiles, custodial role, academic instruction, music program, volunteer service, and others.

E.00476 Gehring, T. (1982). Zebulon Brockway of Elmira: 19th century correctional education hero. *Journal of Correctional Education 33*, 4–7.

An overview of Zebulon Brockway's career is provided in this reserch article. Using data from Brockway's book, *Fifty Years of Prison Service*, the author focuses on two of Brockway's more notable contributions: the programs that he established, and the influence of the educational experience at Elmira.

E.00477 Pisciotta, A. W. (1994). *Benevolent Repression: Social Control and the American Reformatory-Prison Movement.* New York: New York University Press.

In this book the author provides a historical analysis of the history of the adult reformatory movement. The primary focus, of the author, is the reform efforts of Zebulon Brockway at Elmira Reformatory, in New York between 1876 and 1920. A thorough discussion of indeterminate sentencing and educational programs is provided.

E.00478 Smith, B. A. (1980). The Irish general prisons board, 1877–1885: Efficient deterrence or bureaucratic ineptitude? *Irish Jurist 15*(Summer), 122–136.

The author of this article presents a historical analysis of the Irish General Prison Board from 1877 to 1885. She discusses the report of the Kimberly Commission on Penal Servitude, 1878 through 1879, the

Royal Commission on Irish Prisons, and formation of the General Prisons Board. She acknowledges that parliamentary neglect of needed legislation and generally unforeseen political unrest complicated the task of creating a centralized, humane penal system.

E.00479 Smith, B. A. (1988). Military training at New York's Elmira Reformatory, 1888 - 1920. *Federal Probation 52*(1), 33–40.

Contained in this article is a discussion of the military training model as a correctional management strategy at Elmira Reformatory. Due to an emergency situation at Elmira, the military training model was introduced as a means to organize and discipline inmates. The author indicates that it persisted beyond the crisis and was incorporated into the organizational structure of the institution.

E.00480 Waite, R. G. (1986). From penitentiary to reformatory: Alexander Machonochie, Walter Crofton, Zebulon Brockway, and the road to prison reform - New South Wales, Ireland, and Elmira, New York, 1840 - 1970. In L. A. Knafla, (ed.), *Criminal justice history: An international annual.* Westport, CT: Greenwood.

Presented in this chapter, of an edited book, is a historical analysis of prison reform beginning with the penal facility at New South Wales and ending with Elmira Reformatory. The author discusses the notable contributions of Zebulon Brockway's Elmira Reformatory.

ESCAPES

E.00481 Carlson, K. A. (1990). Prison escapes and community consequences: Results of a case study. *Federal Probation 54(2)*, 36–42.

Presented in this research article are the results of a case study of how inmate escapes impacts a prison's host community. The researcher found that the most notable general effect that the prison had on its host community was economic enhancement. The researcher further reported that the fear of escapes, by community residents, was minimal to none.

E.00482 Herrick, E. (1989). Inmates escapes 87 and 88. *Corrections Compendium 14(4),* 9–12.

Contained in this article are escape statistics for all state prison systems, the District of Columbia, the Federal Bureau of Prisons, and 9 Canadian prison systems for the years 1987 and 1988.

E.00483 Lillis, J. (1994). Prison escapes and violence remain down. *Corrections Compendium 19*(6), 6–21.

The author surveyed 41 State correctional systems, the District of Columbia Department of Corrections, the Federal Bureau of Prisons, and Canadian prison systems to determine the incidence of prisoner escapes and violence for 1992 and 1993. It was determined that he increase in both from 1992 to 1993 was insignificant. Detailed data are provided.

E.00484 Shaffer, C. E., Bluoin, D. & Pettigrew, C. G. (1985). Assessment of prison escape risk. *Journal of Police and Criminal Psychology 1,* 42–48.

Contained in this article are the results of a study which was conducted to measure predictors of escape. This exploratory study involved the examination of 27 variables as possible predictors of prison escapes.

E.00485 Thornton, D. & Speirs, S. (1985). Predicting absconding from young offender institutions. In D. Farrington and R. Tarling (eds.), *Prediction in criminology* (pp. 119–134). Albany, NY: State University of New York Press.

Provided in this edited book chapter are the results of a study of escapes from a youthful offender prison. Youthful-Offender Psychology Unit data on males, who were admitted to the open institution between May 1977 and December 1978, were analyzed. This resulted in the development of a prediction scale for identifying young offenders who are most likely to abscond from open correctional facilities.

EXECUTIONS IN THE UNITED STATES

E.00486 Bedau, H. A. (1982). *The death penalty in America* (3rd Ed.). New York: Oxford University Press.

In this book the author discusses various issues relating to the imposition of the death penalty. Specifically analyzed are execution issues from the following perspectives: historical, sociological, psychological, legal, political, and offender. Included in the legal analysis are Supreme Court decisions relating to executions.

E.00487 Bowers, W. J., Pierce, G. L., & McDevitt, J. (1984). *Legal homicide: Death as punishment in America, 1864–1982.* Boston: Northeastern University Press.

Contained in this book is a historical examination of capital punishment in the United States from 1864 to 1982. The authors present a descriptive analysis of executions prior to *Furman v Georgia* (1972). The analysis of executions after *Furman* is based on fairness, utility, and adherence to contemporary state values.

E.00488 Gallup, A. & Newport, F. (1991). Death penalty support remains strong. *Gallup Monthly Report* (June), 128–132.

Presented in this article are the results of the 1991 Gallup Opinion Poll on the death penalty. Results indicate that public support for the death penalty remains high, with three quarters of Americans now favoring capital punishment as an option in murder cases. This reflects a quarter century of steady growth in support of capital punishment. The low point occurred in 1966 when Gallup found 42 percent in favor of the death penalty and 47 percent opposed.

E.00489 Johnson, R. (1990). *Death work: A study of the modern execution process*. Pacific Grove, CA: Brooks/Cole Publishing.

This book, based on several decades of researching capital punishment, is a comprehensive approach to the subject. The author describes the execution process as a form of torture in which the condemned are psychologically tormented by their powerlessness and isolation. The author discusses the constant problem of suicide as well as the negative impact that death work has on the personnel who do the work, for example, stress reactions, including anxiety and dehumanized personal identities.

E.00490 Schneider, V. & Smykla, J. O. (1991). Summary analysis of executions in the United States, 1608–1987: the Espy file. In R.M. Bohm (ed.), *Death penalty in America: Current Research* (pp. 1–19). Cincinnati: Anderson Publishing.

Contained in this edited book chapter is a discussion of the Espy File, a unique data source on executions in the United States. The file, a comprehensive collection of newspaper and other media accounts, documents 14,570 legal executions which were carried out between 1608 and 1987.

E.00491 Streib, V. L. (1988). Imposing the death penalty on children. In K. C. Haas and J. A. Inciardi (eds.), *Challenging capital punishment: Legal and social science approaches* (pp. 245–267). Newbury Park, CA: Sage Publications.

Contained in this edited book chapter is an overview of sentencing children to death. The author approached the imposition of death penalties for children (under the age of 18 at the time of the crime) from legal and empirical perspectives.

E.00492 Zimring, F. E. & Hawkins, G. (1986). *Capital Punishment and the American Agenda.* Cambridge: Cambridge University Press.

The authors ask if capital punishment fits into the American future and if not, how it can be ended.

F

FEDERAL BUREAU OF PRISONS

F.00493 Hershberger, G. L. (1979). *The development of the Federal Prison System*. Washington, DC: U.S. Government Printing Office.

The author presents the history and development of the Federal Prison System. Beginning with the concept of the penitentiary and progressing to the modern era, the author discusses different penal philosophies and programs employed in federal prisons. Included are photographs and a bibliography.

F.00494 Kline, S. (1992). A profile of female offenders in the Federal Bureau of Prisons. *Federal Prisons Journal 3*(1), 33–36.

Presented in this article is a profile of female inmates incarcerated in federal prisons. The author reports that in the ten year period from 1981 to 1991, the number of female inmates in federal prisons increased 254 percent, from 1,400 to 5,000.

F.00495 Roberts, J. W. (1990). View from the top. *Federal Prisons Journal 1*(4), 27–55.

Presented in this article is an overview of the administration of the Federal Bureau of Prisons under the leadership of five directors. The author notes significant contributions of Sanford Bates, James Bennett, Myrl Alexander, Norman Carlson and J. Michael Quinlan.

FORCE, USE OF

F.00496 Bryan, D. (1994). Dealing with violent inmates: Use of non-lethal force. *Corrections Compendium 19*(6), 1–2, 23.

The author describes two categories of non-lethal force that is used with violent and potentially violent situations in the correctional setting. Details on the use of electric stun guns and spray devices are provided.

F.00497 Henry, P., Senese, J. D. & Smith-Ingley, G. (1994). Use of force in America's prisons: An overview of current research. *Corrections Today 56*(4), 108, 110, 112, 114.

Using data from 424 use of force incident reports and interviews with over 400 correctional officers and inmates, the authors examined the use of force in Florida prisons. The authors then used a national survey to estimate the extent and nature of use of force incidents nationwide. They report that from the nationwide survey they found patterns similar to those in the data from Florida.

Cases

F.00498 *Hudson v. McMillian*, 503 U.S. 1, 112 S.Ct. 995, 117 L.Ed.2d 156 (1992)

Inmate Hudson was beaten by two correctional officers after an argument between one guard and Hudson. The supervisor on staff admonished the guards – "not to have too much fun." Hudson alleged his 8th Amendment rights were violated by this attack. The Court found that "even with minor prison disturbances, guards must balance the need to restore discipline with the risk of harm resulting from the use of force."

F.00499 *Inmates of Attica Correctional Facility v. Rockefeller*, 453 F. 2d 12 (1971)

In this case action was taken by prison inmates, for Federal equitable relief, against correctional personnel who constantly subjected the inmates to unprovoked acts of brutality following a riot. The federal appellate court enjoined state officials from future acts of brutality and torture and authorized the assignment of federal monitors in institutions.

F.00500 *Johnson v. Glick*, 481 F. 2d 1028 (1973).

In this case, civil rights action was brought by a prisoner, Johnson, against Warden Glick and guards of a detention facility for unconstitutional use of force. The Court stated that "management by a few guards of large numbers of men and women, may require and justify the use of a degree of intentional force." Even so the court recognized that under certain circumstances, individual assaults may be actionable. The Court specified the following guidelines for determining if force is actionable: is there need for the application of force, what is the relationship between the need and the amount of force used, what is the extent of injury inflicted, was force applied in a good faith effort to maintain or restore discipline or was it used maliciously and sadistically in order to harm?

F.00501 *Sample v. Ruettgers*, 704 F.2d 491 (1983)

In this case the Court addressed the issue of whether a beating of an inmate constituted a violation of the 8th Amendment? The Court reasoned that if an individual's unauthorized denial of medical treatment can violate the 8th Amendment then it is difficult to understand why a beating would not violate the same Amendment.

F.00502 *Whitley v. Albers*, 475 U.S. 312, 106 S. Ct. 1078, 89 L. Ed. 2d 251 (1986)

Prisoner Whitley was shot in the leg during the quelling of a prison riot and brought a Section 1983 action against prison officials, alleging violation of his Eighth Amendment rights. The Court allowed the use of deadly force to put down a prison riot saying that as long as it is used in a "good faith" effort to maintain order and restore discipline then it is Constitutional.

FORT LEAVENWORTH

F.00503 Cavanaugh, C. G., Jr. (1983). Behind the walls. *Soldiers*, June, 42–52.

The U.S. Disciplinary Barracks at Fort Leavenworth, Kansas was established by Congress in 1874. In this article the author provides a brief history of the institution and insight into the jobs the 672 military correctional staff face each day.

F.00504 Cohen, R. L. (1983). United States Disciplinary Barracks: Overview. *Military Police Journal 10*(4), 18–19.

In this article the author provides historical information about the United States Disciplinary Barracks (USDB) beginning with its establishment in 1874 as the United States Military Prison. Today it is the military's only maximum security prison for U.S. Army, U.S. Air Force and U.S. Marine Corps personnel who receive a court–martial sentence of confinement at hard labor in excess of one year. Through a special agreement the USDB accepts female inmates and U.S. Navy officer inmates.

G

GANGS

G.00505 American Correctional Association. (1994). *Gangs in correctional facilities: A national assessment.* Washington, DC: National Institute of Justice.

Provided in this government publication is an overview of prison gangs in the United States. The publication is based on research funded by the National Institute of Justice to study prison gangs in American prisons.

G.00506 Camp, G. M. & Camp, C. G. (1985). *Prison gangs: Their extent, nature and impact on prisons.* Washington, DC: Department of Justice, Office of Legal Policy.

The authors examine the impact of gangs on prisons, inmates and administrators and identifies strategies used to counter prison gangs. Using survey data from the 50 State prison systems, the District of Columbia, and the Federal Bureau of Prisons, the authors present an overview of the nature and extent of prison gangs.

G.00507 Camp, G. M. & Camp, C. G. (1988). *Management strategies for combating prison gang violence.* South Salem, NY: Criminal Justice Institute.

Contained in this report are management strategies for controlling prison gang violence. It is based on first hand observations and analyses of responses to prison gang violence by five correctional facilities in Washington and Illinois. The researchers propose useful solutions to correctional administrators.

G.00508 Carroll, L. (1974). *Hacks, Blacks and cons: Race relations in a maximum security prison.* Lexington, MA: Heath, Lexington Books.

Contained in this book is a description of race relations in one prison. The author examines race relations through identification of conditions in prison that determine the quality of race relations. The author also analyzes the relationship between race relationships and prison gangs.

G.00509 Irwin, J. & Cressey, D. (1962). Thieves, convicts and the inmate culture. *Social Problems 10*, 142–155.

Presented in this article are the results of an examination of prison subculture. Special emphasis is placed on the inmates and their roles in the prison subculture. The authors discuss the role of alcohol and drugs in the inmate subculture.

G.00510 Pelz, M. E., Marquart, J. W. & Pelz, T. (1992). Right-wing extremism in the Texas prisons: The rise and fall of the Aryan Brotherhood of Texas. *The Prison Journal 71*, 23–37.

The researchers provide a thorough history of the birth, growth and demise of the Aryan Brotherhood of Texas. Right-wing extremism is offered as an approach to understanding the birth and growth of this prison gang.

HOWARD BELDING GILL

G.00511 Gill, H. B. (1962). Correctional philosophy and architecture. *Journal of Criminal Law, Criminology, and Police Science 53*, 312–322.

The author traces the history of penal philosophy in the United States and discusses the influence of penal philosophy on prison architecture and the influence of prison architecture on penal policies.

G.00512 Gill, H. B. (1965). What is a community prison? *Federal Probation 29*, 15–23.

The author discusses the concept of 'community prisons' and identifies four essential characteristics of a community prison. They are 1) normalcy in the interpersonal relationships between officials and staff, 2) small group principle in relation to living quarters, dining, bathing, work programs and leisure time activities, 3) inmate participation – sharing action and responsibility for all institutional activities except disciplinary and financial, and 4) community contacts which include bringing the outside community into the prison and taking the inmates outside the prison whenever possible.

G.00513 Gill, H. B. (1970). A new prison discipline: Implementing the Declaration of Principles of 1870. *Federal Probation 34*, 29–33.

The author states that the Declaration of Principles of 1870 does not need to be revised, however, there needs to be an affirmation of the progress achieved in the last 100 years. He states there needs to be a 'New Prison Discipline.' This model would include two types of discipline, a set of rules and regulations and a way of life.

G.00514 President's Commission on Law Enforcement and the Administration of Justice. (1968). *The challenge of crime in a free society*. Washington, DC: Superintendent of Documents; New York: Avon.

This report of The President's Commission on Law Enforcement and Administration of Justice, established by President Lyndon Johnson, to investigate the causes of crime and delinquency, provides recommendations for preventing crime and delinquency and improving law enforcement and the administration of justice.

GOOD TIME CREDIT

G.00515 Austin, J. (1986). Using early release to relieve prison overcrowding: A dilemma in public policy. *Crime and Delinquency 32(4)*, 404–502.

Presented in this article are the results of an assessment of early release to relieve prison overcrowding. The assessment is based on the early release of over 21,000 inmates from the Illinois Department of Corrections between 1980 and 1983. The inmates were released in response to a prison crowding crisis.

G.00516 Austin, J. (1991). *The consequences of escalating the use of imprisonment: The case study of Florida.* Rockville, MD: National Institute of Justice/National Criminal Justice Reference Service.

In Florida the massive incarceration of drug offenders has resulted in Florida having the highest rate of prison admissions but the shortest length of stay of any prison system in the United States. Because of Florida's drug war and mandatory sentencing practices, the prison system has become chaotic and ineffective.

G.00517 Clear, T. R., Hewitt, J. D. & Regoli, R. M. (1978). Discretion and the indeterminate sentence: Its distribution, control and effect on time served. *Crime and Delinquency 24,* 428–445.

Contained in this article are the results of an evaluation of sentencing reform (determinate sentencing) incorporated in the 1977 Indiana penal code. The authors discuss the demise of good time credit as a result of determinate sentencing.

G.00518 Flanagan, T. J. (1982). Discretion in the prison justice system: A study of sentencing in institutional disciplinary proceedings. *Journal of Research in Crime and Delinquency 19*(2), 216–237.

The author of this article presents findings from a study of institutional disciplinary sentences. The researcher describes how discretion impacts dispositional decisions in disciplinary infraction proceedings in a state prison system. The author notes that the disciplinary committee has the discretion to take an inmate's good time or place the inmate in 'time-out' status, both of which result in more time served by the inmate.

G.00519 Jacobs, J. B. (1982). Sentencing by prison personnel: Good time. *UCLA Law Review 30,* 217–270.

Contained in this law review article are recommendations for changing good time procedures. The author recommends that good time should either be abolished or restricted due to its susceptibility to abuse.

G.00520 Parisi, N. & Zillo, J. A. (1983). Good time: The forgotten issue. *Crime and Delinquency 29,* 228–237.

Contained in this article are recommendations regarding good time when revising sentencing structures. The authors suggest that consideration be given to the function of good time in the actual sentences that inmate serve.

G.00521 Ross, R. R. & Barker, T. G. (1986). *Incentives and disincentives: A review of prison remission systems.* Ottawa, Ontario, Canada: Canada Solicitor General.

The authors review the literature concerning remission systems and come to the conclusion that little research has been devoted to prison remission or incentive systems.

G.00522 Weisburd, D. & Chayet, E. F. (1989). Good time: An Agenda for research. *Criminal Justice and Behavior 16*, 183–195.

Presented in this article is an overview of the research literature on good time. The researchers examine good time policy and research and outline an agenda for systematic review of good time policies and practices.

H

MARY BELLE HARRIS

H.00523 Harris, M. B. (1942). *I knew them in prison* (rev. ed.). New York: The Viking Press.

In this autobiography the author discusses her career in penology from her first position at Blackwell Island, New York through her tenure as warden at the Federal Industrial Institution for Women in Alderson, West Virginia. She discusses various programs and methods that were employed in these institutions during her administration.

H.00524 Schweber, C. (1980). Harris, Mary Belle, Aug, 19, 1874-Feb. 22, 1957: Prison Administrator. *Notable American Women 1950-1975.* Cambridge, MA: Harvard University Press.

Contained in this reference book is a biographical sketch of Mary Belle Harris. Included is information about Ms. Harris's family, educational background, and administrative responsibilities in corrections, including a review of her tenure at the Federal Bureau of Prison's Women's Reformatory at Alderson West Virginia.

JOHN HAVILAND

H.00525 Barnes, H. E. (1927). *The evolution of penology in Pennsylvania: A study in American social history.* Indianapolis, IN: The Bobbs-Merrill Co. (Reprinted, Montclair, NJ, Patterson Smith,1968).

This book is an excellent resource tool for researching the Pennsylvania prison system. The author presents a historical analysis of the development of penology in the Pennsylvania system.

H.00526 Beaumont, G. De & Tocqueville, A. De (1964). *On the penitentiary system in the United States and its application in France.* Carbondale, IL: Southern Illinois University Press. (Originally published in 1833).

Contained in this book is a descriptive assessment of the penitentiary system of the United States. The authors visited prisons in the United States to determine if the American system used any principles or programs that would be applicable in French prisons. The authors proposed that France establish a model prison based on the Pennsylvania System, however, they recognized that because of legal, religious and administrative obstacles, the French government would only be able to utilize a few principles from American corrections.

H.00527 Eriksson, T. (1976). *The reformers: An historical survey of pioneer experiments in the treatment of criminals.* New York: Elsevier North-Holland.

Contained in this book is a historical review of experiments in correctional treatment reform. The researcher provides information on the major reform efforts in Europe and the United States from the 16th century to the present.

H.00528 Johnston, N. B. (1973). John Haviland. In H. Mannheim (ed.), *Pioneers in Criminology* (2nd ed.) (pp. 107–128). Montclair, NJ: Patterson Smith.

Presented in this edited book is a biography of John Haviland. He is regarded by some to be the most prolific and important prison architect of all time.

H.00529 Teeters, N. K. & Shearer, J. D. (1957). *The prison at Philadelphia: Cherry Hill.* New York: Columbia University Press.

The history of the prison at Cherry Hill is presented in this book. It is based on records that were stored in the towers of the prison until 1954. The authors discusses Haviland's design and construction of the prison, and the influence of its architecure on the treatent of prisoners, as well as the general operation of the prison.

H.00530 Vaux, R. (1872). *Brief sketch of the origin and history of the state penitentiary for the eastern district of Pennsylvania at Philadelphia.* Philadelphia: McLaughlin Brothers.

Contained in this book is a short history of the Penitentiary for the Eastern District of Pennsylvania and its system of punishment. The author provides information for those engaged in the study of penal science and of penitenitary discipline. Also presented is a review of early reform and rules for prisoners.

HAWES-COOPER ACT

H.00531 Gildemeister, G. A. (1987). *Prison labor and convict competition with free workers in industrializing America, 1840–1890.* New York: Garland Press.

In this book the author presents a historical analysis of American prison labor in the free market from 1840–1989. The author addresses the following issues: the administrative requirement for prisoners to work, how prison produced goods competed with the products produced in the free world, and how prison contract labor competed with work of free workers.

H.00532 Robinson, L. N. (1931). *Should prisoners work?* New York: John C. Winston Co. International Press.

Contained in this book is an analysis of inmatework policies. Provided is a pro and con approach to prison work programs, including ways that the prison, the general public, and inmates benefit and are harmed from inmate work policies.

H.00533 U.S. Department of Justice. (1987). *Work in American prisons: The private sector gets involved.* Washington, DC: National Institute of Justice.

Presented in this government report is a description of current and historical developments in private-sector prison industries. Included is an analysis of the costs and benefits of private-sector prison industry and suggested strategies for future growth.

HEALTH CARE

H.00534 Anno, B. J. (1992). *Prison health care: Guidelines for the management of an adequate delivery system.* Longmont, CO: National Institute of Corrections Information Center.

Provided in this manual on correctional health care are management guidelines for prison health delivery systems. It is based on the most recent research literature, case law, standards of national prison and medical organizations, and experts correctional health care.

H.00535 Anno, B. J. (1993). Health care for prisoners: How soon is soon enough? *The Journal of the American Medical Association 269*(5), 633–634.

According to the author of this research article, during the 1970s the American Medical Association developed a set of standards for health care in jails. This program was expanded during the 1980s to include prisons and juvenile detention centers. Even so, increases in prison populations, incidences of infectious disease, and budget constraints, have continued the persistent problem of prisoners are not receiving adequate medical care.

H.00536 Glaser, J. B. & Greifinger, R. B. (1993). Correctional health care: A public health opportunity. *Annals of Internal Medicine 118*(2), 139-145.

According to the authors, approximately 1.2 million inmates have some type of communicable disease. The researchers argue that it is in the best interest of local health care personnel to test and treat inmate ailments while health care personnel have the opportunity to do so. It is pointed out that because many of the inmates are characterized by risky lifestyles and limited access to health care that without treatment while in prison, their release from prison is expected to result in an escalation of communicable diseases. Thus, in the long run, providing health care for inmates is regarded as a protective measure for society.

H.00537 Kay, S. L. (1991). *The constitutional dimensions of an inmate's right to health care.* Chicago: The National Commission on Correctional Health Care.

Provided in this booklet are references to the law, as it applies to correctional health settings. It is written for the legal, correctional, and medical professional.

H.00538 Koren, E. I. (1993). Status report: State prisons and the courts, January 1, 1993. *National Prison Journal 8*(1), 3–11.

Contained in this article is a review of the current conditions of the state correctional systems in the United States. The author focuses on their compliance with court corders and consent decrees that limit inmate populations and improve prison conditions.

H.00539 McConnell, Elizabeth H. (1992). Avoiding court ordered prison health care: Policy considerations for the prison administrator. *Journal of the American Criminal Justice Association, 10*(2), 35-47.

The author provides a thorough review of prison health care law suits with an explanation of the legal principles established in each case. Suggested are prison health care policies that meet constitutional guidelines.

H.00540 National Commission on Correctional Health Care. (1992). *Standards for health services in prisons.* Chicago: National Commission on Correctional Health Care.

Presented in this document are the 68 standards of the National Commission on Correctional Health Care, i.e., the minimum requirements. for health services in prisons. Issues addressed are governance and administration, managing a safe and healthy environment, health promotion and disease prevention, special needs and services, personnel and training, health care services support, and inmate care and treatment.

H.00541 Weiner, J. & Anno, B. J. (1992). The crisis in correctional health care: The impact of the National Drug Control Strategy on correctional health services. *The Annals of Internal Medicine 117*, 71–77.

This article stems from a paper that received recognition from the American College of Physicians, the National Commission on Correctional Health Care, and the American Correctional Association. The researchers provide an analysis of the impact of the National Drug Control Strategy (NDCS) on correctional health services and offer recommendations for improvements in this area of health care.

Cases

H.00542 *Bell v. Wolfish*, 441 U.S. 520, 99 S.Ct. 1861, 60 L.Ed.2d 447 (1979)

This case was litigated when inmates of a short-term facility challenged the facility's double-celling procedure. The facility, designed to house pre-trial defendants, placed two inmates in a room that was designed to house one occupant. An important outcome of the case was that standards which are developed by professional associations are advisory and do not necessarily define what is minimally required by the Constitution.

H.00543 *Estelle v. Gamble*, 429 U.S. 97, 97 S.Ct. 285, 50 L.Ed.2d 251 (1976)

The Supreme Court ruled that "deliberate indifference" of prison officials or personnel to the serious medical needs of inmates constitutes cruel and unusual punishment, thus violating the Eighth Amendment. In this case the Court recognized that adequate health care is a right that must be extended to all inmates, that it is not a privilege which is subject to the discretion of correctional personnel.

HISTORY OF PRISONS

I. The Jacksonian Era

H.00544 Atherton, A. L. (1987). Journal retrospective: 1845–1986. *The Prison Journal 67*, 1–37.

In this article the author provides an overview of major issues confronting the Pennsylvania Prison Society and the Pennsylvania correctional system from 1845 to 1986.

H.00545 Fogel, D. (1975). *We are the living proof.* Cincinnati: Anderson.

Contained in this book are the author's recommendation for replacement of current correctional treatment models with a Justice in Administration model. According to the author, the "justice model" assures fair treatment to all prisoners.

H.00546 Foucault, M. (1977). *Discipline and punish: The birth of prisons* (trans. Alan Sheridan). New York: Pantheon.

Contained in this book is a historical analysis of punishment from the French perspective. The author describes the movement away from torture, beginning in the 17th century, and toward incarceration as punishment for criminal misconduct.

H.00547 Howard, J. (1977). *State of the prisons in England and Wales.* London: J.M. Dent.

Originally published in 1777, presented in this book are observations about conditions in English and Welsh jails and prisons.

H.00548 Rothman, D. J. (1971). *The discovery of the asylum: Social order and disorder in the New Republic.* Boston: Little, Brown and Co.

Contained in this book is a functionalist perspective on asylums and the social structure. Rothman proposes that society's institutions, whether social, political, or economic, cannot be understood apart from the society in which they exist. The author argues that asylums and society are interdependent, each supporting the other. Also discussed is the relationship between features of the medical model, such as diagnostics, and society's acceptance of asylums as appropriate facilities for those labeled deviant.

H.00549 Teeters, N. K. (1937). *They were in prison: A history of the Pennsylvania Prison Society, 1787–1937*. Philadelphia, PA: John C. Winston.

The book is a chronicle of the Pennsylvania prison system. The author discusses the main differences between the Auburn and Pennsylvania systems. This reference book contains excerpts from prison records.

II. The Progressive Era

H.00550 Adamson, C. (1984). Toward a Marxian penology: Captive criminal populations as economic threats and resources. *Social Problems 31*(4), 435–458.

This article is based on an analysis of penology in the United States during the 19th century. The author emphasizes the influence of business and the supply of labor on the development of penology.

H.00551 American Correctional Association. (1983). *The American prison: From the beginning: A pictorial history*. Laurel, MD: American Correctional Association.

Presented in this book is a pictorial history of American prisons. Short, descriptive narratives support each picture.

H.00552 Bartollas, C. & Conrad, J. P. (1992). *Introduction to corrections* (2d ed.). New York: HarperCollins Publishers.

Contained in this textbook is a comprehensive and objective overview of American corrections.

H.00553 Dean-Myrda, M. C. & Cullen, F. T. (1985). The panacea pendulum: An account of community as a response to crime. In L. F. Travis III, (ed.). *Probation, parole, and community corrections* (pp. 9–29). Prospect Heights, IL: Waveland.

Throughout the history of American correctional philosophy the concept of community has been prominent. Even so there has never been a consensus of whether community is within the larger society or within an institution or if community should be benign or punitive. The authors discuss the role of the community to corrections.

H.00554 Rothman, D. J. (1980). *Conscience and convenience: The asylum and its alternatives in progressive America*. Waltham, MA: Little, Brown and Co.

Contained in this book is an exploration of the origins and consequences of programs that dominated criminal justice, juvenile justice, and mental health in the 20th century. The author discusses the similarities between penitentiaries and state mental institutions, demonstrating that both are asylums in the United States.

H.00555 Shane-DuBow, S., Brown, A. P. & Olsen, E. (1985). *Sentencing reform in the United States: Histories, content, and effect.* Washington, DC: Government Printing Office.

The authors present a review of the major changes in State sentencing statutes that occurred between 1971 and 1982.

H.00556 Sullivan, L. E. (1990). *The prison reform movement: Forlorn hope.* Boston: Twayne Publishers.

The author traces the prison reform movement from its origins in the late nineteenth century through the 1980s. Included are discussions of the Age of Progressive Reform, riot and rebellion, the decline of treatment programs, inmate violence and revolt, and the current philosophy of repression.

III. The Modern Era: 1960 to the Present

H.00557 Bureau of Justice Statistics. (1992). *Prisoners in 1991.* Washington, DC: U.S. Department of Justice.

This government publication contains inmate statistics for 1991. The data is based on a census of inmates in American prisons.

H.00558 Bureau of Justice Statistics. (1993). *Survey of state prison inmates in 1991.* Washington, DC: U.S. Department of Justice.

Provided in this government publication is statistical information on individuals incarcerated in American prisons. The data were collected in lengthy interviews with prisoners. The report is a valuable resource containing profiles of the nation's prisoners and the crimes they committed.

H.00559 Camp, G. M. and Camp, C. G. (1993). *The Corrections Yearbook 1993.* South Salem, NY: Criminal Justice Institute.

Contained in this annual publication arestatistics on offenders and practitioners in adult corrections. Also provided is a population profile for the United States and Canadian adult correctional system as well as statistical data on administration and staff. The data reported in this volume were obtained through surveys that were mailed to State and

Federal adult correctional agencies in the United States and the Correctional Service of Canada.

H.00560 Murton, T. O. (1976). *The dilemma of prison reform.* New York: Holt, Rinehart and Winston.

In this book the author examines the role and nature of corrections in the United States. Also explored is the nature of reform movements and why prison reform has not been attained. Many of the author's personal experiences as a prison administrator are shared. Those relating to his experiences in the Arkansas Department of Corrections are especially compelling.

H.00561 Nagel, W. G. (1973). *The new red barn: A critical look at the modern American prison.* New York: Walker.

The author provides a comprehensive overview of state of the art physical designs for correctional facilities. Included are critical discussions by architects, psychologists, social scientists and correctional administrators, about how physical design meets the needs of treatment, rehabilitation, and security.

H.00562 Sykes, G. M. (1958). *Society of captives: A study of a maximum security prison.* Princeton: Princeton University Press, (reprinted, 1971).

This book is based on a classic study of a maximum security prison from a sociological perspective. The researcher examined the prison's organizational dysfunctions and their consequent effects.

Cases

H.00563 *Bell v. Wolfish,* 441 U.S. 520, 99 S.Ct. 1861, 60 L.Ed.2d 447 (1979)

This case was litigated when inmates of a short-term facility challenged the facility's double-celling procedure. The facility, designed to house pre-trial defendants, placed two inmates in a room that was designed to house one occupant. An important legal principle established by the case is that standards developed by professional associations are advisory and do not necessarily define what is minimally required by the Constitution.

H.00564 *Ruffin v. Commonwealth,* 62 Va. (21 Grat.) 790, 796 (1871)

As a result of this case, the Court recognized that inmates do not have the same rights as free citizens. In fact, the Court found that inmates not only forfeit their liberty, but all personal rights except those accorded by law.

According to the Court, inmates are 'slaves' of the state.

H.00565 *Ruiz v. Estelle*, 503 F. Supp. 1265 (S.D. Texas, 1980), Cert. denied, 103 Ct. 1438

This case, brought by inmate Ruiz, became the most comprehensive civil action in correctional law. The plaintiff alleged that the Texas Department of Corrections had unconstitutionally exposed prisoners to physically deteriorated, dangerous, and overcrowded conditions, the court concurred.

H.00566 *Wolff v. McDonnell*, 418 US 539, 94 S.Ct. 2963, 41 L.Ed.2d 935 (1974)

In this 6-to-3 decision, the Court held that the 'due process clause' of the 14 Amendment provides inmates with procedural protection if they are facing a loss of good time or confinement because of an institutional disciplinary action. Some of the specific procedural requirements are advance written notice of charges, written explanation of the findings, and opportunities to call witnesses and to present case.

HOMICIDE

H.00567 Abbott, J. (1991). *In the belly of the beast: Letters from prison*. New York: Vintage Books/Random House.

This book is a chronicle of the author's life in prison. It is based on letters written by the author, a convicted murderer, to Norman Mailer. The letters contain details about the author's home life as a child, personal experiences in a juvenile correctional institution beginning at the age of 12, as well as the impact of incarceration as an adult. A common theme in all these experiences is the presence of violence and how, in the author's opinion, it negatively impacted his life.

H.00568 Braswell, M., Dillingham, S. & Montgomery, R. (1985). *Prison violence in America*. Cincinnati: Anderson.

Presented in this book are several perspectives on prison violence. In the book's eleven chapters the authors describe some of the more common types and causes of prison violence. They also offer prevention and coping strategies for administrative consideration.

H.00569 Earle, W. (as told to). (1992). *Final truth: The autobiography of mass murder/serial killer, Donald "Pee Wee" Gaskins*. Atlanta: Adept.

In this book serial killer Donald Gaskins tells his life story and discusses how and why he killed dozens of people.

H.00570 Fox, V. (1972). Prison riots in a Democratic society. *Police 16*, 33–41.

Contained in this article is an analysis of the development patterns in prison riots, including the role of violence in riots. The author also presents the results of a survey of the public's reaction to the Attica riot.

H.00571 Herrick, E. (1989). The surprising direction of violence in prison. *Corrections Today 14*, 1, 4–17.

This article is based on a survey conducted to measure violence in prisons in the United States. The author concluded that violent deaths in prison dropped between 1984 and 1988, but that physical assaults on staff increased.

H.00572 Ralph, P. H. & Marquart, J. W. (1992). Gang violence in Texas prisons. *The Prison Journal 71*(2), 38–49.

Detailed in this article is the history of inmate gangs and gang violence in Texas prisons. The authors discuss the Texas Department of Corrections' current strategy of administrative segregation of gang members and its impact on gang violence.

H.00573 Rochman, S. (1991). Alternatives to prison violence. *Corrections Compendium 16*(6), 1, 6–8.

This article, reprinted from the *Ithica, New York Times,* is a description of how the Alternatives to Violence Project (AVP) was employed to curb rising levels of violence. The first AVP program was started in 1975 at the Green Haven Correctional Facility in Stormville, New York. AVP programs are currently operating in approximately 30 percent of the prisons in New York state.

H.00574 Stone, W. G. (1982). *The hate factory*. Agoura, CA: Dell Publishing.

Chronicled in this book is the author's eyewitness account of the riot at the New Mexico State Penitentiary on February 2, 1980. The author, an inmate in the prison, provides a vivid description of the violence that contributed to the 33 deaths during the 36 hour riot.

I

ILLEGAL IMMIGRANTS IN PRISON

I.00575 Bureau of Justice Statistics. (1993). *Survey of state prison inmates, 1991.* Washington, DC: U.S. Department of Justice.

Provided in this government publication is statistical information for individuals incarcerated in American prisons. The data were collected in lengthy interviews with prisoners. The report is a valuable resource that contains profiles of the nation's prisoners and the crimes they committed as well as statistical information on illegal immigrant offenders.

I.00576 McShane, M. D. (1987). Immigration processing and the alien inmate: Constructing a conflict perspective. *Journal of Crime and Justice 10*(1), 171–194.

Contained in this article is an analysis of the handling of illegal immigrants in correctional institutions in the United States. The author demonstrates the benefits of focusing on structural factors rather than process factors when conducting conflict-oriented research.

INDETERMINATE SENTENCES

I.00577 Alschuler, A. W. (1978). Sentencing reform and prosecutorial power: A critique of recent proposals for 'fixed' and 'presumptive' sentencing. *University of Pennsylvania Law Review 126*(3), 550–577.

Presented in this law review article is an examination of sentencing reform issues. The author notes that most sentencing reforms occur with little or no consideration given to decisions that are made prior to sentencing. For example, the prosecutor's discretion in charging the defendant and in plea bargaining. According to the author this area of discretion provides opportunities to circumvent the 'presumptive' sentence.

I.00578 Cullen, F. T. & Gilbert, K. E. (1982). *Reaffirming rehabilitation.* Cincinnati: Anderson Publishing.

In this book, the authors criticize the present movement to eliminate rehabilitation programs from prisons and institute the 'justice model' with its attendant presumptive sentencing. Their conclusions stem from an analysis of the classical and positivist schools of criminology, 'justice model,' problems caused by determinate sentencing, and effects of new sentencing laws.

I.00579 Glaser, D. (1985). Who gets probation and parole: Case study versus actuarial decision making. *Crime and Delinquency 31*(3), 367–378.

In this article the author presents the results of his analysis of two methods which are used to decide suitability for probation or parole. The methods are actuarial tables, which are based on risk-prediction formulas, and case studies. The author concludes that risk prediction scores, based on actuarial tables, are more accurate than case studies in predicting future risk of recidivism.

I.00580 Griset, P. L. (1991). *Determinate sentencing: The promise and the reality of retributive justice.* Albany, NY: State University of New York Press.

Contained in this book is the author's investigation of the "myth of determinate sentencing." The author questions the reality of determinate sentencing by addressing the following questions, what happens when a sentencing model ignores crime control purposes of the criminal sanction and fails to allocate sentencing authority among criminal justice decision makers and what has happened to the determinate sentencing model?

I.00581 Morris, N. & Tonry, M. (1990). *Between prison and probation: Intermediate punishments in a rational sentencing system.* New York: Oxford University Press.

In this book the authors discuss the need for a system of intermediate punishments. They suggest that the current options of either imprisonment or probation do not provide enough choice. They support the development of intermediate punishments which they say could provide rational alternatives to the two extremes of probation and prison.

INDUSTRY

I. History

I.00582 American Correctional Association. (1986). *A study of prison industry: History, components, and goals.* U.S. Department of Justice, National Institute of Corrections. Washington, DC: U.S. Government Printing Office.

This report is based on data that the American Correctional Association collected from 39 federal, state, and Canadian jurisdictions through mailed surveys. The study was conducted to examine the evolution, goals, components, and organizational approaches of prison industries.

I.00583 Cullen F. & Travis, L. F. (1984). Work as an avenue of prison reform. *New England Journal of Criminal and Civil Confinement 10 (Winter)*, 45–64.

In this article an overview of work as a rehabilitative tool is presented. The authors believe that prisoners should work for decent wages while in prison. The researchers suggest that this ideal should be pursued by correctional administrators because it promotes the work ethic and contributes to the social order in a positive way, for both prisoners and custodial staff.

I.00584 Flanagan, T. (1989). Prison labor and industry. In L. Goodstein and D. L. MacKenzie (eds.), *The American prison: Issues in research and policy.* New York: Plenum Press.

This edited book chapter contains the author's cautions with regard to renewed interest in prison labor programs. The author argues that prison labor offers many benefits for the total correctional community, including the offenders, the correctional system, and society. However, the author suggests that in order to ensure the success and acceptability of prison work programs, policy makers need to carefully examine past mistakes, present limitations, and reasonable expectations of prison labor programs.

I.00585 Funke, G.S., Wayson, B.L. & Miller, N. (1982). *Assets and liabilities of correctional industries.* Lexington, MA: D.C. Heath and Company.

Contained in this book is a thorough discussion of prison industries. The authors' pro and con approach to the subject stems from the following perspectives: historical, economic, philosophical, and legal. Included in their discussion are recommendations regarding prison industry programs.

I.00586 Hawkins, G. (1983). Prison labor and prison industries. In M. Tonry and N. Morris (eds.), *Crime and justice: An annual review of research* (Vol. 5). Chicago: University of Chicago Press.

This chapter, in an edited volume, contains the author's views on prison labor and prison industries. The author addresses the negative impact that the 'principle of less eligibility' has on the development and implementation of prison industries.

I.00587 Hiller, E. T. (1914). Labor unionism and convict labor. *Journal of Criminal Law and Criminology 5*, 851–879.

Discussions about convict labor and how it relates to competition of free labor are presented in this article. The author explains labor unions' arguments against the use of convict labor in prison industry.

I.00588 Lewis, W. D. (1965). *From Newgate to Dannemora: The rise of the penitentiary in New York, 1796–1848*. Ithaca, NY: Cornell University Press.

In this book is an overview of the history of penology in the state of New York. The author explains the process through which the New York prison system evolved, from mild correctional practices to a harsh and repressive system. The changing role of prison industry is also discussed.

I.00589 McKelvey, B. (1935). The prison labor problem: 1875–1900. *Journal of Criminal Law and Criminology 25*, 254–271.

Contained in this article is a historical account of prison labor from 1875 through 1900. The author places primary emphasis on legislation regarding prison labor during this period.

I.00590 McKelvey, B. (1936). *American prisons: A history of good intentions*. Chicago: University of Chicago Press. (Reprinted, Montclair, NJ: Patterson Smith, 1968, 1977).

Presented in this book is a historical account of the American prison system from 1835 through 1977. The author presents detailed information on changing standards, reform movements, criminological theories, and confrontations in penology. Included in the material is a discussion of the inmate lease system.

I.00591 Miller, M. B. (1980). At hard labor: Rediscovering the 19th century prison. In T. Platt and P. Takagi (eds.), *Punishment and penal discipline*.

Berkeley, CA: Crime and Social Justice.

In this edited book chapter is a description of the evolution of prison labor. The author examines the administrative practices surrounding work in prison, including using work as punishment.

I.00592 Mohler, H. C. (1924). Convict labor policies. *Journal of Criminal Law and Criminology 15*, 530–597.

The author presents a comprehensive overview of convict labor in the United States in this article. Included is a historical account of the evolution of convict labor policies, a survey of the principal systems of convict employment, a review of convict labor in the United States before the Civil War, a description of the leasing system, an analysis of organized labor's objections to convict labor, and a summary of the progress of convict labor since 1900.

I.00593 Teeters, N. K. (1955). *The cradle of the penitentiary: The Walnut Street Jail at Philadelphia, 1773–1835*. Philadelphia, PA: Pennsylvania Society.

In this book the author provides a historical account of the development of the Walnut Street Jail in Philadelphia. The author examines the reforms that lead to the jail becoming a prison. The time period examined is 1773 to 1835.

I.00594 Wines, E. C. & Dwight, T. W. (1867). *Report on the prisons and reformatories of the United States and Canada*. Albany, NY: Van Benthuysen and Sons' Steam Printing House. (Reprinted, New York: AMS, 1973).

The authors visited and studied the prisons and reformatories of 18 northern states and Canada in 1866. The authors discovered many deficiencies such as prisons being part of the political machinery of the state, the incarceration of youths with hardened criminals, and the lack of positive rehabilitation and reward. The authors presented their findings and recommendations to the New York Legislature in 1867.

I.00595 Wines, F.H. (1910). *Punishment and reformation: A study of the penitentiary system*. New York: Thomas Y. Crowell Company. (Reprinted, New York: AMS, 1919, 1975).

This book, compiled from a series of lectures the author gave at the University of Wisconsin in the 1890s, chronicles changes in the law that reflect a reformatory approach toward criminals during the nineteenth century. Discussed is, what constitutes crime, retribution and punishment, mental factors and delinquency, treatment programs, inmate self-government, and a look at what will evolve in the future.

II. Current Programs

I.00596 Criminal Justice Associates. (1985). *Private sector involvement in prison–based businesses: A national assessment*. Rockville, MD: National Institute of Justice/National Criminal Justice Reference Service.

Identified in this book are the strengths and weaknesses of current private sector involvement in prison-based businesses. The authors collected their data using mail surveys, site visits, and statute reviews.

I.00597 Flanagan, T. J. (1989). Prison labor and industry. In L. Goodstein and D. L. MacKenzie (eds.), *The American prison: Issues in research and policy* (pp.135–161). New York: Plenum Press.

Contained in this edited book chapter are the author's cautions with regard to renewed interest in prison labor programs. The author argues that prison labor offers many benefits for the total correctional community, including the offenders, the correctional system, and society. However, the author suggests that in order to ensure the success and acceptability of prison work programs, policy makers need to carefully examine past mistakes, present limitations, and reasonable expectations of prison labor programs.

I.00598 Logan, C. H. (1990). *Private prisons: Cons and pros*. New York: Oxford University Press.

Discussed this article are the positive and negative attributes of privatization of prisons. In this critical examination, the author suggests that comparisons of privately run facilities with government operated facilities, must include the following, propriety, cost, quality, quantity, flexibility, security, liability, accountability, corruption, and dependence. Above all, the author suggests, that one must insure that the overall goal of any plan is to provide a safe, humane, efficient and just system.

I.00599 Miller, R., Sexton, G. E. and Jacobsen, V. J. (1991). *Making jails productive: Research in brief*. Rockville, MD: National Institute of Justice, National Criminal Justice Reference Service.

This government publication stems from the Jail Industries Initiatives. The authors report that the initiatives resulted in many innovative and creative correctional programs which reduced violence in prison and defrayed the cost of incarceration by engaging prisoners in work programs.

I.00600 Sexton, G. E., Farrow, F. C. & Auerbach, B. J. (1985). *The private sector and prison industries*. Washington, DC: National Institute of Justice.

Contained in this government report is a summary of a survey of private sector involvement in prison industries. The authors provide 1) examples of how the private sector is involved in prison industry, 2) details on how private firms can participate in prison industry, and 3)recommendations for prison officials when designing such plans.

INMATE SELF-GOVERNANCE

I.00601 Baker, J. E. (1974). *The right to participate: Inmate involvement in prison administration*. Metuchen, NJ: Scarecrow Press.

Contained in this book is a historical account of inmate involvement in the administration of prisons. The author bases this analysis of inmate participatory management on assessment of participatory management in correctional facilities from 1793 to 1973.

I.00602 Baker, J. E. (1977). Inmate self-government and the right to participate. In R. M. Carter, D. Glaser and L. T. Wilkins (eds.), *Correctional institutions* (2nd ed.).

Included in this edited book chapter is an examination of past experiments and experiences of inmate self-government. The author includes the views of present correctional facility administrators on inmate self-government.

I.00603 Burdman, M. (1974) Ethnic self-help groups in prison and on parole. *Crime and Delinquency 20*, 39–47.

An evaluation of the relationship between ethnic self-help groups and broader social movements is presented in this article. The author discusses the results of an examination of ethnic self-help groups that assist inmates in prison and parolees on parole.

I.00604 Fox, J. G. (1982). *Organizational and Racial Conflict in Maximum Security Prisons*. Lexington, MA: Lexington Books.

This book is based on the author's study of racial and organizational conflicts in five state maximum security prisons. The researcher collected attitudinal data about racial conflicts from prison administrators, guards, and inmates.

I.00605 Helfman, H. M. (1950). Antecedents of Thomas Mott Osborne's mutual welfare league in Michigan. *Journal of Criminal Law, Criminology, and Police Science 40*, 597–600.

In this article the author presents historical data to support the argument that nineteenth century developments in the penal administration of the Detroit House of Correction and the Michigan State Prison are the origins of the concept of inmate self-government.

I.00606 Huff, C. R. (1974). Unionization behind prison walls. *Criminology 12*, 597–600.

The author of this article presents thorough discussion and description of unionization in prison. Specifically addressed are the following topics: history of the movement, goals and objectives of inmates, legal issues, and reactions of the administration.

I.00607 Kasinsky, R. G. (1977). A critique of sharing power in the total institution. *Prison Journal 57(Autumn/Winter)*, 56–61.

In this article, the author discusses three models of participatory management. Included in the discussion are prison reform programs which exemplify each model, and the basic objectives of democratic decision making.

I.00608 Murton, T. (1971). Inmate self-government. *University of San Francisco Law Review 6*(October), 87–101.

In this article the author presents an overview of inmate self-government. Included in the presentation is the medical model, prison management, the inmate as a change agent, the democratic model, management of Tucker State Prison Farm, and the inmate as healer.

I.00609 Murton, T. & Baunach, P. J. (1975). *Shared decision-making as a treatment technique in prison management.* New York: Haworth Press.

Contained in this book are the results of a one-year study where use and effects of participatory management in prison were examined. Evaluated was inmate participatory management in prisons in the United States.

I.00610 Osborne, T. M. (1917). Self-government by the prisoner. Part I –
Self-government in a state prison. In J. K. Jaffray (ed.), *The prison and
the prisoner: A symposium* (pp. 99–106). Boston: Little, Brown and
Company.

The author spent a week incarcerated in Auburn to study the system and
the methods used by the prison administration to govern its inmates. The
author found that the 'good conduct league,' made up of prisoners, was
an effective tool in managing the prisoners because it allowed the
prisoners a voice in how the institution was run.

I.00611 Scharf, P. & Hickey, J. (1977). Thomas Mott Osborne and the limits of
democratic prison reform. *Prison Journal 57(Autum/Winter)*, 3–15.

In this article the authors describe the evolution of the mutual welfare
league at Sing Sing prison.

INMATE SUPERVISION: NEW GENERATION PHILOSOPHY

I.00612 Farbstein, J. & Wener, R. E. (1989). *A comparison of "direct" and
"indirect" supervision correctional facilities, final report.* Washington,
DC: National Institute of Corrections.

In this publication are the results of a comparative study of direct and
indirect supervision in correctional institutions. Data were collected
via a mail survey and case studies of direct and indirect supervision in jails
and prisons. The two approaches were compared on the basis of cost,
impact on staff, safety and security, inmate behavior in relationship to the
physical environment, design issues, and overcrowding.

I.00613 Jackson, P. G. (1992). *Detention in transition: Sonoma County's new
generation jail.* Washington, DC: National Institute of Corrections.

Using inmate and staff questionnaires the author determines how well
Sonoma County's (California) new 1.5 million-dollar, podular style, direct
supervision facility is working.

I.00614 Johnson, B. R. (1994). Exploring direct supervision: A research note.
American Jails 8(1), 63–64.

Reported in this article are the author's findings from a survey of 43
administrators of direct-supervision facilities. In general, the results
indicate considerable support among new-generation jail administrators

for the direct-supervision approach. One of the strongest arguments supporting this approach is that it helped to reduce stress for both inmates and staff as well as the amount of inmate-on-inmate violence.

I.00615 Lovrich, N. P. & Associates. (1991). *Staff turnover and* stress *in new generation jails*: Key implementation issues for a significant correctional policy innovation, final report. Washington, DC: National Institute of Corrections.

Presented in this report are the results of a personnel survey in which issues and attributes associated with staff turnover were assessed. Among the issues examined were salary, organizational commitment, promotion opportunities, and job satisfaction. The data were collected from New Generation Jail personnel.

I.00616 Nelson, W. R., O'Toole, M., Krauth, B. & Whitemore, C. G. (1983). *New generation jails*. Boulder, CO: Library Information Specialists.

Contained in this book is a comprehensive review of new generation jails in the United States. The authors compare "podular/direct supervision" jail designs and management to the concepts of "linear/intermittent surveillance" and "podular/remote surveillance." They also present an overview of the principles of "podular/direct surveillance," discuss its growing acceptance by correctional administrators, and suggest its implications for correctional planning.

I.00617 Senese, J. D., Wilson, J., Evans, A. O., Aquirre, R. & Kalinich, D. (1992). Evaluating inmate infractions and disciplinary response in a traditional and a podular/direct supervision jail. *American Jails 6*(4), 14–23.

In this research article the researchers report the effects of inmate management and control in a traditional jail and a podular/direct supervision jail. The focus of their analysis is on inmate rule violations. Two important conclusions were derived. First, correctional officers in the podular/direct supervision jail wrote up only the most serious rule violations and second, there was an overall reduction in inmate violence and contraband.

I.00618 Zupan, L. L. (1991). *Jails: Reform and the new generation philosophy*. Cincinnati: Anderson Publishing Co.

Contained in this book is an overview of new generation jail reform. The author discusses how the new generation, "podular/direct supervision," jail philosophy is implemented in the architectural design and inmate management style of jails. Also addressed is how the quality of life within the institution, for both the inmates and staff, is influenced by such reform.

I.00619 Zupan, L. L. (1993, March-April). The need for research on direct inmate supervision. *American Jails: The Magazine of the American Jail Association*, 21-22.

In this article, the author presents arguments for research of second generation correctional facilities. Aguments supoorting the research are that direct supervision facilities have changed the dynamics of incarceration, billions of dollars have been spent on the model, and little or no scientific research exists in which the model has been evaluated.

Cases

I.00620 *Cooper v. Pate*, 378 U.S. 546, 84 S.Ct. 1733, 12 L.Ed.2d 1030 (1964)

In this case the Court determined that Section 1983 Civil Rights violation cases can be filed by state prisoners who can articulate clear constitutional claims against state officials or employees.

I.00621 *Estelle v. Gamble*, 429 U.S. 97, 97 S.Ct. 285, 50 L.Ed.2d 251 (1976)

The Supreme Court ruled that "deliberate indifference" of prison officials or personnel to the serious medical needs of inmates constitutes cruel and unusual punishment, thus violating the Eighth Amendment.

I.00622 *Holt v. Sarver*, 442 F.2d 308 (8th Cir. 1971)

In this case Arkansas prisoners alleged savage treatment and inhumane conditions. The Federal Court declared the entire Arkansas State Prison system to be in violation of the Eighth Amendment.

I.00623 *Wolff v. McDonnell*, 418 US 539, 94 S.Ct. 2963, 41 L.Ed.2d 935 (1974)

In this 6-to-3 decision, the Court held that the due process clause of the 14 Amendment provides inmates with procedural protection if they are facing a loss of good time or confinement because of an institutional disciplinary action. Some of the specific procedural requirements are, advance written notice of charges, written statement explaining the findings, and opportunities to call witnesses and present case.

INTERSTATE COMPACT AGREEMENT

I.00624 Abadinsky, H. (1991). *Probation and parole: Theory and practice.* Englewood Cliffs, NJ: Prentice Hall.

Contained in this textbook is an overview of probation and parole in the United States, including a historical account, as well as the current functions of these practices. The author presents a thorough discussion of the interstate compact agreement.

I.00625 Cromwell, P. & Killinger, G. (1994). *Community-based corrections: Probation, parole, and intermediate sanctions,* 3rd ed. St. Paul, MN: West.

In this textbook the authors present a thorough discussion of the relationship between interstate compacts and probation. They describe the more significant problems associated with interstate compact agreements for offenders on probation.

I.00626 Ferdico, J. N. (1992). *Ferdico's criminal law and justice dictionary.* New York: West Publishing Company.

This book is a legal dictionary. It consists of criminal law and justice terms and definitions, including interstate compact agreement.

I.00627 McShane, M. D. & Krause, W. (1993). *Community corrections.* New York: Macmillan Publishing Company.

Provided in this textbook is an overview of community corrections in the United States. The authors address such topics as probation, parole, and other community-based alternatives. They also provide a thorough discussion of the interstate compact agreement.

J

JAILHOUSE LAWYERS

J.00628 Aylward, A. & Thomas, J. (1984). Quiescence in women's prison litigation: Some exploratory gender issues. *Justice Quarterly 1*, 253–276.

Presented in this research article are the results of an examination of prison litigation for gender differences. The authors found that in spite of female inmates being subjected to poor living conditions, overcrowding, little job training, disciplinary problems and an unbalanced representation of racial minorities, they filed lawsuits significantly less often than their male counterparts. The authors also addressed the role of jailhouse lawyers in penal institutions.

J.00629 Jacobs, J. J. (1979). *Individual rights and institutional authority: Prisons, mental hospitals, schools, and military*. Indianapolis, IN: Michie/Bobbs-Merrill Co., Inc.

Contained in this book is an overview of federal court decisions, research notes, and other materials that express legal rights of individuals and institutions such as prisons, mental hospitals, schools, and the military. The role of the jailhouse lawyer is explained.

J.00630 Thomas, J. (1988). *Prisoner litigation: The paradox of the jailhouse lawyer*. Totowa, NJ: Rowman and Littlefield.

A comprehensive assessment of jailhouse lawyers is presented in this book. The author examines the claim that prisoner lawsuits are basically frivolous. Thomas admits that the number of prisoner lawsuits have increased, but also acknowledges that many of these suits are not frivolous and that the courts are not "soft" on prisoners. In the second part of the book, Thomas describes prisoners, their attitudes regarding lawsuits, and life in prison as it relates to lawsuits.

Cases

J.00631 *Bounds v. Smith*, 430 U.S. 817 (1977)

In this case the Court determined that prison officials are obligated to establish either a legal services program or a law library even when prison policy permits mutual legal assistance among inmates. The legal services program and law library are essential to meet the needs of the inmate population.

J.00632 *Ex parte Hull*, 312 U.S. 546 (1940)

An inmate sued, alleging that his constitutional rights were violated by a prison regulation which required that prison officials review all legal documents of inmates before they are filed with the court. The Supreme Court found the prison regulation to be unconstitutional.

J.00633 *Johnson v. Avery*, 393 U.S. 483 (1969)

The legal principle established in this case is that jailhouse lawyers must be permitted to assist other inmates with filing habeas corpus petitions unless the state provides other reasonable assistance to the inmates.

J.00634 *Ruffin v. Commonwealth*, 62 Va. (21 Grat.) 790, 796 (1871)

As a result of this case, the Court recognized that inmates do not have the same rights as free citizens. In fact, the Court found that inmates not only forfeit their liberty, but all personal rights except those accorded by law. According to the Court, inmates are 'slaves' of the state.

J.00635 *Smith v. Rowe*, 761 F.2d 360 (7th Cir. 1985)

In this case the Court upheld a jury verdict in favor of a prisoner who refused to accept a new job assignment because her removal from the assistant prison librarian position was wrongfully terminated. The prison was ordered to reinstate her.

JUDICIAL INTERVENTION

J.00636 Chilton, B. S. (1991). *Prisons under the gavel: The Federal Court* *takeover of Georgia Prisons.* Columbus, OH: Ohio State University Press.

This book is based on a case study of the Georgia Prison system. The author provides a concise, descriptive account of the lawsuits filed against the system and the years of monitoring by the courts.

J.00637 Cooper, P. J. (1988). *Hard judicial choices: Federal District Court judges and state and local officials.* New York: Oxford University Press.

Provided by this book is insight into the sometimes strained relationship between federal district court judges and state and local prison officials.

J.00638 Crouch, B. M. & Marquart, J. W. (1989). *An appeal to justice: Litigated reform of Texas prisons.* Austin, TX: University of Texas Press.

In this book the authors describe how the Texas Department of Corrections (TDC) was transformed by the decision in *Ruiz v. Estelle,* one of the most sweeping class–action suits in correctional law. Data for the study were collected using archival resources and personal interviews with hundreds of prisoners, administrators, and correctional staff. One of the many issues litigated was the TDC's use of inmates as building tenders (inmate guards) to police housing facilities.

J.00639 DiIulio, J. J., Jr. ed. (1990). *Courts, corrections and the Constitution: The impact of judicial intervention on prisons and jails.* New York: Oxford Press.

Presented in this edited book are submissions from fourteen academic and practicing social scientists and lawyers. Topics discussed include judicial intervention in the administration of prisons and jails. Detailed case studies of judicial intervention in state prison systems in Texas, Georgia, West Virginia, New Jersey and in the New York City jails is presented. The contributors provide a review of the research literature on intervention.

J.00640 Fiss, O. M. (1979). The Supreme Court, 1978 term – foreword: The forms of justice. *Harvard Law Review 93*(1), 1–58.

The author discusses the cases considered and decisions rendered by the United States Supreme Court during the 1978 term. Included in the discussion are judicial intervention cases from prison and jail systems in the United States.

J.00641 Fuller, L. (1978). The forms and limits of adjudication. *Harvard Law Review 92*, 353–409.

Contained in this law review article is an examination of the types and limitations of adjudication. The author specifically addresses judicial intervention in a broad framework that includes the concepts of social order, rationality, and rule of law.

J.00642 Harris, M. K. & Spiller, D. P. (1976). *After decision: Implementation of judicial decrees in correctional settings.* Washington, DC: American Bar Association.

Contained in this book are the results of a debate about the effectiveness of prisoner litigation as a method of generating social change. The authors conclude that the value of judicial intervention as a means of affecting social change depends on who one asks.

J.00643 Harvard Center for Criminal Justice. (1972). Judicial intervention in prison discipline. *Journal of Criminal Law and Criminology 63*, 200–228.

In this article the results of an examination of the fairness of judicial intervention in prison disciplinary hearings is presented. Fairness of judicial intervention is evaluated by examining the court's effectiveness in guiding administrative decision-making.

J.00644 Jacobs, J. B. (1977). *Stateville: The penitentiary in mass society.* Chicago: University of Chicago Press.

The author presents a historical overview of the Stateville Maximum Security Penitentiary in Chicago, Illinois. Beginning with its construction in 1925 through the judicial intervention in the late 1960s and early 1970s, the author presents a look at all phases of prison life, including inmates and staff perspectives.

J.00645 Jacobs, J. B. (1980). The prisoner's rights movement and its impact, In N. Morris and M. Tonry (eds.), *Crime and justice: An annual review of research*, Volume 2. Chicago: The University of Chicago Press.

In this edited book chapter the author presents a comprehensive overview of the relationship between judicial intervention and the prisoner's rights movement. The author discusses how the movement has impacted the administration of prisons. Also discussed is the significance of judicial intervention to society as a whole.

J.00646 Martin, S. J. & Ekland-Olson, S. (1987). *Texas prisons: The walls came tumbling down*. Austin, TX: Texas Monthly Press.

The authors of this book provide the reader with a practical example of judicial intervention, i.e. the period of time that the Texas Department of Corrections was under court order. The authors provide an analysis of the personalities and events that were involved in the Court's reform of the Texas prison system from 1967 through 1987. Generally addressed in the book are the changes brought about by *Ruiz v. Estelle*.

J.00647 Yackle, L. W. (1989). *Reform and regret: The story of federal judicial involvement in the Alabama Prison System*. New York: Oxford University Press.

Provided in this book is a detailed history of prison reform in the Alabama prison system. The reform is a direct result of judicial intervention. The author discusses the strengths and weaknesses of the reform effort.

Cases

J.00648 *Cooper v. Pate*, 378 U.S. 546, 84 S.Ct. 1773, 12 L.Ed.2d 1030 (1964)

In this Section 1983 Civil Rights case the Court determined that suits can be filed by state prisoners who can articulate clear constitutional claims against state officials or employees.

J.00649 *Holt v. Sarver*, 309 F.Supp. 362 (1970).

In this case Arkansas prisoners alleged savage treatment and inhumane conditions. The Federal Court agreed with the inmates' suit and declared the entire Arkansas State Prison system to be in violation of the Eighth Amendment.

J.00650 *Monroe v. Pape*, 365 U.S. 167, 81 S.Ct. 473, 5 L.Ed.2d 492 (1961)

In this case the Supreme Court ruled that citizens can bring Section 1983 law suits against the state officials in Federal Courts without first exhausting state judicial remedies.

J.00651 *Morris v. Travisono*, 310 F.Supp 857 (1970)

The Rhode Island prison's disciplinary and classifications systems were challenged in this case. The Court provided specific guidelines for the prison system to follow in its classification procedures and disciplinary policies.

J.00652 Palmigiano v. Garrahy, 443 F.Supp 956 (1977)

This is a class action suit, filed for prisoners and pretrial detainees, alleging that confinement conditions at the Rhode Island prison system violated the eighth and fourteenth amendments. The Court concluded that the "totality of conditions of confinement . . . do not provide a tolerable living environment."

J.00653 *Pugh v. Locke*, 406 F.Supp. 318 (M.D.Ala. 1976)

The Court determined that Classification Systems should be used to protect inmates from assaults. Specifically, inmates who pose a risk for homosexual behavior should be identified in the classification process and assigned in an effort to limit assaults in prison.

J.00654 *Ruffin v. Commonwealth*, 62 Va. (21 Grat.) 790, 796 (1871)

As a result of this case, the Court recognized that inmates do not have the same rights as free citizens. In fact, the Court found that inmates not only forfeit their liberty, but all personal rights except those accorded by law. According to the Court, inmates are 'slaves' of the state.

J.00655 *Ruiz v. Estelle*, 503 F. Supp. 1265 (S.D. Texas, 1980), Cert. denied, 103 Ct. 1438

This case, brought by inmate Ruiz, became the most comprehensive civil action in correctional law. The plaintiff alleged that the Texas Department of Corrections had unconstitutionally exposed prisoners to physically deteriorated, dangerous, and overcrowded conditions, the Court concurred.

J.00656 *Wolff v. McDonnell*, 418 US 539, 94 S.Ct. 2963, 41 L.Ed.2d 935 (1974)

In this 6-to-3 decision, the Court held that the due process clause of the 14 Amendment provides inmates with procedural protection if they are facing a loss of good time or confinement because of an institutional disciplinary action. Some of the specific procedural requirements are, advance written notice of charges, written statement by fact finders explaining the findings, and opportunity to call witness and present case.

L

LEASE SYSTEM

l.00657 Ayers, E. L. (1984). *Vengeance and justice: Crime and punishment in the 19th-century in the American South.* New York: Oxford University Press.

The author presents his work into two parts: antebellum criminal justice and crime and punishment in the South from the beginning of the Civil War until about 1900. His discussion of southern criminal justice encompasses the social and cultural influences of the time. Of particular note is a thorough discussion of the plantation model for leasing inmates, a model pioneered by southern rural prisons.

L.00658 McConville, S. (1981). *A history of English prison administration, Volume I 1750–1877.* London: Routledge and Kegan Paul.

Using the Prison Commission Files of the Public Record Office and Prison Blue Books, the author has written a thorough history of the English prison system from 1750 to 1877. Inmate lease systems are described.

L.00659 McKelvey, B. (1936). *American prisons: A history of good intentions.* Chicago: University of Chicago Press. (Reprinted, Montclair, NJ: Patterson Smith, 1968, 1977).

Contained in this book is a historical account of the American prison system from 1835 through 1977. The author presents detailed information on changing standards, reform movements, criminological theories, and confrontations in penology. Included in the material is a discussion of the inmate lease systems.

L.00660 Melossi, D. and Pavarini, M. (1981). *The prison and the factory: Origins of the penitentiary system* (G. Cousin, Trans.). London: Macmillan.

The authors discuss the development of the prison as a social institution. They employ a Marxian framework to trace and analyze the correlates of the rise of capitalism and the rise the prison. They argue that the emergence of different types of punishment, for example manual labor, is related to economic conditions in society. Also discussed is the relationship between the need for manual labor and the emergence of inmate lease models.

L.00661 Rothman, D. J. (1971). *The discovery of the asylum: Social order and disorder in the New Republic*. Boston: Little, Brown and Co.

Contained in this book is a functionalist perspective on asylums and the social structure. Rothman proposes that society's institutions, whether social, political, or economic, cannot be understood apart from the society in which they exist. The author argues that asylums and society are interdependent, each supporting the other. He discusses the interdependent relationship between correctional systems and those who lease inmates.

L.00662 Sellin, J. T. (1976). *Slavery and the penal system*. New York: Elsevier North/Holland.

Provided by the author of this book are insights about the influence of slavery on the evolution of penal systems and practices in Europe and the United States. The author presents an overview of the inmate lease system and how slavery encouraged its use.

L.00663 Wines, E. C. & Dwight, T. W. (1867). *Report on the prisons and reformatories of the United States and Canada*. Albany, NY: Van Benthuysen and Sons' Steam Printing House.

The authors visited and studied the prisons and reformatories of 18 northern states and Canada in 1866. The authors discovered many deficiencies such as prisons being part of the political machinery of the state, the incarceration of youths with hardened criminals, and the lack of positive rehabilitation and reward. The authors presented their findings and recommendations to the New York Legislature in 1867.

LEGAL ISSUES

I. Historical

L.00664 Bronstein, A. J. (1980). Prisoners' rights: A history. In G. P. Alpert (ed.),

Legal rights of prisoners (pp. 19–45). Newbury Park, CA: Sage Publications, Inc.

In this edited book chapter, the author reviews recent court cases relating to the legal rights of prisoners. Issues addresses in the cases are due process, punishment, jail conditions, communications, discrimination, political activities, privacy, appearance, treatment, and probation.

L.00665 Jones, C. & Rhine, E. (1985). Due process and prison disciplinary practices: From *Wolff* to *Hewitt*. *New England Journal on Criminal and Civil Confinement 11*(Winter), 44–122.

In this law review article, the authors trace the development of due process in prison disciplinary cases. Included in the article is a discussion of cases relating to prison disciplinary issues, for example *Wolff v. McDonnell, Morissey v. Brewer, Estelle v. Gamble, Gagnon v. Scarpelli, Jones v. North Carolina Prisoners Labor Union, Pell v. Procunier, Meachum v. Fano, Montanye v. Haynes,* and *Hewitt v. Helms.*

L.00666 Manville, D. E. (1983). *Prisoners' self-help litigation manual.* New York: Oceana Publications.

Contained in this prisoners' manual is basic information to assist prisoners in bringing lawsuits regarding prison conditions and practices, parole matters, detainers, post conviction proceedings such as writs of habeas corpus, and other legal issues.

L.00667 Potuto, J. (1991). *Prisoner collateral attacks: Federal habeas corpus and federal prisoner motion practice.* Deerfield, IL: Clark, Boardman and Callaghan.

In this book the author provides a thorough discussion of habeas corpus and motions suits, both of which are types of collateral attacks used by prisoners. The author examines the technical and substantive differences between writs and motions and concludes that the operating laws and principles are generally the same for both Federal and state prisoners. The U.S. Supreme Court supports the same view.

L.00668 Schwartz, M. A. & Kirklin, J. E. (1991). *Section 1983 litigation: Claims, defenses, and fees.* New York: John Wiley and Sons, Inc.

In this book the authors present a comprehensive review of the major legal issues involving Section 1983 suits. The authors provide practical information regarding the cases, including defenses and fees.

II. Constitutional Issues in Prison Operations

L00669 Alexander, R. (1994). Hands-off, hands-on, hands-semi-off: A discussion of the current legal test used by the United States Supreme Court to decide inmates' rights. *Journal of Crime and Justice 17*(1), 103–128.

The author of this article suggests that a 1987 U.S. Supreme Court decision restricting prisoner rights has indirectly reintroduced a partial hands-off doctrine.

L.00670 Bronstein, A. J. (1985). Prisoners and their endangered rights. *Prison Journal 65*(1), 3–17.

Contained in this article is an analysis of court decisions regarding prisoners' rights. The author suggests that prisoners' rights have eroded in recent years and that the basis of the erosion is changes in the philosophy of the court, political leadership, and public education.

L.00671 Collins, W. C. (1993). *Correctional law for the correctional officer.* Laurel, MD: American Correctional Association.

The author of this book discusses many of the legal issues which confront correctional officers during the course of their employment. Of particular note are the discussions relating to liability and prisoners' rights.

L.00672 del Carmen, R. V., Ritter, S. E. & Witt, B. A. (1993). *Briefs of leading cases in corrections.* Cincinnati: Anderson Publishing Company.

The authors present briefs of the leading court cases relating to prison law, probation, parole, the death penalty, juvenile justice, and sentencing.

L.00673 Dunn, A. (1994). Flood of prisoner rights suits brings effort to limit filings. *New York Times*, March 21, A-1, B-12.

Even though prisoner civil rights law suits have made a tremendous impact on corrections systems and forced improvements in prison medical care, legal access, and inmate treatment, the author points out that more and more law suits are being filed that are based on trivial issues. It is recognized that the volume of such cases in recent years has burdened the courts and overwhelmed state attorneys. The author suggests ways to reduce such cases.

L.00674 Vaughn, M. S. & del Carmen, R. V. (1993). Smoke-free prisons: Policy dilemmas and constitutional issues. *Journal of Criminal Justice 21*(2),

151–170.

In this article the authors discuss smoking or no-smoking policies in correctional facilities. Of particular interest is their discussion of the dangers of second-hand smoke versus the constitutional rights of prisoners.

III. Prison Crimes

L.00675 Finizio, S. (1992). Prison cells, leg restraints, and "custodial interrogaation": *Miranda's* role in crimes that occur in prison. *University of Chicago Law Review 59*, 719–748.

In this law review article the author explores what role the Supreme Court's decision in *Miranda v. Arizona* should play in crimes that occur in prison. Included in the discussion are the principles of *Miranda*, the evolution of the *Miranda* doctrine and it's implications for prison, current approaches to *Miranda* in the prison setting, and problems with the traditional custodial interrogation approach in prisons.

L.00676 LaFave, W. R. (1987). *Search and seizure: A treatise on the fourth amendment* (2d ed.). St. Paul, MN: West Publishing.

In this book, the author provides a comprehensive examination of the Fourth Amendment protection against unreasonable search and seizure. The author presents a thorough discussion of the current state and trends in search and seizure laws. Included in the discussion are legal precedents for search and seizure in correctional settings.

L.00677 Robbins, I. P. (1982). Legal aspects of prison riots. *Harvard Civil Rights–Civil Liberties Law Review 16*, 735–776.

In this law review article is an overview of prison riots from the perspective of attorneys, prisoners, and correctional staff. In particular, the author discusses legal issues that stem from prison riots.

L.00678 Ulshen, R. Z. & Burke, R. J. (1992). Prisoners' substantive rights. *Georgetown Law Journal 80*, 1677–1725.

In this law review article, the authors acknowledge that a prison regulation that infringes on a prisoner's constitutional rights is valid only if it is reasonably related to legitimate penal interest. The authors discuss the four relevant factors in determining the reasonableness of a prison regulation. They also discuss prisoners' substantive rights, such as, right of access to courts, freedom of speech, association and religion, rights to personal privacy, rights relating to living conditions, medical care, and disciplinary treatment and rights to procedural due process.

IV. Employees

L.00679 Hood, J. B. & Hardy, B. A. Jr. (1983). *Workers' compensation and employee protection laws in a nutshell.* St. Paul, MN: West Publishing Company.

The authors present an overview of the laws relating to employee and employment issues. Of particular note are the legal guidelines for workers' compensation and employee protections.

Cases

L.00680 *American Federation of Government Employees v. Roberts*, 9 F.3d 1464 (9th Cir. 1993)

The issue addressed in this case a policy of random urinalysis (drug testing) for correctional employees. The District Court ruled that random testing of prison employees could only be done for those employees in primary law enforcement positions who in the course of their regular duties are issued or given access to firearms. This case is currently being appealed.

L.00681 *Anderson v. Creighton*, 483 U.S. 635, 107 S.Ct. 3034, 97 L.Ed.2d 523(1987)

The issue is whether a warrantless search of a bank robbery suspect's house is constitutional. An FBI agent participated in the search because the officers believed the suspect might be in his home. The court denied any 14th Amendment violations on summary judgement. The appellant court ruled that the lawfulness of the search could not be determined on summary judgement.

L.00682 *Angarita et al. v. St. Louis County*, 981 F.2d 1537 (8th Cir. 1993)

This case involves a complaint to seek damages and equitable relief. Three officers alleged they were deprived of their property rights and continued employment when they were forced to resign from their positions with the St. Louis Police Department. The jury found in favor of the officers.

L.00683 *Baxter v. Palmigiano*, 425 U.S. 308, 96 S.Ct. 1551, 47 L.Ed.2d 810 (1976)

In this case the Court ruled that whether or not to allow inmates to confront witnesses, as part of a disciplinary hearing, is within the discretion of prison officials.

L.00684 *Bell v. Wolfish*, 441 U.S. 520, 99 S.Ct. 1861, 60 L.Ed. 2d 447 (1979)

This case was litigated when inmates of a short-term facility challenged the facility's double-celling procedure. The facility, designed to house pre-trial defendants, placed two inmates in a room that was designed to house one occupant.

L.00685 *Bienvenu v. Beauregard Parish Police Jury*, 705 F.2d 1457 (5th Cir. 1983)

Prisoner at Louisiana's Hunt Corrections Center alleged that the conditions at the Louisiana parish jail had caused him severe harm. The issue before the court is whether Bienvenu had a constitutional right to appointed counsel to represent him on his appeal. The motion was denied.

L.00686 *Block v. Rutherford*, 468 U.S. 576, 104 S.Ct. 3227, 82 L.Ed.2d 438 (1984)

The Supreme Court held that a county jail's practice of conducting random shakedown searches of pretrial detainee's cells in the absence of the detainees is a reasonable response by jail officials to legitimate security concerns and does not violate any of the inmate's constitutional rights. The Court also found that contact visits with spouses, relatives, children and friends be allowed for low risk pretrial detainees who are incarcerated for a month or more.

L.00687 *Blockburger v. United States*, 284 U.S. 229, 76 L.Ed. 306 (1932)

The petitioner was charged with violating provisions of the Harrison Narcotic Act by allegedly selling morphine. Five counts of such action were contained in the indictment. The jury returned a verdict against the petitioner upon the second, third, and fifth counts only. Each of these counts charged a sale of morphine hydrochloride to the same purchaser.

L.00688 *Bounds v. Smith*, 430 U.S. 817, 97 S.Ct. 1491, 52 L.Ed.2d 72 (1977)

This case addressed initial proceedings and focused on how the inmate can present his/her claim in the first instance to a court. Without meaningful implementation of the right to access inmates could not be able to put before a judge sufficient information to enable the court to determine whether the case had merit.

L.00689 *Brady v. Maryland*, 373 U.S. 83, 83 S.Ct. 1194, 10 L.Ed.2d 215 (1963)

The legal principle established in this case is the prosecutor's duty, when prosecuting criminal cases, to disclose exculpatory evidence to defendants' attorneys.

L.00690 *Brown v. Miller*, 631 F.2d 408 (5th Cir, 1980)

In this case, the defendants, the mayor of a municipality and a corporation substantially owned by him, were found to have taken a police officer's property without due process. The mayor acting 'under color of law' deprived the plaintiff of his due process rights [when the mayor took the police officer's paychecks to pay overdue phone bills.] On appeal, the mayor claimed that the lower court erred in three areas: 1) the mayor was not acting under 'color of law' when he seized the paychecks; 2) certain evidence presented to the court should have been excluded; and 3) the punitive damages awarded to the plaintiff was excessive. The court affirmed the district court's judgment as to liability but reversed the award of damages and remanded to the lower court for a new trial on that issue.

L.00691 *City of Cleburne* v. *Cleburne Living Center, Inc.*, 473 U.S. 432, 105 S.Ct. 3249, 87 L.Ed.2d 313 (1985)

The Cleburne Living Center filed a suit against the city of Cleburne because they were denied a zoning permit which they said violated residents' 14th Amendment rights. A group home for the mentally retarded was to be built in Cleburne. Before construction a zoning permit needed to be obtained. After a public hearing, the city council denied the permit. The District Court held the ordinance and its application were constitutional. The Court of Appeals reversed, holding that the ordinance was invalid as currently applied. The Court maintained that mental retardation is a "quasi-suspect" classification which calls for a more exact standard of judicial review than is normally afforded economic and social legislation.

L.00692 *Cook v. Rhode Island Department of Mental Health*, 10 F.3d 17 (1st Cir. 1993)

In this case the Court addressed the prohibition against discrimination of those covered by Section 504 of the Rehabilitation Act of 1973, for example, mentally and physically impaired people.

L.00693 *Cookish v. Powell*, 945 F.2d 441 (1st Cir. 1991).

In this case the plaintiff alleged that his 4th Amendment rights were violated by a prison procedure where female correctional officers supervised and/or observed him during a visual body cavity search. The prison officials denied any violation of the inmate's 4th Amendment rights and claimed they had qualified immunity. The court ruled in favor of prison officials stating that such a procedure was protected by qualified immunity.

L.00694 *Cruz v. Beto*, 405 U.S. 319, 92 S.Ct. 1079, 31 L.Ed.2d 263 (1972)

In this case inmate Cruz alleged that his right to practice the religion of his choice was violated by the Texas Department of Correcitons. The Court ruled that disruptive attorneys can be removed from the penitentiary and that "freedom of religion extends only as far as the umbrella of equal protection can shelter it."

L.00695 *Daniels v. Williams*, 474 U.S. 327, 106 S.Ct. 662, 88 L.Ed.2d 662, (1986)

An inmate housed in a Richmond, Virginia jail slipped on a pillow which had been negligently left on a stairway by a sheriff's deputy. The inmate claimed that such negligence violated his rights to freedom from bodily injury "without due process of law" within the meaning of the due process clause of the 14 Amendment. The court held that the due process clause was not violated by the officials negligent act causing unintended loss of or injury to life, liberty, or property.

L.00696 *Darden v. Wainwright*, 477 U.S. 168, 106 S.Ct. 2464, 91 L.Ed.2d 144 (1986)

During *voir dire*, the trial judge in this case asked "Do you have any moral or religious, conscientious moral or religious principles in opposition to the death penalty so strong that you would be unable without violating your own principles to vote to recommend a death proceeding regardless of the facts?" The Court found that the record of the voir dire process, viewed in its entirety, shows that the court's decision to remove a juror was proper.

L.00697 *Durmer v. O'Carroll*, 991 F.2d 64 (3rd Cir. 1993)

Inmate Durmer claimed that the department of corrections exhibited "deliberate indifference" to his medical needs during his time of incarceration in the New Jersey correctional system. The District Court found no deliberate indifference. The Appellant Court reversed and remanded.

L.00698 *Estelle v. Gamble* (429 U.S. 97, 97 S.Ct. 285, 50 L.Ed.2d 251 (1976)

The Supreme Court ruled that "deliberate indifference" of prison officials or personnel to the serious medical needs of inmates, constitutes cruel and unusual punishment, thus violating the Eighth Amendment.

L.00699 *Ex parte Hull*, 312 U.S. 546 (1940)

The Supreme Court found a prison regulation, requiring the filing of all legal documents with the institution for review by prison officials prior to their filing in court, to be unconstitutional.

L.00700 *Farmer v. Brennan*, 114 S.Ct. 1970, 128 L.Ed. 1034 (1941)

Inmate Farmer claimed that he was beaten and raped by another inmate after being transferred to a penitentiary where he was placed in the general population. The inmate was a preoperative transsexual. The Court held that prison officials could only be liable under the 8th Amendment for acting with "deliberate indifference" to inmate health and safety only if they know that inmates face a substantial risk of serious harm and disregards that risk by failing to take reasonable measures to abate it.

L.00701 *Foulds v. Corley*, 833 F.2d 52 (5th Cir, 1987)

In this case, Foulds, an inmate at the Montgomery County, Texas jail claimed his constitutional rights were violated. Other inmates had attempted to escape and Foulds claimed he was being punished because he would not tell authorities anything about those inmates. He said he was held in solidary confinement for 15 days which was cold and rat-infested. The trial court dismissed his claim. On appeal, the court ruled that the trial court dismissed the case prematurely and reversed and remanded the case.

L.00702 *Fraire v. Arlington*, 957 F.2d 1268, 1273 (5th Cir. 1992)

In this case, it was alleged that unconstitutionally excessive force was used by the correctional system in the shooting death of inmate Fraire. The District Court said Lowery (the person who shot Fraire) was qualifiedly immune. The Court of Appeals affirmed.

L.00703 *Francis v. Henderson*, 425 U.S. 536, 96 S.Ct. 1708, 48 L.Ed.2d 149 (1976)

The Court found that a federal prisoner who failed to timely challenge an alleged unconstitutional composition of his grand jury was not entitled to an overturn on the state conviction. The Court of Appeals affirmed the lower court decision that the constitutional challenges to the grand jury must be made before the trial begins.

L.00704 *Gibson v. Collins*, 947 F.2d 780 (5th Cir. 1991) cert. denied, 113 S.Ct. 102 (1992)

In this case the inmate's writ of habeas corpus was denied. The inmate alleged his burglary conviction was unconstitutional because he was denied due process because the conviction was not supported by sufficient evidence. The Court of Appeals affirmed the District Court's order.

L.00705 *Gilmore v. Lynch*, 319 F.Supp 105 (N.D. Ca. 1970)

In this case the Court determined that jailhouse lawyers may retain their clients'(other inmates) papers until the clients' cases are completed.

L.00706 *Gregg v. Georgia*, 428 U.S. 153, 96 S.Ct. 2909, 49 L.Ed.2d 859 (1976)

Torture and barbaric modes of physical punishment are considered cruel and unusual punishment, however, the death penalty does not constitute cruel and unusual punishment in and of itself. The decision in this case resulted in reinstating the death penalty, thus eliminating the moratorium on the death penalty that began with *Furman v. Georgia.*

L.00707 *Grummett v. Rushen*, 779 F.2d 491 (9th Cir. 1985)

As a result of this case the Court determined that routine pat-down searches conducted by female guards, which include the groin area of male inmates, do not violate inmates' rights to privacy.

L.00708 *Guajardo v. Estelle*, 580 F.2d 748 (5th Cir. 1978)

In this case the Court ruled that prisoners in solidary confinement are restricted or prohibited from receiving reading materials during this punitive confinement.

L.00709 *Guiney v. Police Commissioner*, 582 N.E.2d 523, 411 Mass. 328 (Mass. 1991)

This case was litigated on the basis that random drug testing of police officers is unconstitutional. The Court determined that random drug testing of police officers without consent and without concrete, substantial governmental interest are considered unreasonable search and seizures.

L.00710 *Hamm v. De Kalb County*, 774 F.2d 1567 (11th Cir. 1985)

In this case the Court ruled that the same standards established in *Estelle* for adequate medical care for sentenced prisoners are also applicable to pretrial detainees.

L.00711 *Harlow v. Fitzgerald*, 457 U.S. 800, 102 S.Ct. 2727, 73 L.Ed.2d 396 (1982)

In this case the Court extended the defense of absolute immunity to government officials whose special functions or constitutional status requires complete protection from suits or damages.

L.00712 *Hay v. Waldron*, 834 F.2d 481, 486 (5th Cir. 1987)

The Court determined that strip searches of inmates in administrative segregation are not subject to the "least restrictive means" test. If strip searches are reasonably related to legitimate institutional objectives, then they are not unconstitutional and are not in violation of the 4th Amendment.

L.00713 *Helling v. McKinney*, 509 U.S. ___, 113 S.Ct. 2475, 125 L.Ed.2d 22 (1993)

In this case the Court determined that inmates do not have to wait for harm to occur for a court to find that serious needs are unmet.

L.00714 *Hill v. Lockhart*, 474 U.S. 52, 106 S.Ct. 366, 88 L.Ed.2d 203 (1985)

In this case an inmate entered a guilty plea for the crime of theft. He alleged his lawyer did not tell him that as a second time offender he would be required to serve one–half of his sentence before he was eligible for parole. The inmate alleged that his guilty plea was involuntary because he had ineffective counsel. The District Court denied habeas relief without a hearing. The Court of Appeals affirmed the District Court's position.

L.00715 *Houchins v. KQED*, 438 U.S. 1, 98 S.Ct. 2588, 57 L.Ed.2d 553 (1978)

In this case the media alleged that their 'freedom of speech' was violated by local jail administrators. The Court determined that the press has no constitutional rights to visit and photograph a jail in connection with a press investigation of conditions where a pretrial detainee committed suicide.

L.00716 *Howell v. Burden,* 12 F.3d 190 (11th Cir. 1994)

This is the second appeal of the case involving inmate Howell, a chronic sufferer of asthma. He died after a severe asthmatic attack while incarcerated in the Augusta Correctional and Medical Institution. His widow brought suit against the prison alleging that the defendants violated Howell's 8th Amendment rights by being deliberately indifferent to Howell's health. The Court of Appeals reversed and remanded the case.

L.00717 *Hudson v. McMillian,* 503 U.S. 1, 112 S.Ct. 995, 117 L.Ed.2d 156 (1992).

The Court determined from this case that in order for an 8th Amendment violation to occur, a prisoner must suffer a "serious" injury.

L.00718 *Hudson v. Palmer,* 468 U.S. 517, 104 S.Ct. 3194, 82 L.Ed.2d 393 (1984)

The plaintiff filed suit against the corrections system alleging that his Fourth Amendment right to privacy was violated when guards searched his cell. The Court disagreed and placed limitations on inmates' right to privacy in their cells.

L.00719 *Hutto v. Finney,* 437 U.S. 678, 98 S.Ct. 2565, 57 L.Ed.2d 522 (1978)

Prior to the present case, the Court found that the manner in which the Arkansas state prison system operated constituted cruel and unusual punishment. The court specifically outlined remedies to these violations. The present case is an appeal of two of the remedies identified by the Court: 1) an maximum limitation of 30 days in solidary confinement; and 2) an award of attorney fees to be paid by the Department of Corrections. The Court found these remedies to be valid.

L.00720 *Illinois v. Perkins,* 496 U.S. 292, 110 S.Ct. 2394, 110 L.Ed.2d 243 (1990)

In this case, an undercover agent was placed in a prison to discover information about a murder in the prison. The agent was housed next to inmate Perkins. When the agent asked Perkins if he had ever killed anyone, Perkins began making statements implicating himself in the murder the agent was investigating. The trial court ruled that the confession was not admissible because the agent never identified himself as an agent. On appeal the court found that an undercover law enforcement officer need not give Miranda warnings to an incarcerated suspect before asking questions which may incriminate the inmate.

L.00721 *Jackson v. Cain, 864 F.2d 1235 (5th Cir. 1989)*

An inmate filed a suit alleging that the employees of the Louisiana Department of Corrections violated his civil rights. The District Court granted summary judgement on all issues. The Appellate Court upheld the summary judgements on the issues of handcuffing, mail tampering, and medical treatment. But, the other summary judgements, i.e., cruel and unusual punishment, retaliation claims, failure to follow punishment limitations, and procedural due process claims were found to be in error. The Court remanded the case to the district court for discovery and trial on these issues.

L.00722 *Jackson v. Gates*, 975 F.2d 648 (9th Cir, 1992)

This legal action resulted after Jackson, a police officer, was dismissed from his employment for refusing to comply with an order to provide sample of urine for drug testing. The court found that such dismissal violated Jackson's Fourth Amendment rights.

L.00723 *Jackson v. Virginia*, 443 U.S. 307, 99 S.Ct. 2781, 61 L.Ed.2d 560 (1979)

In this case the petitioner, convicted of first-degree murder after a bench trial in a Virginia Court, petitions for the sentence to be set aside because there was insufficient evidence of premeditation, a necessary element of first-degree murder. The court found that the lower court must consider not whether there is any evidence to support the state-court conviction but whether there is sufficient evidence to support such a verdict.

L.00724 *Johnson v. Avery*, 393 U.S. 483, 89 S.Ct. 21, L.Ed.2d 718 (1969)

In this case the Court established inmates' right of access to jailhouse lawyers. The Court ruled that jailhouse lawyers are permitted to aid inmates with the filing of habeas corpus petitions in the absence of other counsel.

L.00725 *Johnson v. Glick*, 481 F.2d 1028 (2nd Cir. 1973)

An inmate in the House of Detention in Manhattan, NY, alleged that his civil rights were violated when a correctional officer reprimanded Johnson inappropriately. He alleged that the officer assaulted him. The lower court said it could not substantiate the validity of the attack and therefore refused to hear it. On appeal the Court found that ruling was in error.

L.00726 *Jordan v. Gardner*, 986 F.2d 1521 (9th Cir. 1993)

The court held that cross gender clothed body searches were in violation of the 8th Amendment because of psychological effects such searches would have on the inmates.

L.00727 *Kentucky v. Thompson*, 490 U.S. 454, 109 S.Ct. 1904, 104 L.Ed.2d 506 (1989)

A consent decree settling a class action suit brought by the Kentucky penal inmates provided specific instructions for the prison. The inmates appealed the regulation that qualified who could be placed on the visitors list. The court ruled that the "Kentucky regulations do not give state inmates a liberty interest in receiving visitors that is entitled to the protections of the due process clause."

L.00728 *Kirby v. Illinois*, 406 U.S. 682, 92 S.Ct. 1877, 32 L.Ed.2d 411 (1972)

In this case the Court ruled that the exclusionary rule does not apply to pre–indictment confrontations.

L.00729 *Lavernia v. Lynaugh*, 845 F.2d 493 (5th Cir. 1988)

In this case, a prisoner appealed his conviction of aggravated rape. The court found that the trial court did not err when it rejected the defendants six claims regarding the case.

L.00730 *Lee v. Washington*, 390 U.S. 333, 88 S.Ct. 994, 19 L.Ed.2d 1212 (1968)

In this case inmates alleged that they were victims of descrimination as a result of racial segregation in prison. The Court ruled that racial segregation in prisons is unconstitutional.

L.00731 *Local 194A v. Bridge Cmsn*, 572 A.2d 204 (N.J. App. Div. 1990)

The court held that "drug testing of public employees physically involved in the opening and closing of bridges which cross the Delaware River may be conducted as part of an annual physical examination."

L.00732 *L.W. v. Grubbs*, 974 F.2d 119 (9th Cir. 1992)

A nurse working in a correctional institution was raped and terrorized by an inmate. She sued the institution but the Court dismissed her case on the basis that she was an employee and knowlingly accepted the risks. On appeal the Court reversed. It was determined that her suit could not be dismissed just because she was employed in the institution and knew the risks.

L.00733 *Madyun v. Franzen,* 704 F.2d 954 (7th Cir 1983), cert denied, 104 S.Ct 493 (1983)

The Court ruled that inmate searches by female guards of male prisoners is not unconstitutional. However, limitations on practice of religion are constitutional if supported by an important governmental objective and if the ban was reasonably adopted to achieve this objection.

L.00734 *Mathis v. United States,* 391 U.S. 1, 88 S.Ct 1503, 20 L.Ed.2d 381 (1968)

The findings of the Court in this case emphasize the relevance *Miranda* warnings but in a prison setting. The Supreme Court found a Miranda violation to exist when an unwarned prisoner was questioned by an Internal Revenue Service agent conducting a tax investigation. The inmate was later prosecuted based on the information obtained from the interviews. The Court found that the Miranda warning does not extended to routine prison investigations.

L.00735 *McClesky v. Kemp,* 481 U.S. 279, 107 S.Ct. 1756, 95 L.Ed.2d 262 (1987)

In this case, an inmate was sentenced to death for killing a police officer. After exhausting all appeals, the inmate filed a habeas corpus suit alleging, based on a scientific study which showed the death penalty was applied discriminately, that he should have his conviction reversed. The Court found the study to be valid but that the statistics were insufficient to demonstrate unconstitutional discrimination.

L.00736 *McCleskey v. Zant,* 499 U.S. 467, 111 S.Ct. 1454, 113 L.Ed.2d 517 (1991)

Prior to this case the petitioner was convicted of murder and a related crime by a jury and sentenced to death. McCleskey claimed that the state created a situation to induce him to make incriminating statements about the murder without the assistance of counsel in violation of the *Massiah* v. *United States.* The petitioner failed to raise this issue in his unsuccessful petitions. In his second Federal habeas petition he raised this challenge. The court declared "McCleskey's failure to raise his Massiah claim in his first federal habeas petition constituted abuse of the writ."

L.00737 *McDonnell v. Hunter*, 809 F.2d 1302 (8th Cir, 1987)

In this class action suit, the employees challenged the constitutionality of an Iowa Department of Corrections policy which subjects employees to vehicle searches and person searches including urine, blood, or breath testing. The District Court ruled that the Department of Corrections officials and their agents could enforce this search policy only in limited situations. The search must be based on a reasonable suspicion. The present court affirmed.

L.00738 *McMann v. Richardson*, 397 U.S. 759, 90 S.Ct. 1441, 25 L.Ed.2d 763 (1970)

The defendants were found guilty in state court after they plead guilty on the advise of counsel. They said they pleaded guilty because their counsel told them their confession would be admissible. The confession was not admitted and the petitioners seek collateral relief. The Court of Appeals reversed in each case but the Supreme Court granted the petition for certiorari.

L.00739 *Miranda v. Arizona*, 384 U.S. 436, 86 S.Ct. 1602, 16 L.Ed.2d 694 (1966)

The Supreme Court ruled that any time police begin to question a suspect after he is taking into custody they must first warn the suspect of his rights including – The suspect has the right to remain silent, that any statement he does make may be used as evidence against him, and that he has a right to an attorney, either retained or appointed.

L.00740 *Monell v. Department of Social Services*, 436 U.S. 658, 98 S.Ct. 2018, 56 L.Ed.2d 611 (1978).

In this class action suit, female employees sued stating their civil rights were violated by a policy which forced pregnant workers to take unpaid leaves of absence before leaves were required for medical reasons. The District Court found that the petitioners' civil rights had been violated but barred the recovery of back pay. On appeal, the court reversed the back pay issue.

L.00741 *Monroe v. Pape*, 365 U.S. 167, 81 S.Ct. 473, 5 L.Ed.2d 492 (1961)

The Supreme Court held that prisoners could use the civil rights statute (42 USC Section 1983) as a procedural vehicle for challenging prison conditions and practices.

L.00742 *Murray v. Giarratano*, 492 U.S. 1, 109 S.Ct. 2765, 106 F.2d 279 (1989)

Virginia death row inmates brought a civil rights suit against various officials of the Commonwealth of Virginia. They claimed the constitution required they be provided with counsel at the expense of the institution to assist with collateral proceedings related to their convictions and sentences. On appeal, the court reversed and remanded the case.

L.00743 *Murray v. Maggio*, 736 F.2d 279 (5th Cir. 1984)

Inmate Murray was convicted of armed robbery by a jury and sentenced to 25 years in the Louisiana Department of Corrections. He sought a petition of habeas corpus claiming inadequate counsel. The Federal District Court denied his petition. On appeal, the court affirmed that there was no error in the carefully reasoned report and recommendations declared at trial and adopted by the District Court.

L.00744 *Newman v. Alabama*, 559 F.2d 283 (5th Cir. 1977)

This case resulted in one of many court decisions in which prisons were made to expand prison programs including educational, vocational, and work study/work release programs for inmates.

L.00745 *North Carolina v. Alford*, 400 U.S. 25, 91 S.Ct. 160, 27 L.Ed.2d 162 (1970)

The appellee plead guilty to second-degree murder, even though he said he did not commit the crime, because he was afraid of getting the death penalty if the charge of first-degree murder was substantiated. He was sentenced to 30 years in prison. The Court of Appeals found that the plea was involuntary because it was motivated by fear of the death penalty. On appeal, the court held that the trial judge did not commit any constitutional errors in accepting the appellee's guilty plea.

L.00746 *Ohio v. Johnson*, 467 U.S. 493, 104 S.Ct. 2536, 81 L.Ed.2d 425 (1984)

The respondent plead guilty to involuntary manslaughter and grand theft. At the arraignment, the court granted the motion to dismiss the remaining charges based on the grounds that double jeopardy prohibited further prosecution. The Court held that the double jeopardy clause does not prohibit the State from continuing its prosecution of the respondent on the remaining charges.

L.00747 *O'Lone v. Estate of Shabazz*, 482 U.S. 342, 107 S.Ct. 2400, 96 L.Ed.2d

282 (1987)

Inmates have the right to practice their religion while incarcerated. However, the court maintained that when a "prison regulation impinges on inmate's constitutional rights, the regulation is only valid if it is reasonably related to legitimate penological concerns."

L.00748 *Pell v. Procunier*, 417 U.S. 817, 94 S.Ct. 2800, 41 L.Ed.2d 495 (1974)

In this case the Court found that inmates do not relinquish all constitutional rights when they are incarcerated.

L.00749 *Pennsylvania v. Finley*, 481 U.S. 551, 107 S.Ct. 1990, 95 L.Ed.2d 539 (1987)

The Court found that all inmates, not only those who can afford it, have the right to access the court.

L.00750 *Picard v. Connor*, 404 U.S. 270, 92 S.Ct 509, 30 L.Ed.2d 438 (1971)

This case involves an inmate who was referred to as "John Doe" until he was identified. He claimed that the indictments used in this fashion violated his civil rights. The District Court disagreed but the Appellate Court found that the procedure used to bring the defendant to trial violated the equal protection clause. On appeal, the Court ruled that the defendant did not exhaust all state remedies before filing a federal habeas corpus writ. Therefore, the case was reversed and remanded.

L.00751 *Plyler v. Doe*, 457 U.S. 202, 102 S.Ct. 2382, 72 L.Ed.2d 786, *reh. den.*, 458 U.S. 1131 (1982)

In this case, the court examined whether the state of Texas could deny undocumented school-age children free public education using the Equal Protection clause of the 14th Amendment as a basis for the denial. The Court said Texas could do so, but Justice Marshall dissented stating that "It continues to be my view that a class-based denial of public education is utterly incompatible with the Equal Protection Clause of the 14th Amendment."

L.00752 *Preiser v. Rodriques*, 411 U.S. 475, 93 S.Ct. 1827, 36 L.Ed.2d 439 (1973)

The Court maintained its 'hands off' approach to becoming involved in the daily operations of the prison.

L.00753 *Procunier v. Martinez*, 416 U.S. 396, 94 S.Ct. 1800, 40 L.Ed.2d 224 (1974)

The court ruled that prison mail censorship is constitutional only when the practice furthers government interests in security and rehabilitation. The mail censorship (restrictions) cannot be any greater than that necessary to meet the government interest, i.e., to provide security for the institution.

L.00754 *Procunier v. Navarette*, 434 U.S. 555, 98 S.Ct 855, 55 L.Ed.2d 24 (1978)

This case was brought against prison officials for violating an inmate's civil rights by interfering with his outgoing mail. The District Court granted summary judgement for petitioners on this claim based on their asserted qualified immunity from liability for damages under section 1983. The Court of Appeals subsequently reversed, holding that inmates are entitled to 1st and 14th amendment protections for outgoing mail and that the summary judgement was incorrect. The Supreme Court held that the Appellant court erred in reversing the summary judgement.

L.00755 *Rhodes v. Chapman*, 452 U.S. 337, 101 S.Ct. 2392, 69 L.Ed.2d 59 (1981)

Inmates do not give up all their constitutional rights when incarcerated. However, the Court ruled that overcrowding in a prison, in and of itself, is not cruel and unusual punishment.

L.00756 *Riggins v. Nevada*, 504 U.S. 127, 112 S.Ct. 1810, 118 L.Ed.2d 479 (1992)

This case was litigated when inmates were forced to take antipsychotic drugs. The Court ruled that forcing inmates to take antipsychotic drugs is unconstitutional absent an overriding justification and a determination of medical appropriateness.

L.00757 *Rubio v. Estelle*, 689 F.2d 533 (5th Cir. 1982)

Rubio was convicted of possession of heroin. Because she had two previous convictions, her sentence was enhanced to life imprisonment. She filed for habeas corpus relief challenging that her due process rights were violated. She said she had inadequate counsel, that she had problems understanding the English language, and that the confidential informant should have been confronted. The Court found that her due process rights had not been violated and she needed to raise the issues in this case during the actual trial.

L.00758 *Ruiz v. Estelle*, 679 F.2d 1115 (5th Cir. 1982) Opinion amended in part and vacated in part, 688 F.2d 266 (5th Cir. 1982) 460 U.S. 1042 (1983).

This case, brought by inmate Ruiz, became the most comprehensive civil action in correctional law. The plaintiff alleged that the Texas Department of Corrections had unconstitutionally exposed prisoners to physically deteriorated, dangerous, and overcrowded conditions, the Court concurred.

L.00759 *Saahir* v. *Collins*, 956 F.2d 115 (5th Cir. 1992)

The District Court dismissed the petitioners' successive federal habeas corpus petitions for abuse of the writ. Because Saahir failed to show a fundamental miscarriage of justice, the court affirmed the District Court's order dismissing the petition with prejudice.

L.00760 *Sawyer v. Whitley*, 505 U.S. 333, 112 S.Ct. 2514, 120 L.Ed.2d 269 (1992)

This case involved a defendant sentenced to death for murder. The defendant claimed he had inadequate counsel because records of his mental stautus were not admitted at his trial and that he was actually innocent of the crime. The Court held "to show actual innocence one must show by clear and convincing evidence that but for a constitutional error, no reasonable juror would have found the petitioner eligible for the death penalty under the applicable state law."

L.00761 *Saxbe v. Washington Post*, 417 U.S. 843, 94 S.Ct 2811, 41 L.Ed.2d 514 (1974)

The Court ruled that the media does not have a right to interview inmates. The availability of inmates for interviews by the media is based on prison discretion and the willingness of the inmate. The Court found that the denial was not arbitrary nor discriminatory.

L.00762 *Simon and Schuster v. Members of the New York State Crime Victims Board*, 502 U.S. 105, 112 S.Ct. 501, 116 L.Ed.2d 476 (1991)

The Court found that New York had a compelling interest to deprive criminals of their profits of their crimes and to use these funds to compensate victims. The court would not allow criminals to profit from their crimes even if the money would subsequently go to the victims.

L.00763 *Skillern v. Estelle*, 720 F.2d 839, 852 (5th Cir. 1983), *cert. denied*, 469 U.S. 873 (1984)

The petitioner Skillern was found guilty of murdering a state narcotics agent and was subsequently sentenced to death. He argued for reversal on his appeal because of three issues:"the death penalty was unconstitutionally imposed in the absence of sufficient evidence of his own personal culpability for the unexpected act of his codefendant; 2) the District Court denied him an evidentiary hearing; and 3) the evidentiary error was of constitutional magnitude, rendering the sentencing hearing fundamentally unfair and violative of due process." The Court found no error under these circumstances.

L.00764 *Smith v. Bennett*, 365 U.S. 708, 81 S.Ct. 895, 6 L.Ed.2d 39 (1961)

The court held that a filing fee for a writ of habeas corpus is unconstitutional. In this case, the $4.00 billing fee for the habeas petition was unconstitutional.

L.00765 *Stone v. Powell*, 428 U.S. 465, 96 S.Ct. 3037, 49 L.Ed.2d 1067 (1976)

The legal principle established in this case is that the 'exclusionary rule' does not extent to habeas corpus hearings.

L.00766 *Strickland v. Washington*, 466 U.S. 668, 104 S.Ct 2052, 80 L.Ed.2d 674 (1984)

The Court found that in order for a defendant's counsel to be considered ineffective, the defendant must show first that "the counsel's performance was deficient and second that the deficient performance prejudiced the defense so as to deprive the defendant of a fair trial."

L.00767 *Superintendent, Massachusetts Correctional Institution, Walpole v. Hill*, 472 U.S. 445, 105 S.Ct. 2768, 86 L.Ed.2d 356 (1985)

The issue is whether judicial review of disciplinary hearings is constitutional. The state argued that this hearing is sufficient to satisfy due process demands. The Supreme Court decided to decline to answer the question until it had an actual case where judicial review of the disciplinary hearing was barred by law.

L.00768 *Teague v. Lane*, 489 U.S. 288, 109 S.Ct. 1060, 103 L.Ed.2d 334 (1989)

The Court found that the Uniformed Criminal Extradition Act (UCEA) which introduces a new rule regarding a pretrial transfer hearing is not to be applied retroactively to cases involving previous UCEA.

L.00769 *Thornburgh v. Abbott*, 490 U.S. 401, 109 S.Ct. 1874, 104 L.Ed.2d 459 (1989)

The Supreme Court ruled that prison restrictions of inmate publications from the outside are constitutional (do not violate the 1st Amendment) as long as the restrictions are based on a legitimate penological interest.

L.00770 *Timm v. Gunter*, 917 F.2d 1093 (8th Cir. 1990)

Pat–down searches of male inmates by female officers which are performed in a professional manner and do not include instructions to deliberately search inmates' genitals and anal areas are considered constitutional.

L.00771 *Trop v. Dulles*, 356 U.S. 86, 78 S.Ct. 590, 2 L.Ed.2d 630 (1958)

The basis of this case was the 8th Amendment. In its decision the Court argued that the 8th Amendment takes its meaning from the "evolving standards of decency that mark the progress of a maturing society."

L.00772 *Turner v. Safley*, 482 U.S. 78, 107 S.Ct. 2254, 96 L.Ed.2d 65 (1987)

This case dealt with two rules at a Missouri State Prison - a ban on correspondence between inmates in the prison system and prohibiting inmates to marry while incarcerated. The lower court struck down both rules but the Supreme court overturned this decision, stating it had serious reservations about an overly aggressive role of the Federal Courts in prison cases.

L.00773 *Udey v. Kastner*, 805 F.2d 1218 (5th Cir. 1986)

The court ruled that "special diets of organically grown produce washed in distilled water is not required where costs of providing them are over $15,000 per year and where granting the requests will give rise to many fraudulent claims for similar treatment."

L.00774 *United States v. Flores*, 981 F.2d 231 (5th Cir. 1993)

Flores appealed his conviction of 240 months incarceration for distributing heroin. He filed a motion to have his sentence "vacated, set aside, or corrected" under 28 USC @ 2255. The District Court denied the motion. The Appellate Court affirmed the District Court's motion.

L.00775 *United States v. Gouveia*, 467 U.S. 180, 104 S.Ct. 2292, 81 L.Ed.2d 146 (1984)

The Supreme Court held that prisoners in administrative segregation were not entitled to legal counsel until an adversary judicial hearing had been initiated against the inmate. Merely placing an inmate in segregation prior to such proceedings was insufficient to warrant legal representation.

L.00776 *Walker v. Rowe*, 791 F.2d 507 (7th Cir. 1986)

Family members of deceased correctional officers filed suit against the Pontiac Correctional Center. A disruption occurred when officers were bringing inmates back to their cells after an exercise period. Three officers were killed, other inmates were injured, and part of the prison was set on fire. The families alleged that the prison officers denied the workers (prisoners) their constitutional right to a safe working environment. The jury found in favor of the plaintiffs. This case is on appeal.

L.00777 *Waller v. Florida*, 397 U.S. 387, 90 S.Ct. 1184, 25 L.Ed.2d. 435 (1970)

The court ruled that the Court of Appeals had erred when it said there was no double jeopardy when the defendant was tried a second time in a state court for the same offense. The court held that the State of Florida and its municipalities are not separate sovereign entities each entitled to impose punishment for the same alleged crime.

L.00778 *Washington v. Harper*, 494 U.S.210,110 S.Ct.1028, 108 L.Ed.2d 178 (1990)

The Supreme Court said that the unwanted administration of antipsychotic drugs violates the due process clause of the 14 Amendment.

L.00779 *Whitley v. Albers*, 475 U.S. 312, 106 S.Ct. 1078, 89 L.Ed.2d 251 (1986)

The issue addressed in this case is excessive force. The Court found that prison officials will not be held liable under the constitution for actions taken to restore order in face of a riot even if in hindsight the behavior was unreasonable. Only when deliberately set out to cause harm or acting in such a way to completely disregard inmate safety will the actions be viewed as unconstitutional.

L.00780 *Williams v. Steele*, 194 F.2d 32 (8th Cir. 1952)

A prisoner in the United States Medical Center, Springfield, Missouri alleged he was mistreated by the prison system. The Court dismissed the petition stating that the inmate was lawfully detained, and although the Court believed the inmate had been mistreated, the Court could not interfere because it lacked jurisdiction over the matter.

L.00781 *Wilson v. Seiter*, 501 U.S. 294, 111 S.Ct. 2321, 115 L.Ed.2d 271 (1991)

An Ohio prison inmate, Wilson, filed suit alleging certain conditions of his confinement constituted cruel and unusual punishment in violation of the 8th Amendment. He claimed that the prison officials, once notified of the problems, refused to take remedial action. The District Court granted summary judgement, and the Court of Appeals affirmed. The Supreme Court vacated and remanded because the Court of Appeals erred in failing to consider Wilson's claims under the deliberate indifference standard.

L.00782 *Wolff v. McDonnell*, 418 US 539, 94 S.Ct. 2963, 41 L.Ed.2d 935 (1974)

In this 6-to-3 decision, the Court held that the due process clause of the 14 Amendment provides inmates with procedural protection if they are facing a loss of good time or confinement because of an institutional disciplinary action. Some of the specific procedural requirements are, (1) advance written notice of charges, (2) written statement by fact finders explaining the findings, and (3) opportunity to call witness and present case.

LIFE WITHOUT PAROLE

L.00783 Cheatwood, D. (1988). The life-without-parole sanction: Its current status and a research agenda. *Crime and Delinquency 34*(1), 43–59.

The author discusses the problems created by life without parole sanctions and presents a research agenda to prepare for these problems before they arise.

L.00784 Martin, S. E. (1983). Commutation of prison sentences: Practice, promise, and limitation. *Crime and Delinquency 29*(4), 593–612.

Presented in this article is an overview of the legal and administrative structures, policies, and actual usage of sentence commutation in the United States.

L.00785 Steward, J. & Lieberman, P. (1981). What is this new sentence that takes away parole? *Student Lawyer* (October), 14–17, 39.

Contained in this article is an overview of life-without-parole legislation. The authors report that only a few states had enacted legislation of this type in 1975, however, 21 states now have some form of a life-without-parole sentence. Opponents of the sentence suggest   that it will create a new breed of super inmate, one prone to violence who is uncontrollable. Supporters of the sentence suggest that it has put some of the most notorious burglars out of business. According to prison officials, the legislation will result in prison expansion or overcrowding.

L.00786 Wright, J. H. (1990). Life-without-parole: An alternative to death or not much of a life at all? *Vanderbilt Law Review 43*(2), 529–568.

The author sees life-without-parole as the ultimate penalty which is being used by states as a method to curtail violent crime and to change the public's perception that the criminal justice system has failed.

LONG-TERM PRISONERS AND LIFERS

L.00787 Banister, P. A., Smith, F. V., Heskin, K. J. & Bolton, N. (1973). Psychological correlates of long-term imprisonment: I. Cognitive variables. *British Journal of Criminology 13*, 312–323.

The authors found that the longer prisoners were incarcerated, the slower their psychomotor skills became. They found no evidence that imprisonment is associated with general intellectual decline.

L.00788 Bureau of Justice Statistics. (1993). *Survey of State Prison Inmates, 1991*. Rockville, MD: National Institute of Justice/National Criminal Justice Reference Service.

This report is based on in-depth interviews with 13,968 State prison inmates and represents the largest database resource for evaluating the effectiveness of correctional policies.

L.00789 Cheatwood, D. (1988). The life-without-parole sanction: Its current status and a research agenda. *Crime and Delinquency 34*(1), 43–59.

This article is based on an analysis of the problems inherent in the contemporary life-without-parole sanctions. The author suggests a possible research agenda that could prepare prison administrators for these problems before they occur.

L.00790 Cobden, J. & Stewart, G. (1984). Breaking out: A perspective on long-term imprisonment and the process of release. *Canadian Journal of Criminology 26*, 500–510.

The authors of this research article present data from case studies of long-term inmates. They report that long-term prisoners go through three phases during their sentence, resigning one's self to the term of imprisonment, planning for release, and adjusting to freedom. Each phase is characteristically distinct and requires difficult adjustment. Prisoners must choose whether or not they will adjust to each phase. Graduated release and other alternate forms of community resources for long-term prisoners are recommended.

L.00791 Davis, S. P. (1990). Survey: Number of lifers up 45 percent in two years. *Corrections Compendium 15*(8), 1, 8–16.

The article is based on research which was conduced to determine sanctioning patterns as exemplified in state, federal, and Canadian correctional systems. The author indicates that between 1988 and 1990, the number of inmates serving life sentences, in the institutions surveyed, increased by 45 percent.

L.00792 Flanagan, T. J. (1981). Dealing with long-term confinement: Adaptive strategies and perspectives among long-term prisoners. *Criminal Justice and Behavior 8*(2), 201–222.

In this article, the author suggests that an inmate's ability to use various adaptive strategies may alleviate some of the negative impacts of long-term confinement.

L.00793 Flanagan, T. J. (1985). Sentence planning for long-term inmates. *Federal Probation 44*(3), 23–28.

Proposed in this article is the belief that the growing number of inmates with long-term sentences is creating another inmate class with special needs. The author recommends that correctional administrators consider this emerging inmate class in its planning and development of management policies and programs.

L.00794 Flanagan, T. J., Clark, D. D., Aziz, D. W. & Szelest, B. P. (1990). Compositional changes in a long-term prisoner population, 1956–1989. *Prison Journal 80*(1), 15–34.

This article stems from an evaluation of New York state's inmate population over a 34-year period, from 1956 through 1989. Specifically, the authors compared characteristics of the total inmate population with characteristics of long-term prisoner subgroups.

L.00795 Herrick, E. (1988). Number of lifers in U.S. jumps nine percent in four years. *Corrections Compendium 12*(10), 9–11.

In this article it is reported that there are just over 41,000 inmates serving life sentences in U.S. prisons. This represents a nine percent increase in the past four years. This is Part I of a survey of lifers in American correctional institutions.

L.00796 Herrick, E. (1988). Survey: Lifers eligible for parole in most states. *Corrections Compendium 12*(11), 9–13.

Indicated in Part II of this article, a survey on lifers in American correctional institutions, is that most inmates who are serving life sentences can expect to be eligible for parole at some point.

L.00797 Heskin, K. J., Bolton, N., Smith, F. V. & Banister, P. A. (1974). Psychological correlates of long-term imprisonment, III: Attitudinal variables. *British Journal of Criminology, Delinquency, and Deviant Social Behavior 14*(2), 150–157.

In this research article, the authors report the results of a study in which the relationship between the length of time served in prison and prisoners' attitudes toward select concepts was examined. The purpose of the research was to determine if the length of time an inmate is incarcerated impacted the inmate's attitude and if so, how.

L.00798 MacKenzie, D. L. & Goodstein, L. (1985). Long-term incarceration impacts and characteristics of long-term offenders: An empirical analysis. *Criminal Justice and Behavior 12*(4), 395–414.

The article stems from a comparative analysis of long-term versus short-term inmates' adjustment to incarceration. The researchers discuss the differences and their relevance for correctional administrators.

L.00799 MacKenzie, D. L., Robinson, J. W. & Campbell, C. S. (1989). Long-term incarceration of female offenders: Prison adjustment and coping. *Criminal Justice and Behavior 16*(2), 223–238.

Contained in this article are the results of a study which was conducted to compare long-term versus short-term female inmates' adjustment to incarceration. The authors discuss the results of a survey administered to

141 female offenders serving either short-term or long-term prison sentences in Louisiana. The researchers compared the two groups in terms of jail time served, length of sentence, and overall adjustment to prison life.

L.00800 MaGuire, M., Pinter, F. & Collis, C. (1984). Dangerousness and the tariff: The decision-making process in release from life sentences. *British Journal of Criminology 24*(3), 250–268.

Contained in this article are the results of an evaluation of England's new policy for releasing prisoners serving life sentences. The authors conclude that the policy will impact the balance of power among those who are consulted about release and the principles and assumptions which had been used in previous decision making.

L.00801 Palmer, W. R. T. (1984). Programming for long-term inmates: A new perspective. *Canadian Journal of Criminology 26*(4), 439–457.

This article is based on an evaluation of a group program for long-term inmates. The author discusses 'Lifeservers,' a program at Warkworth Institution in Ontario for long-term prisoners.

L.00802 Toch, H. (1977). *Living in prison: The ecology of survival*. New York: Free Press.

In this book the author documents how men adapt to the stress of living in prison. The author discusses the personal impact that loss of security has on individual inmates.

L.00803 Toch, H. (1984). Quo vadis? *Canadian Journal of Criminology*, October, 511–514.

According to the author, the field of corrections is experiencing a vacuum with regard to goals. He suggests that with the rejection of the rehabilitation goal, there has been no other goal espoused. As a result, organizations that do not have goals, cannot define their mission. He recommends that to adequately determine the mission, we must have more knowledge of what prison does to people. The author suggests that long-term inmates could be beneficial in helping to define this mission.

L.00804 Wormith, J. S. (1984). Controversy over the effects of long-term incarceration. *Canadian Journal of Criminology 26*(4), 423–437.

In this literature review, the author reports research findings that reflect the impact of long-term incarceration on inmates.

L.00805 Zamble, E. (1992). Behavior and adaptation in long-term prison inmate: Descriptive longitudinal results. *Criminal Justice and Behavior 19*(4), 409–425.

This article stems from an evaluation of behavior and adaptation of long-term inmates. The author gathered longitudinal data on twenty-five long-term prisoners over a seven year period to evaluate their adaptation to prison. The researcher based the assessment on a comprehensive set of measures of behavior, emotional states, and inmate cognition.

L.00806 Zamble, E. & Porporino, F. J. (1988). *Coping, behavior, and adaptation in prison inmates*. Secaucus, NJ: Springer-Verlag.

Contained in this book are the results of a study which was conducted to examine how male inmates cope with incarceration. The authors based their study on data collected in interviews with 133 inmates in institutions in Ontario, Canada.

M

AUSTIN HARBUTT MacCORMICK

M.00807 Barlett, A. (1934). The four-eyed kid: Austin MacCormick. *New Yorker*, May 26, 24–27.

This article was written shortly after MacCormick's raid on Welfare Island. The author describes MacCormick as an administrator who believed in humane methods: however, he had the ability to be firm with prisoners and rude to people who disagree with him. His instructions prior to the Welfare Island raid were not to engage in rough stuff unless it was necessary, but if was necessary, make it good and rough. He advocated using force as a deterrent for the other inmates.

M.00808 Barlett, A. (1934). Welfare Island raid aids prison reform: Commissioner MacCormick's 'new broom' assault on the corruption of New York's gangster-ruled penitentiary. *The Literary Digest 2*(1), 5–6.

In this article, the author describes the notorious corruption in the prison system in New York in 1934. According to the author, MacCormick's attack on corruption at Welfare Island marked the beginning of prison reform in the United States.

M.00809 Barlett, A. (1940). M'Cormick to quit corrections post. *The New York Times*, January 12, 15.

Contained in this newspaper article is the announcement of Austin MacCormick's January 12, 1940 resignation as Commissioner of New York State's Correction Facilities to become the director of the Osborne Association. According to the article, MacCormick set the standard for prison reform; the basis of which was frequent prison raids and a record of stiff policies.

M.00810 Barlett, A. (1951). Austin H. MacCormick. In *Current Biography*. New York: H.W. Wilson.

Highlighted in this biographical sketch of Austin MacCormick are his significant contributions to corrections. According to MacCormick, the public's apathy to inadequate jail systems stems from their lack of knowledge of jail conditions and widespread feelings that the usual jail inmate is a dirty and depraved person who deserves little sympathy and is not worth trying to help. MacCormick was particularly interested in alcoholics whom he considered sick persons in need of scientific and sociological treatment.

RICHARD A. McGEE

M.00811 Conrad, J. P. (1981). *Justice and consequences*. Lexington, MA: Lexington Books.

In this book, based on Conrad's evaluation of the goals and philosophies of incarceration, the author suggests ways to improve institutional life and provides an overview of Richard McGee's influence on correctional administration.

M.00812 McGee, R. A. (1981). *Prisons and politics*. Lexington, MA: Lexington Books.

Contained in this book is a historical analysis and the personal experiences of a corrections administrator. The author analyzes the impact that politics has had on correctional policy and offers correctional administrators suggestions for dealing with the political aspects of administration. Most of the analysis is based on the penal system in California.

M.00813 Warren, E. (1977). *The memoirs of Chief Justice Earl Warren*. Garden City, NY: Doubleday.

The author, a former Chief Justice of the United States Supreme Court, chronicles personal experiences in this role. The author discusses his personal relationship with Richard McGee.

MARION PENITENTIARY

M.00814 Dickey, C. (1990). A new home for Noriega? *Newsweek*, January 15, 66–69.

In this news article, the author discusses the Marion Illinois Federal Prison where Manuel Noriega is housed. The author describes the inmates at Marion as the most dangerous, most escape-prone, and most threatening inmates in the Federal Prison System. The author points out that correctional officers at Marion agree that their prisoners are the worst in the federal prison system.

M.00815 Earley, P. (1992). *The hot house: Life inside Leavenworth Prison*. New York: Bantam Books.

In this book the author describes life inside the United States' oldest Federal penitentiary. He bases the book on the lives of several inmates and staff and provides a chilling account of the day-to-day life they share inside Fort Leavenworth.

M.00816 Holt, R. & Phillips, R. (1991). Marion: Separating fact from fiction. *Federal Prisons Journal 2*(2), 28–36.

The Federal Bureau of Prisons adopted a new classification system in 1978 and since then Marion Correctional Institution (Illinois) has been the institution where inmates classified as level-six security are housed. The authors discuss the rationale and effectiveness of classification policy.

MEDICAL EXPERIMENTS

M.00817 Bettag, O. (1957). Use of prison inmates in medical research. *American Journal of Correction 19*(3), 4–6, 26–29.

In this article, the author discusses the ethical issues surrounding the use of prisoner in medical experiments.

M.00818 Gettinger, S. & Krajick, K. (1979). The demise of prison medical research. *Corrections Magazine 5*(4), 4–14.

Contained in this article is a discussion of medical research in which inmates are subjects. The authors provide details on the benefits and costs of such research, and explains how past practices were supported. The authors conclude that most medical research, in which inmates are experimental subjects, is no longer permitted.

M.00819 Healy, M. (1994, January 8). Science of power and weakness. *The Los Angeles Times*, A:1, A:12.

In this newspaper article, the author discusses the use of prisoners as research subjects in medical experiments. Also addressed are the ethical issues associated with such research. The author specifically recounts the use of prisoners in human radiation studies.

M.00820 Krajick, K. and Moriarty, F. (1979). Life in the lab: Safer than the cellblocks? *Corrections Magazine 5*(4), 15–20.

Contained in this article is a discussion of the ethical issues of using inmates as subjects in medical experiments. The authors provide details on many medical research facilities which are located at various state institutions.

M.00821 Mills, M. and Morris, N. (1974). Prisoners as laboratory animals. *Society 11*(5), 60–66.

In this article the authors discuss how medical research, with prisoners as subjects, can be beneficial to society, the prison system, and the prisoners themselves, as long as minimum safeguards are maintained.

MENTALLY ILL PRISONERS

M.00822 Adams, K. (1983). Former mental patients in a prison and parole system: A study of socially disruptive behavior. *Criminal Justice and Behavior 10*(3), 358–384.

Presented in this article is an examination of the socially disruptive behavior of prisoners who have been diagnosed as mentally ill. The author examines prison behavior as well as behaviors while being supervised in the community. The author analyzes the differences in these prisoners and the general population in relation to prison disciplinary infractions and post-prison adjustment.

M.00823 Cameron, J. (1988). Balancing the interests: The move towards less restrictive commitment of New York's mentally ill. *New England Journal on Criminal and Civil Confinement 14*, 91–106.

In this law review article, the author acknowledges some of the legal issues associated with involuntary commitment of the mentally ill. Issues addressed in the article are the state's power of involuntary commitment, movement towards increased protection of individual rights, movement away from the 'strict dangerous standard,' and New York states mental hygiene laws.

M.00824 Clingempeel, W. G., Mulvey, E. & Reppucci, N. D. (1980). National study of ethical dilemmas of psychologists in the criminal justice system. In J. Monahan (ed.), *Who Is the client?* Washington, DC: American Psychological Association.

In this article the authors present the findings of a Task Force empaneled by the American Psychological Association in 1976 to study the ethical dilemmas of psychologists working in the criminal justice system. One of the areas addressed is mentally ill prisoners.

M.00825 Collins, W. C. (1988). Medicating the jailed mentally ill: Some legal concerns. *Corrections Today 50*(7), 46–50.

In this article the author discusses legal issues of medicating a person who is mentally ill and incarcerated. The issue of adequate mental health care is discussed in light of an inmate's refusal to be medicated. The author specifically addresses the test of 'deliberate indifference to serious medical needs,' the inmate's right to refuse treatment, and involuntarily medicating inmates.

M.00826 Dix, D. L. (1845). *Remarks on prisons and prison discipline in the United States* (reprinted from the 2nd ed., 1967). Montclair, NJ: Patterson Smith.

This book is the result of a four year investigation that the author conducted into all of the prisons in the New England and Middle Atlantic states. The author found these prisons characterized by cruelty, injustice and laxity of punishment. She concluded that although the Pennsylvania System is not perfect it is the most perfect prison system that man has produced.

M.00827 Kay, S., Wolkenfeld, F. & Murrill, L. (1988). Profiles of aggression among psychiatric patients. *Journal of Nervous and Mental Disease 176*(9), 539–548.

In this research article, the authors describe their assessment of the nature and prevalence of aggression in a psychiatric population. The data were collected from two cohorts of 114 and 150 in-patients. Chronic patients showed the lowest incidence of assault and aggression. Gender differences and daily variations were not significant.

M.00828 McShane, M. D. (1989). Bus stop revisited: Discipline and psychiatric patients in prison. *Journal of Psychiatry and law 17*(3), 413–433.

In this article the author concluded that inmates with extensive psychiatric problems are one of the more difficult inmate populations to administer services to in terms of manpower, resources, and potential liabilities.

M.00829 Monahan, J. (1984).The prediction of violent behavior: Toward a second generation of theory and policy. *American Journal of Psychiatry 141*(1), 10–15.

This article is based on an evaluation of research studies on the prediction of violent behavior. After examining the first wave of research focusing on predicting violent behavior, the author concludes that predicting violent behavior is highly inaccurate. The author also addresses the unique problem of predicting violent behavior in individuals characterized by mental illness.

M.00830 Pye, M. & Potter, E. (1980). Dangerous side–effects of neuroleptic drugs. *International Journal of Offender Therapy and Comparative Criminology 24*, 290–292.

In this article the authors conclude that for years mentally ill prisoners have been given medications to control their behavior. Now, scientists are finding that some of these medications cause permanent damage to the central nervous system. The authors argue that other medications should be used for controlling mentally ill inmates.

M.00831 Toch, H. (1986). The disturbed disruptive inmate: Where does the bus stop? In K. C. Haas and G. P. Alpert (eds.), *Dilemmas of punishment* (pp. 100–115). Prospect Heights, IL: Waveland Press.

Contained in this edited book chapter are arguments that prisons need a better, more stable plan to handle mentally ill inmates. The author suggests that in the past, inmates with mental problems have been shuttled back and forth between mental institutions and the prison and that this policy often enhances mental disturbance.

M.00832 Toch, H. and Adams, K. (1986). Pathology and disruptiveness among prison inmates. *Journal of Research in Crime and Delinquency 25*(1), 7–21.

This article stems from a study which was conducted to examine the degree to which mentally unstable inmates were characterized by disciplinary problems. The researcher conducted the study by assessing the relationship between custodial violations and the mental health of the inmates who were characterized by custodial violations.

M.00833 Toch, H. and Adams, K. (1987). The prison as dumping ground: Mainlining disturbed offenders. *Journal of Psychiatry and Law 15*, 539–554.

In this article the authors acknowledge that many offenders sentenced to prison are emotionally disturbed at the time of their offense and continue to be disturbed during their admission to prison. These offenders have difficulties adjusting to imprisonment and can create problems for the staff. The authors suggest that these inmates might be better served through diversion programs that involve interagency cooperation.

M.00834 Toch, H. and Adams, K. (1989). *The Disturbed Violent Offender*. New Haven, CT: Yale University Press.

Contained in this book is an analysis of data from samples of inmates convicted of violent offenses who entered the New York State prison system in 1985. Presented is an analysis of the relationship between mental disorder and criminal violence in individuals that are both disturbed and violent.

M.00835 Wiehn, P. J. (1982). Mentally ill offenders: Prison's first casualties. In R. Johnson and H. Toch (eds.), *The pains of imprisonment* (pp. 221–237). Newbury Park, CA: Sage Publications.

Provided in this edited book chapter is an overview of the adjustment problems experienced by mentally ill inmates. The author explains how the added difficulty of mental illness contributes to victimization and isolation. The author then describes an outpatient treatment program in Connecticut which is an alternative to imprisonment for the mentally ill.

Cases

M.00836 *Bee v. Greaves*, 744 F.2d 1387 (10th Cir. 1984)

In this case the court ruled that pretrial detainees have the right to refuse medication.

M.00837 *Estelle v. Gamble* (429 U.S. 97, 97 S.Ct. 285, 50 L.Ed.2d 251 (1976)

The Supreme Court ruled that "deliberate indifference" of prison officials or personnel to the serious medical needs of inmates constitutes cruel and unusual punishment violating the Eighth Amendment.

M.00838 *Vitek v. Jones,* 445 U.S. 480 (1980)

In this case the court recognized that due process protections must be intact prior to transferring inmates from prison to mental hospitals.

MUTILATION

M.00839 Bennum, I. (1983). Depression and hostility in self-mutilation. *Suicide and Life Threatening Behavior 13,* 71–84.

Presented in this article is an examination of self-mutilation by people who are suffering from severe depression. The author suggests that these individuals usually try to render a limb inoperable and employ unique ways to attempt suicide.

M.00840 Beto, D. R. & Claghorn, J. (1968). Factors associated with self-mutilation within the Texas Department of Corrections. *American Journal of Corrections 30,* 25–27.

The authors of this research article report the results of their study that was conducted to determine the causative factors leading to self-mutilation of incarcerated inmates and to identify predictive factors. Data were collected from 100 male inmates in the Wynne Treatment Center of the Texas Department of Corrections. The significant predictive factors discovered are race, family size, narcotic addiction, family type, occupation, and religion.

M.00841 Franklin, R. K. (1988). Deliberate self-harm: Self-injurious behavior within a correctional mental health population. *Criminal Justice and Behavior 15*(2), 210–218.

The article stems from a study of self-mutilation by prisoners who are characterized by mental health problems. The author found that suicide is not always the purpose of 'self-harm,' sometimes referred to as self-mutilation or self-injurious behavior. This is especially true for prisoners.

M.00842 Johnson, E. H. (1973). Felon self-mutilation: Correlate of stress in prison. In B. Danto (Ed.), *Jail house blues: Studies of suicidal behavior in jail and prison.* Orchard Lake, MI: Epic Publications, Inc.

In this edited book chapter the author describes how the criminally insane feel about their imprisonment and how they come to the conclusion to commit suicide.

M.00843 Jones, A. (1986). Self-mutilation in prison: A comparison of mutilators and non-mutilators. *Criminal Justice and Behavior 13*(3), 286–296.

This article is based on a comparison of two groups of prisoners, one consisting of 67 self-mutilating inmates and the other consisting of 68 randomly selected non-mutilating inmates. Inmate-case records were the source of data for the 15 variables that the researchers used for making comparisons.

M.00844 Lloyd, C. (1990). *Suicide and self-injury in prison: A literature review.* London: Her Majesty's Stationery Office.

Contained in this book is a review of the research literature on suicide in British prisons. The author found that the suicide rate in British prisons is higher than that of the general population. This has caused concern because suicide is believed to be preventable in closed institutions. Also the state is responsible for inmates and prison conditions which may contribute to suicide.

M.00845 Ross, R. R. & MacKay, H. B. (1979). *Self-Mutilation.* Lexington, MA: Lexington Books.

In this book the authors report results from a study of self-mutilation among adolescent females in a Canadian training school. The study was subsequently curtailed when people became aware that the subjects were assisting in the operation of a treatment program to halt self-mutilation.

M.00846 Schaffer, C., Carroll, J. & Abramowitz, S. (1982). Self-mutilation and the borderline personality. *Journal of Nervous and Mental Disease 170*, 468–473.

This research article is based on data collected from 14 self-mutilators and 14 psychiatric controls matched for age, sex, and in-patient/out-patient status. Subjects were administered the Diagnostic Interview for Borderline. The self-mutilators scored significantly higher on impulse-action patterns, affects, psychoticism, and interpersonal relations as well as on the total borderline index.

M.00847 Simpson, M. (1980). Self-mutilation as indirect self-destructive behavior. In N. Forberow (ed.), *The many faces of suicide.* New York:

McGraw Hill.

This edited book chapter contains the author's findings that self-mutilation should not be classified as attempted suicide. The author indicates that in many cases, people cut themselves knowing that it is not fatal, to see the blood, and because it feels good.

N

NATIONAL PRISON PROJECT

N.00848 Berger, A. B. (1992). *Wilson v. Seiter:* An unsatisfying attempt at resolving the imbroglio of Eighth Amendment prisoners' rights standards. *Utah Law Review* (Spring), 565–599.

The author provides a history of the Cruel and Unusual Punishment Clause from biblical times up until its adoption in the United States Constitution. He then examines the development of the clause in the United States by studying precedent from the early days of the Republic up through current Supreme Court decisions. By presenting an examination of the Court's ruling in *Wilson,* the author argues that the Court contravene precedents which are often impractical. He suggests that the Court's earlier method of adjudicating prisoners' suits presented a fairer balance between the rights of prisoners and society.

N.00849 Bronstein, A. J. (1985). Prisoners and their endangered rights. *The Prison Journal 65,* 3–17.

In this article, the author provides an analysis of recent judicial decisions regarding rights of prisoners. The author concludes that the progress made in this area is being eroded and that the future of such rights depends on political leadership and public education, as well as the philosophy of the court.

N.00850 Chilton, B. S. & Nice, D. C. (1993). Triggering federal court intervention in state prison reform. *The Prison Journal 73,* 30–46.

In this article, the authors examine data from all the states except Alaska and Hawaii to determine what triggers federal court intervention in prison reform litigation. Data were gleaned from the following sources, U.S. Census Bureau, (2) *The Book of the States*, and (3) *Statistical Abstracts*.

N.00851 Conrad, J. P. (1985). The view from the witness chair. *The Prison Journal 65*, 18–25.

In this article, the author chronicles past and present institutional disciplinary procedures for inmates. It is suggested that prison litigation challenging these procedures has benefitted prisoners. Even so, the author recommends that further efforts should target eliminating unacceptable conditions in prisons.

N.00852 Donahue, W. A. (1991). The new agenda of the ACLU. *Society 28*(2), 5–14.

The author argues that the ACLU's politicized agenda is not new. However, its boldness in using Constitutional arguments to reform the nature of American economic life is new. It is argued that the "ACLU has made a decisive shift away from traditional civil libeterian concerns toward a new agenda of legalizing collectivist economic programs." The article also contains a historical overview of the development of the ACLU.

N.00853 O'Manique, J. O. (1992). Development, human rights and law. *Human Rights Quarterly 14*, 383–408.

Explored in this article are the foundations of positive law and its relationship to the development of human rights. The author hypothesizes that human rights are universal and are the basis for positive law. He discusses natural law and positivism, neo-Darwinian theory, the origins of rights and law, Thomas Hobbes' vision of the world, international law, and world order theories.

N.00854 Rudovsky, D. (1973). *The rights of prisoners: The basic ACLU guide to a prisoner's rights*. New York: Discus Books.

This book is designed for use by inmates and non-specialists. The author explains prisoners' rights and provides a guide on how to protect those rights.

N.00855 Ryan, M. (1992). Reports and surveys: The Woolf report, on the tread-mill of prison reform? *Political Quarterly 63*, 50–57.

This is a summary of the Woolf Report on prison disturbances that occurred in England in the early 1990s. It contains background information, an explanation of the disturbances, an overview of England's community prisons and the remand population as well as a section on prison officers.

Cases

N.00856 *Bell v. Wolfish*, 441 U.S. 520, 99 S.Ct. 1862, 60 L.Ed.2d 447 (1979)

This case was litigated when inmates of a short-term facility challenged the facility's double-celling procedure. The facility, designed to house pre-trial defendants, placed two inmates in a room that was designed to house one occupant.

N.00857 *Palmigiano v. Garrahy*, 443 F.Supp. 956, (D.R.I. 1977)

In this class action suit, representing prisoners and pretrial detainees, it was alleged that confinement conditions at the Rhode Island prison system violated the Eighth and Fourteenth Amendments. The Court concluded that the "totality of conditions of confinement . . . do not provide the tolerable living environment."

N.00858 *Rhodes v. Chapman*, 452 U.S. 337, 101 S.Ct. 2392, 69 L.Ed.2d 59 (1981)

The Supreme Court ruled that double-celling in and of itself is not unconstitutional.

NEWGATE PRISON

N.00859 Durham, A. M. (1989). Newgate of Connecticut: Origins and early days of an early American prison. *Justice Quarterly* 6(1), 89–116.

In this article, the author makes a case that the Walnut Street Jail is not the first American prison. It is suggested that other earlier institutions pre-date the Philadelphia facility. The author also provides an overview of the Newgate prison and its place in colonial penology.

N.00860 Durham, A. M. (1990). Social control and imprisonment during the American revolution: Newgate of Connecticut. *Justice Quarterly* 7(2), 293–323.

Provided in this article is a historical account of the pre-revolutionary history of Connecticut, including an explanation of the formal and informal methods used to control Loyalist behavior. A discussion of Newgate is presented, including the population it served, conditions of the institution, and problems with security.

N.00861 Erikson, K. T. (1966). *Wayward puritans: A study in the sociology of deviance.* New York: John Wiley and Sons.

This book is based on the classic sociological study of witches as form of deviancy. The author applies traditional Durkheimian ideas to historical data to assess research hypotheses about deviance. The author reviews the Quaker invasion and their pursuit of witches in Salem. The purpose of the research is to study the problem of group identities and boundaries, stabilities and instabilities in rates of deviance, and the functions of deviance for the integration of groups.

NEWS MEDIA

N.00862 Dulaney, W. L. (1970). The news media and corrections. *Federal Probation 34*, 63–66.

In this article, the author points out the reasons why the mass media does not cover significant problems in corrections. Analyzing the goals of the correctional system and that of the mass media, the author suggests ways to increase the coverage, thus making it more comprehensive.

N.00863 Jacobs, J. B. & Brooks, H. A. (1983). The mass media and prison news. In J.B. Jacobs (ed.), *New perspectives on prisons and imprisonment.* Ithaca, NY: Cornell University Press.

In this edited book chapter, the author focuses on the relationship between the mass media and correctional institutions. This chapter is one of twelve that contain analyses of contemporary prison issues from socio-legal perspectives.

N.00864 Marsh, H. L. (1986). The media and correctional administrators: The time for mutual cooperation and understanding has come. *Criminal Justice Research Bulletin 2*(4), 1–4.

In this article, the author profiles the potentially explosive relationship between the mass media and prison administrators. The author provides suggestions on ways to improve the relationship.

N.00865 McGee, R. A. (1981). *Prisons and politics.* Lexington, MA: Lexington Books.

This book stems from the author's experiences as a correctional administrator. The author conducts a historical analysis of the impact of politics on correctional policy, special attention is directed at prison policy in on California.

N.00866 Turnbo, C. (1994). News at eleven: Correctional accountability and the media. *Federal Prisons Journal 3*(3), 47–50.

Today in the United States, the news media is the best means for the average American to hear an intelligent discourse on corrections; however, media reporting on corrections is too often influenced by sensationalism and not reality.

NORFOLK PRISON

N.00867 Barnes, H. E., & Teeters, N. K. (1943). *New horizons in criminology.* New York: Prentice Hall, Inc.

Contained in this book is a comprehensive discussion of crime, criminals, punishment, and prisons. The authors also offer suggestions for future reforms in the repression of crime and the treatment of criminals. They provide information on the evolution of correctional officers.

N.00868 Commons, W. H., Yahkub, T. & Powers, E. (1940). *A report on the development of penological treatment at Norfolk Prison Colony in Massachusetts.* New York: Bureau of Social Hygiene.

The authors present a history of Norfolk Prison. Included is the official manual of the prison colony, a policy statement, a breakdown of the prison buildings, an organizational breakdown and illustrations of the individualized treatment plans developed for the inmates.

N.00869 Gill, H. B. (1931). The Norfolk state prison colony at Massachusetts. *Journal of Criminal Law and Criminology 22*(May), 107–112.

In this article, the author describes the general governance of Norfolk Prison. He describes the board of inspectors, their appointment and responsibilities. He also provides an overview of general regulations and discipline. Sections of the article include the Norfolk plan, group system of housing and supervision, community organization as a basis for joint-responsibility and individual programs for treatment.

N.00870 Gill, H. B. (1962). Correctional philosophy and architecture. *Journal of Criminal Law, Criminology, and Police Science 53*, 312–322.

The author traces the history of penal philosophy in the United States and discusses the influence of penal philosophy on prison architecture and the influence of prison architecture on penal policies.

N.00871 Gill, H. B. (1970). A new prison discipline: Implementing the Declaration of Principles of 1870. *Federal Probation 34*, 29–33.

The author states that the Declaration of Principles of 1870 does not need to be revised but that there needs to be an affirmation of the progress achieved in the last 100 years. He states there needs to be a 'New Prison Discipline.' The new discipline consists of two types, a set of rules and regulations and a way of life.

N.00872 McKelvey, B. (1936). *American prisons: A history of good intentions.* Chicago: University of Chicago Press. (Reprinted, Montclair, NJ: Patterson Smith, 1977).

Contained in this book is a historical account of American prisons from 1835 through 1977. The author presents detailed information on changing standards, reform movements, criminological theories, and confrontations in penology. The author provides a short discussion of the role of Norfolk Prison in the history of American prisons.

O

THOMAS MOTT OSBORNE

O.00873 Bacon, C. (1974). *Foundations of criminal justice: Prison reform*. New York: AMS Press.

Contained in this book is a comprehensive review of prison reform in the United States. The author discusses Thomas Mott Osborne's role in prison reform.

O.00874 Bates, S. (1936). *Prisons and beyond*. New York: Books for Libraries Press. (Reprinted 1971, New York: Macmillan).

Bates, the first director of the Federal Bureau of Prison, presents a thorough discussion of the following: the structure and administration of the Federal Penal System, the administration of county prisons, what is wrong with the prison system, how the Federal system recognizing its deficiencies used science to build a model system, practical problems of administration, what prisoners think about, an examination of the parole system, can prisons fulfill a useful function, can we afford the price of good prisons, will the future prison be based on the present model, and the fundamental importance of community efforts at prevention. The author's intent is to prove that a prison system utilizing rehabilitation provides the best protection to society. Bates also acknowledges Osborne's contributions to penology.

O.00875 Haynes, F. E. (1939). *The American prison system*. New York: McGraw-Hill Book Company, Inc.

In this book, the author describes the American prison system from an operational perspective. Also included is a discussion of Thomas Mott Osborne's impact on penology.

O.00876 Lewis, O. F. (1922). *The development of American prisons and prison customs*. New York: Prison Association of New York.

Contained in this book is a historical analysis of the evolution of American prisons. The author includes an extensive presentation on Philadelphia's Walnut Street Prison of 1790 and the New York State Prison of 1796. The Auburn State System is also discussed and contrasted with the two former systems. The author discusses the role of Thomas Mott Osborne in the evolution of American prisons.

O.00877 Osborne, T. M. (1916). *Society and prisons: Yale lectures on the responsibilities of citizenship*. New Haven, CT: Yale University Press.

Contained in this book is a collection of lectures delivered at Yale University on the responsibilities of citizenship. Topics addressed in the series include crime and criminals, courts and punishment, the old prison systems, the mutual welfare league, and the new penology.

P

PANOPTICAN

P.00878 Bentham, J. (1787, 1791). *Panoptican: Or, the inspection house.* 3 vols. Dublin: T. Payne.

Contained in these three volumes are Bentham's complete works on the Panoptican. Some of the issues discussed by Bentham include the inspection principle, penitentiary inspection house plan, essential points and advantages of the plan, safe custody, economy, contract, trades, labor, liberated persons, houses of correction, mad houses, hospitals, schools, and chapels.

P.00879 Hawkins, R. & Alpert, G. P. (1989). *American prison systems: Punishment and justice.* Englewood Cliffs, NJ: Prentice-Hall.

In this book, the authors provide a historical account of the origins and goals of incarceration in the United States. They discuss the relationship between actual experiences of inmates and punishment theory. The authors describe the historical significance of the Panoptican to penology.

P.00880 Howard, E. (1965). *Garden cities of tomorrow.* Cambridge: MIT Press.

This book is a useful text for anyone interested in city planning. The original was published in 1898 and is considered a classic for the ideas presented. Some ideas are outdated, others however, have become entrenched in modern city design. The Panoptican design is discussed.

PAROLE BOARDS

P.00881 Bottomley, A. K. (1990). Parole in transition. A comparative study of origins, developments, and prospects for the 1990s. In M. Tonry and N. Morris (eds.), *Crime and Justice: A Review of Research* (pp. 319–374). Chicago: University of Chicago Press.

This article is a chronicle of parole in England, the United States, and Canada. The author discusses its origins and precursors, challenges to the theory and practice of parole during the 1970s, and options and prospects for the future of parole.

P.00882 Bureau of Justice Statistics. (1991). *Probation and parole. 1990.* Rockville, MD: National Institute of Justice/National Criminal Justice Reference Service.

The author provides probation and parole statistics for 1990 showing that the number of people on probation and parole increased and that an estimated 1.7 percent of all adults in the United States were on probation or parole.

P.00883 Cavender, G. (1982). *Parole: A critical analysis.* Port Washington, NY: Kennikat Press.

In this book, the author chronicles the development and practice of parole in the United States. He discusses the current debate about the rehabilitative value of parole.

P.00884 Gottfredson, D., Wilkins, L. T. & Hoffman, P. B. (1978). *Guidelines for parole and sentencing.* Lexington, MA: Lexington Books.

Contained in this book is an overview of parole and sentencing. The authors discuss the need to improve procedures for parole decision-making. They suggest developing and implementing an explicit policy regarding parole decision-making.

P.00885 Rhine, E. E., Smith, W. R., Jackson, R. W., Burke, P. B. & LaBelle, R. (1991). *Paroling authorities: Recent history and current practice.* Laurel, MD: American Correctional Association.

This book is based on an American Correctional Association Task Force evaluation of parole. Data from the 50 states and Canada were analyzed to determine the status of parole practices in the United States and Canada.

P.00886 Rothman, D. J. (1980). *Conscience and convenience: The asylum and its alternatives in progressive America.* Waltham, MA: Little, Brown and Co.

The author provides an overview of the programs that have dominated criminal justice, juvenile justice, and mental health in the 20th century. There is a discussion of how penitentiaries and state mental hospitals are similar.

P.00887 Rhine, E. E., Wetter, R. E. & Runda, J. C. (1994). *The practice of parole boards.* Lexington, KY: Association of Paroling Authorities, International.

The authors studied parole boards to determine the structure and powers of paroling authorities, the parole hearing, the role of the victim in the parole process, issues of parole supervision, HIV policies, and the parole violation and revocation process. Using the data collected, the authors present statistical data, primarily frequency distributions and percentages.

P.00888 Simon, J. (1993). *Poor discipline: Parole and the social control of the underclass, 1890–1990.* Chicago: University of Chicago Press.

The author discusses the history of parole and identifies two distinct models, disciplinary parole and clinical parole, that were used prior to 1970. From the early 1970s until the present a new model of parole has emerged, managerial parole.

P.00889 Tonry, M. H. (1987). *Sentencing reform impacts.* Rockville, MD: National Institute of Justice/National Criminal Justice Reference Service.

The author evaluates the literature on the impact of sentencing changes in the United States and notes that a uniform sentencing system has is in fact a several sentencing systems.

P.00890 von Hirsch, A. (1976). *Doing justice: The choice of punishments, report of the Committee for the Sudy of Incarceration.* New York: Hill and Wang.

The author discusses the use of imprisonment as a device to give serious criminals what they deserve. The author believes that lesser criminals should not receive imprisonment but some lesser disposition.

P.00891 von Hirsch, A. & Hanrahan, K. J. (1979). *The question of parole: Retention, reform or abolition.* Cambridge: Ballinger.

In this book, the authors examine parole and make recommendations to modify it, including altering supervision practices and changing the role of parole boards.

Cases

P.00892 *Gagnon v. Scarpelli*, 411 US 778, 93 S.Ct 1756, 36 L.Ed.2d 656 (1973)

In this case the Court decided that probationers and parolees have a constitutionally limited right to counsel in revocation hearings. This case resulted in providing some control over the unlimited discretion, which had been exercised in the past, by probation and parole personnel in revocation proceedings. The court held that right to counsel would be decided on a case-by-case basis and that the responsible agency would make the decision. The Court also applied the due process standards established in the Morrissey parole case.

P.00893 *Greenholtz v. Inmates of the Nebraska Penal and Correctional Complex*, 442 US 1 (1979)

In this case the Court reviewed the rights of inmates to secure due process at parole hearings. The Court held that early release on parole was a privilege and not a right and that this act of 'grace' did not entitle inmates to receive the full complement of due process rights, i.e., they were not accorded the right to counsel or to call witnesses.

P.00894 *Morrissey v. Brewer*, 408 US 471, 92 S.Ct 2593, 33 L.Ed. 288 (1972)

In this case the Court established due process procedures for parole revocation hearings. The specific due process requirements are, written notice of the claimed violations, disclosure of evidence against the parolee, opportunity to confront and cross examine witnesses, opportunity to be heard and present witnesses and documentary evidence, a "neutral and detached" hearing body, and a written explanation of by the fact finders as to the evidence relied on and reasons for revoking parole.

PATUXENT INSTITUTION

P.00895 Boslow, H. M. (1959). The Maryland defective delinquent law. *British Journal of Delinquency 10*, 5–13.

In this article, the author explains Maryland's 'defective delinquent law,' a law that provides for treatment of chronic juvenile offenders who are dangerous. The author discusses the impact of the law on Patuxent, Maryland's long-term treatment facility for "dangerous" offenders.

P.00896 Carney, F. L. (1974). The indeterminate sentencing at Patuxent. *Crime and Delinquency 20*, 135–143.

In this article, the author examines the Maryland law that provides for treatment of dangerous, chronic juvenile offenders. The treatment is usually part of an indeterminate sentence, sometimes served at Patuxent Institution. The author indicates that the law has been criticized in light of the indeterminate sentencing mandate.

P.00897 Contract Research Corporation. (1977). *The evaluation of Patuxent Institution: Final report.* Belmont, CA: Contract Research Corporation.

Presented are the results of an evaluation that was conducted to determine the feasibility of continuing the indeterminate sentencing of defective delinquents to Patuxent Institution. The researchers recommended the repeal of indeterminate sentencing and the 'defective delinquent law.'

P.00898 Courtless, T. F. (1989). The rehabilitative ideal meets an aroused public: The Patuxent experiment revisited. *Journal of Psychiatry and Law 12*, 607–626.

In this article the author recognizes changes in Maryland's Patuxent Institution that resulted from the 1988 revisions in the state's Article 31B Statute, also known as the "Defective Delinquency Statute." He discusses the statute, the crisis it generated, and the revision process.

P.00899 Hodges, E. (1971). Crime prevention by the indeterminate sentence law. *American Journal of Psychiatry 128*, 291–295.

In this article, the author describes the practice of the first eleven and a half years of the Maryland defective delinquent statute. The statue is meant to provide treatment to those juveniles who are chronic, dangerous offenders. The author suggests that a great deal of crime prevention has resulted from use of the law.

P.00900 Wilkins, L. T. (1976). Treatment of offenders: Patuxent examined. *Rutgers Law Review 29*, 1102–1116.

In this law review article, the author questions the recidivism statistics reported by Patuxent Institution and further questions the comparisons made between Patuxent and other treatment facilities. The conceptualization of recidivism is also thoroughly discussed.

P.00901 Zenoff, E. H. & Courtless, T. (1977). Autopsy of an experiment: The Patuxent experience. *Journal of Psychiatry and Law 5*, 531–550.

In this article, the authors report that the Maryland law, which allowed chronic, dangerous juvenile offenders to receive treatment on an indeterminate sentencing plan, has been repealed. The Patuxent Institution is trying a new plan for dangerous offenders.

PENNSYLVANIA SYSTEM

P.00902 Ackroyd, P. (1990). *Dickens*. New York: HarperCollins.

This book is a biography of the writer, Charles Dickens. Ackroyd explains how Dickens' description of debtors prison and other social problems of the day provide insight about the establishment of a humanitarian approach to incarceration, i.e, the Pennsylvania System.

P.00903 Foucault, M. (1978). *Discipline and punish: The birth of the prison.* Translated by A. Sheridan. New York: Pantheon Books.

The author states that prisons cannot be separated from the societies in which they are found. Prisons serve as the model for other institutions in society, for example, schools, hospitals, and factories.

P.00904 Gibbons, D. C. (1992). *Society, crime, and criminal behavior* (6th Ed.). Englewood Cliffs, NJ: Prentice-Hall.

In this text book, the author provides a historical account of criminology and examines and profiles crime in modern society. He also discusses criminological theory and the criminal justice system. The author describes the historical significance of the Pennsylvania System.

P.00905 Irwin, J. & Austin, J. (1994). *It's about time: America's imprisonment binge.* Belmont, CA: Wadsworth Corporation.

The authors believe that prisons are not the answer to the crime problem in the United States and suggest an overhaul of the current approach to sentencing and imprisonment.

P.00906 Rothman, D. J. (1971). *The discovery of the asylum: Social order and disorder in the New Republic.* Boston: Little, Brown and Co.

Contained in this book is a functionalist perspective on asylums and the social structure. Rothman proposes that society's institutions, whether social, political, or economic, cannot be understood apart from the society in which they exist. The author argues that asylums and society are interdependent, each supporting the other. Also provided is a detailed account of Pennsylvania System penology and the role Quakers played in its development.

P.00907 Teeters, N. K. (1955). *The cradle of the penitentiary: The Walnut Street Jail at Philadelphia, 1773–1835.* Philadelphia, PA: Pennsylvania Prison Society.

In this book the author provides a historical account of the development of the Walnut Street Jail in Philadelphia. The author examines the reforms that lead to the jail becoming a prison and the role of the Quakers in its development. The time period examined is 1773 to 1835.

PHILADELPHIA SOCIETY FOR ALLEVIATING THE MISERIES OF PUBLIC PRISONS

P.00908 Babcock, W. G. & Leban, J. A. (eds.). Journal retrospective, 1845–1986: 200 years of prison society history as reflected in the *Prison Journal. Prison Journal 67*(1), 1–42.

The Pennsylvania Prison Society has worked for the improvement of prisons and the betterment of prisoners from 1845 to the present through the publication of the Prison Journal.

P.00909 Teeters, N. K. (1937). *They were in prison: A history of the Pennsylvania Prison Society, 1787–1937.* Chicago: John C. Winston.

This book is a chronicle of the Pennsylvania prison system. The author discusses the main differences between the Auburn and Pennsylvania systems. This reference book contains excerpts from prisons' records.

P.00910 Teeters, N. K. (1962). Citizen concern and action over 175 years. *Prison Journal: The Pennsylvania Prison Society, 175th Anniversary Issue 42*(Spring), 5–36.

In this article the author discusses the following: contributions of the Prison Society to corrections, the first acts of the Society, visits by Bishop White and Dr. Rogers, operations of the Society, the New Dispensation, dissenegration of Walnut Street Jail, solitary confinement, vagrants and discharged prisoners, beginnings of parole, emergence of the professional approach and Society staff through the years.

PRERELEASE PROGRAMS

P.00911 Bartollas, C. & Conrad, J. P. (1992). *Introduction to corrections* (2d ed.). New York: Harper Collins Publishers.

Contained in this text book is a comprehensive and objective overview of American corrections.

P.00912 Bronick, M. J. (1989). Relieving subpopulation pressures. *Federal Prisons Journal 1*(2), 17–21.

According to this researcher, the Federal Bureau of Prisons' practice of placing specific subpopulations in privately contracted institutions can relieve overcrowding and provide better care for subpopulations with special needs.

P.00913 Buckley, M. (1972). Enter – The ex-con. *Federal Probation 36*(4), 24–30.

The author traces the evolution of Project Re-Entry, a pre-release program conducted by successful ex-inmates at the Massachusetts Correctional Institution in Norfolk.

P.00914 Frank, B. (1973). Graduated release. In B. Frank (ed.), *Contemporary corrections: A concept in search of content* (pp. 225–241). Reston, VA: Reston Publishing Co.

The author examines the various forms of graduated release used in corrections to aid the inmate in his/her return to society. Discussed are pre-release programs, work release programs and halfway houses.

P.00915 Holt, N. & Renteria, R. (1969). Prerelease program evaluation: Some implications of negative findings. *Federal Probation, 33*(June), 42-44. Also, in R.M. Carter, D. Glaser, and L.T. Wilkins (Eds.), *(1977). Correctional Institutions* (2nd ed.). Philadelphia: J. B. Lippincott.

The authors report the findings from their evaluation of a prerelease program in one of California's institutions. The program began in 1965 as an instructional program to prepare inmates for reentry into society.

P.00916 LeClair, D. P. & Guarino–Ghezzi, S. (1991). Does incapacitation guarantee public safety? Lessons from the Massachusetts furlough and prerelease programs. *Justice Quarterly 8*(1), 9–36.

The authors surveyed three samples of male inmates released during the 1970s from The Massachusetts Department of Corrections' facilities to determine if there was an identifiable intervention effect on recidivism rates.

P.00917 President's Commission on Law Enforcement and the Administration of Justice. (1967). *Task force report: Corrections.* Washington, DC: U.S. Government Printing Office.

This task force report on corrections contains recommendations for new roles the Federal Government should play in corrections.

PRESIDENT'S COMMISSION ON LAW ENFORCEMENT AND THE ADMINISTRATION OF JUSTICE, *TASK FORCE REPORT: CORRECTIONS*

P.00918 President's Commission on Law Enforcement and the Administration of Justice. (1967). *The challenge of crime in a free society.* Washington, DC: U.S. Government Printing Office.

Contained in this report is an overview of the President's Commission on Law Enforcement and the Administration of Justice. President Johnson established the Commission on Law Enforcement and Administration of Justice on July 23, 1965 to address the causes of crime and delinquency. Provided in this summary report are 200 plus recommendations for preventing crime and delinquency and for improving law enforcement and the administration of criminal justice.

P.00919 President's Commission on Law Enforcement and the Administration of Justice. (1967). *Task force report: Corrections.* Washington, DC: U.S. Government Printing Office.

This task force report on corrections contains recommendations for new roles the Federal Government should play in corrections. The Commission was established by President Johnson on July 23, 1965 to research the causes of crime and delinquency in America. Provided in this report are the Commission's findings regarding the state of American corrections.

P.00920 Stojkovic, S. (1994). The President's Crime Commission recommendations for corrections: The twilight of the idols. In J. A. Conley (ed.), *The 1967 President's crime commission report: Its impact 25 years later* (pp. 37–55). Cincinnati: Anderson Publishing Co.

In this book chapter the author identifies the significant recommendations of the President's Crime Commission, examines which of these recommendations were implemented and why, presents and examination of why some recommendations were not implemented, and explores the importance of the recommendations for the present and the future.

PRISONIZATION

P.00921 Berk, B. B. (1966). Organizational goals and inmate organization. *American Journal of Sociology, 71*, 522-534. Also in R. G. Leger and J. R. Stratton (eds.). *(1977). Sociology of corrections: A book of readings 1977.* New York: John Wiley and Sons.

In this article, the author examines a variety of correctional settings in order to assess the relationship between organizational goals and informal organizations. Included is a discussion of the Prisonization process.

P.00922 Garabedian, P. G. (1963). Social roles and processes of socialization in the prison community. *Social Problems 11*, 139–152.

In this research article on Prisonization, the author reports the results of data collected from 1700 convicted adult felons in a western state's maximum custody prison. The researcher tests Wheeler's model of the Prisonization process. The findings were consistent with those of Clemmer and Wheeler.

P.00923 Giallombardo, R. (1966). *Society of women: A Study of women's prison.* New York: John Wiley and Sons.

Contained in this book are the results of an exploratory study of women's prisons from a sociological perspective. The author discusses the Prisonization process experienced by female inmates.

P.00924 Glaser, D. (1964). *Effectiveness of a prison and parole system.* New York: Bobbs–Merrill. (Abridged edition published, 1969).

Contained in this book are the results of a study on the rehabilitative effects of prisons and parole agencies. The primary focus of the study was differences in recidivism between inmates who had been incarcerated in federal prison and inmates who had been incarcerated in federal prison and then paroled. Glaser discusses the relationship of Prisonization to success after release.

P.00925 Grusky, O. (1959). Organizational goals and the behavior of informal leaders. *American Journal of Sociology 65*, 59–67.

In this research article, Grusky examines the goal of treatment and its effect on processes of social control with regard to unofficial inmate leaders. Interview and questionnaire data indicate that inmate leaders were likely to receive higher adjustment ratings and to manifest more favorable attitudes toward camp officials, its programs of treatment, and the camp itself when compared to non-leaders. Leaders were less likely to request transfer, to be transferred for disciplinary reasons, or to escape from the institution.

P.00926 Hawkins, G. (1976). *The prison: Policy and practice*. Chicago: University of Chicago Press.

In this book the author discusses prison management. The author focuses on the status of institutions, and use of imprisonment as a method of punishment. Included is a discussion of the prisonization process.

P.00927 Heffernan, E. (1972). *Making it in prison: The square, the cool, and the life*. New York: John Wiley and Sons.

In this book the author examines three groups of inmates – the squares, the cools, and the lifers – in relationship to their adjustment to prison, including their responses to the pressures of incarceration.

P.00928 Irwin, J. & Cressey, D. (1962). Thieves, convicts, and the inmate culture. *Social Problems, 10*, 142-133. Also in R. G. Leger and J. R. Stratton (eds.), (1977). *Sociology of Corrections*. New York: John Wiley and Sons.

The authors present the results of an examination of prison subculture. Special emphasis is placed on the inmates and their roles in the prison subculture. The authors discuss the role of alcohol and drugs in the inmate subculture as well as the overall impact of the prisonization process.

P.00929 Jacobs, J. (1974). Street gangs behind bars. *Social Problems 21*(3), 395–409.

This book is based on a participant observation study of street gangs in prison. The researcher studied street gangs in the maximum security prison in Stateville, Illinois in an effort to determine their role in the prison social structure. The author discusses the impact of the prisonization process on inmates at Stateville.

P.00930 Simmons, I. L. (1975). *Interaction and leadership among female prisoners.* Unpublished Dissertation, Ann Arbor: Xerox University Microfilms.

The author presents an examination of the leadership and interaction patterns of the informal inmate social structures of a state correctional institution for women.

P.00931 Sykes, G. M. (1958). *Society of captives: A study of a maximum security prison.* Princeton, NJ: Princeton University Press.

This book is based on a classic study of a maximum security prison from a sociological perspective. The researcher examined the prison's organizational dysfunctions and their consequent effects, for example, the prisonization of inmates.

P.00932 Sykes, G. M. & Messinger, S. L. (1977). The inmate social system. In R. G. Leger and J. R. Stratton (eds.), *Sociology of corrections: A book of readings 1977.* New York: John Wiley and Sons.

This edited book chapter contains a discussion of the norms, attitudes, and beliefs found in a social system within prisons, i.e., prison subculture. The authors provide a thorough explanation of the categories of social relationships that exist among inmates in penal systems. The categories of social relationships exemplifying the prisonization process are discussed.

P.00933 Welch, M. (1995). *Corrections: A critical approach.* New York: McGraw–Hill.

In this textbook, the author provides an overview of corrections from a critical perspective in the analysis of problems and issues associated with corrections. Welch links corrections, crime, and social problems together. Chapters in this text include a critical approach to crime, a social history of punishment and corrections, a social history of America's correctional experience, traditional and critical perspectives on corrections, the social world of imprisonment, jails and detention, women, juveniles, and minorities in corrections, the death penalty, violence and riots, prisoner rights and litigation, alternatives to incarceration, and current and future trends in corrections.

P.00934 Wheeler, S. (1961). Socialization in correctional communities. *American sociological review 26*, 697–712.

In this paper, Wheeler examines the concept of prisonization and provides the results of an empirical test of the processes that Clemmer described. This data from a western state reformatory is consistent with Clemmer's analysis when length of time served is used as the relevant time variable. However, Wheeler presents evidence of a recovery process and a shedding of the prison culture when inmates are classified into phases of their institutional career.

PRIVACY

P.00935 Alpert, G. P. & Crouch, B. M. (1991). Cross-gender supervision, personal privacy, and institutional security: Perceptions of jail inmates and staff. *Criminal Justice and Behavior 18*(3), 304–317.

This article is based on a study which was conducted to determine if cross-gender supervision of prisoners is a positive management strategy. The authors studied male and female prisoners and staff at the Orange County, Florida Division of Corrections. The authors examined the feasibility of the plan as well as what effect it had on prison conflict. Their discussion of privacy focused on supervision of inmates by opposite gender officers.

P.00936 Cox, V. C., Paulus, P. B. & McCain, G. (1984). Prison crowding research: The relevance for prison housing standards and a general approach regarding crowding phenomena. *American Psychologist 39*(10), 1148–1160.

In this article, the authors summarize the effects of crowding in correctional institutions, including jails and prisons. A discussion of privacy and its impact from crowding, is presented.

P.00937 Ibrahim, A. I. (1974). Deviant sexual behavior in men's prisons. *Crime and Delinquency 20*(1), 38–44.

Presented in this article is an examination of deviant sexual behavior in male prisons. The researcher examined factors which may cause abnormal sexual behavior and criticized attitudes of prison personnel which accept these behaviors and offered possible solutions to these types of deviant behavior. The author also discussed the relationship between privacy and deviant sexual behavior in prison.

P.00938 Johnson, R. (1987). *Hard time: Understanding and reforming the prison.* Pacific Grove, CA: Brooks/Cole Publishing.

After studying life in male maximum security prisons, the author argues that mature coping is possible and can be further facilitated by staff and programs, thus resulting in possible rehabilitation of offenders. The author discusses inmates' privacy in maximum security prisons.

P.00939 Schaeffer, M. A., Baum, A., Paulus, P. B. & Gaes, G. G. (1988). Architecturally mediated effects of social density in prison. *Environment and Behavior 20*(1), 3–19.

The authors examined the relationship between prison crowding and prisoner illness complaints. They examined self-report and biochemical evidence of architecturally mediated crowding stress in relationship to prisoner illness complaints. They discussed how the lack of privacy, which often results from crowding, enhances stress in inmates.

P.00940 Small, M. A. & Scalora, M. (1991). Assessing mental injury claims arising from privacy invasions. *Forensic Reports 4*, 337–352.

In this research article, the authors discuss the legal context and clinical aspects of mental injuries which stem from privacy invasions. They emphasize mental injury claims that arise from violations of constitutional, common law, and statutory privacy interests. They also discuss issues in the assessment of claims, including proof, severity, causation, and malingering. They suggest future directions for research.

PRIVATE PRISONS

P.00941 Anderson, P., Davoli, C. R. & Moriarty, L. J. (1985). Private corrections: Feast or fiasco? *Prison Journal 45*(2), 32–41.

In this article, the authors suggest that privatization of prisons maybe considered a feast or fiasco depending on the assessment of the pros and cons of privatization outlined in the manuscript. Before such a judgment is made, the authors recommend balancing the benefits and drawbacks of privatization.

P.00942 Borna, S. (1986). Free enterprise goes to prison. *British Journal of*

Criminology 26(4), 321–334.

In this article the author examines three aspects of private prisons in the United States and Great Britain, for example, how local authorities raise capital for construction of private prisons, what corporations are involved in prisons for profit, and the social and judicial issues related to private prisons.

P.00943 Brakel, S. J. (1988). Prison management, private enterprise style: The inmate's evaluation. *New England Journal of Criminal and Civil Confinement 14*(2), 175–244.

The author, using data from the Silverdale Detention Center in Chattanooga, Tennessee, analyzed the operation and workability of private prisons' administrators and management.

P.00944 Crants, R. (1991). Private prison management: A study of economic efficiency. *Journal of Contemporary Criminal Justice 7*(1), 49–59.

In this paper, the author examines the value of the private sector in meeting correctional needs in a cost efficient manner. Crants presents data which indicate that significant cost savings can result from private sector involvement in corrections. The private sector's contribution in alleviating overcrowding is acknowledged.

P.00945 Fenton, J. (1985). Private alternative to public prisons. *Prison Journal 65*(2), 42–47.

The author, a corporate executive with a private prison company, describes how his company has designed a program to improve services to inmates that are placed in protective custody.

P.00946 Gentry, J. T. (1986). The Panoptican revisited: The problem of monitoring private prisons. *The Yale Law Journal 96*, 357–375.

The author finds that the private prison concept dates to Jeremy Bentham in 1791. While the concept is old, it is relatively new in practice, consequently, there is no mechanism in place to monitor and evaluate these private prisons. The author outlines such a mechanism.

P.00947 Hatry, H. P., Brounstein, P. J., Levinson, R. B., Altschuler, D. M., Chi, K. & Rosenberg, P. (1989). *Comparison of privately and publicly operated corrections facilities in Kentucky and Massachusetts.* Washington, DC: Urban Institute.

The authors present results of their grant funded comparison of privately and publicly operated state correctional facilities. Data were collected from two adult minimum security facilities in Kentucky and two secure treatment facilities for violent and troubled youth in Massachusetts. The findings indicate that unit cost of the private Kentucky adult facilities were approximately 10 percent higher than the publicly operated facilities, while program costs in Massachusetts were within one percent of each other. Service quality and effectiveness were also examined.

P.00948 Logan, C. H. (1990). *Private prisons: Cons and pros*. New York: Oxford University Press.

In this book the author argues that with everything being equal, private firms can run prisons more cheaply than public agencies.

P.00949 Logan, C. H. & McGriff, B. W. (1989). *Comparing costs of public and private prisons: A case study*. Rockville, MD: National Institute of Justice/National Criminal Justice Reference Service.

Details of a comparison of the actual costs of public and private operations of a prison facility in Hamilton County, Tennessee are presented in this book. The authors report that contracting with Corrections Corporation of American to operate the 350 bed Hamilton County Penal Farm resulted in an annual savings of between 5 and 15 percent for the county.

P.00950 Matthews, R. (1989). Privatization in perspective. In R. Matthews (ed.), *Privatizing criminal justice* (pp. 1–23). London: Sage Publications.

In this book chapter the author provides an analysis of the debate over prison privatization in Great Britain.

P.00951 Mullen, J., Chabotar, K. J. & Carrow, D. M. (1985). *The privatization of corrections*. Washington, DC: Superintendent of Documents GPO.

The authors identify and discuss the primary trends in the prison privatization movement. Major emphasis is placed on the issues surrounding proposals for private financing, construction, and operations.

P.00952 Schuman, A. M. (1989). Cost of correctional services: Exploring a poorly charted terrain. *Research in Corrections 2*(1), 27–33.

This is a discussion of Douglas C. McDonald's evaluation of problems in cost analysis and costs estimation in corrections.

P.00953 Sechrest, D. K., Pappas, N. & Price, S. J. (1987). Building prisons: Pre-manufactured, prefabricated, and prototype. *Federal Probation 51*(1), 35–41.

The authors present a discussion of the willingness to use modular, premanufactured, and prefabricated products in correctional facility construction without any evidence that these components will meet correctional demands or be of long term use.

P.00954 Sellers, M. P. (1989). Private and public prisons: A comparison of costs, programs and facilities. *international Journal of Offender Therapy and Comparative Criminology 33*(3), 241–256.

In an attempt to discover which is more efficient, the author compares three privately operated prisons with three publicly operated prisons.

P.00955 Weiss, R. P. (1989). Private prisons and the state. In R. Matthews (ed.), *Privatizing criminal justice* (pp. 26–51). London: Sage Publications.

The author recommends that Great Britain carefully consider several issues before reaching its decision to insitute the use of private prisons. In particular, the author suggests that Great Britain correctional administrators study the problems and successes the United States has experienced in privatization of prisons.

PROTECTIVE CUSTODY

P.00956 Hagel-Seymour, J. (1982). Environmental sanctuaries for susceptible prisoners. In R. Johnson and H. Toch (eds.), *The pains of imprisonment* (pp. 267–284). Beverly Hills: Sage Publications.

A prominent feature of prison behavior is that it takes place in restricted prison subsettings. The author discusses various subsettings and how prisoners search out the subsetting that fulfills their specific needs, e.g. segregation provides privacy and safety while honor units provide amenities not available to the general population.

P.00957 Henderson, J. D. (1992). Managing protective custody units. *Federal Prisons Journal 3*(2), 42–47.

Along with an increase in prison populations has come an increase in protective custody units. The management of the units has become more professional but individual management styles vary among institutions.

P.00958 Lockwood, D. (1977). Living in protection. In H. Toch (ed.), *Living in prison: The ecology of survival*. New York: Free Press.

Contained in this edited book chapter is an overview of the research literature on protective custody. The author addresses inmate safety and security by exploring protective custody options used in prisons.

P.00959 Pierson, T. A. (1988). Use of protective custody: How different systems respond. *Corrections Today 50*(4), 150, 151, 154.

Contained in this article are the results of a study of protective custody The author examined protective custody by surveying 67 jurisdictions in North America. All 50 states, the Federal Bureau of Prisons, the District of Columbia, Guam, the Virgin Islands, Correctional Service Canada (CSC), and nine Canadian provinces, participated. These represent 65 of the 67 jurisdictions contacted. Two general types of protective custody were identified, lockup protective custody and protection unit protective custody.

P.00960 Seymour, J. (1977). Niches in prison. In H. Toch (ed.), *Living in prison: The ecology of survival*. New York: Free Press.

Contained in this edited book chapter is a discussion of the effectiveness of environmental stress-reducing supports such as niches and protective custody.

Cases

P.00961 *Walker v. Lockhart*, 713 F.2d 1378 (8th Cir. 1983)

The plaintiff alleged that his confinement in the Arkansas prison system constituted cruel and unusual punishment. Sentenced for killing an Arkansas police officer, the plaintiff became a model prisoner who became very religious. Eventually he was allowed to leave the prison to speak to the public. One speaking engagement resulted in the plaintiff not returning to the prison as scheduled. All furlough privileges were eliminated. The plaintiff believed he was in danger in the prison and wanted to be in protective custody. The court dismissed Walker's claims and said the mere publicity of his case resulted in more protection.

PUBLIC INFORMATION OFFICE AND PUBLIC RELATIONS

P.00962 Fox, V. (1972). *Introduction to corrections*. Englewood Cliffs, NJ:

Prentice-Hall.

In this introductory textbook, the author provides a detailed overview of the client, the institution, and treatment programs in the correctional system. The author also discusses the importance of public relations to correctional administration.

P.00963 Hart, B. L., Friel, C. M., Allie, H. J. & Pennel, R. L. (1981). *Correctional data analysis systems: Correctional datagraphics, a directory of correctional statistical reports*. Rockville, MD: National Institute of Justice/National Criminal Justice Reference Service Microfiche Program.

The authors present a directory of 163 prototypes of correctional statistical reports and cover 15 areas of administrative concern. It is intended to clarify input requirements for managerial reports and to resolve output format issues.

P.00964 Koehler, R. J. (1989). Like it or not: We are news. *Corrections Today 51*(1), 16–17.

The author warns that there is little that people find more interesting than crime and punishment. As a result, corrections will always be in the public eye, the media (newspapers, television, radio) will see to that.

P.00965 Petersilia, J. (1991). The value of corrections research: Learning what works. *Federal Probation 55*(2), 24–26.

In this article, the author reviews the current state of corrections research. A discussion of the emerging importance of policy research which determines what works in corrections is presented. The author concludes by stating that results of policy research should be used in public policy debates.

P.00966 Schwartz, J. A. (1989). Promoting a good public image: Effective leadership, sound practices make the difference. *Corrections Today 51*(1), 38, 40, 42.

The author suggests that much of the responsibility for the negative view the public has of corrections can be attributed to the profession itself and not to the news media.

P.00967 Yurkanin, A. (1989). PIO's rate news media in recent survey. *Corrections Today 51*(1), 80.

The author reports the results of a survey of 50 prison public information officers (PIOs). One of the biggest problems reported was lack of time to develop a complete story before dealing with reporters.

R

RACIAL CONFLICT

R.00968 Ayres, E. L. (1984). *Vengeance and justice: Crime and punishment in the 19th-Century American South.* New York: Oxford University Press.

In this book the author examines the most important cultural and structural components of crime and punishment in the slave South. The author also describes the impact of secession, the Civil War, and how the histories of three specific communities – a city, a plantation county, and an upcountry county influenced Souther culture. Chapter topics include the following: Honor and its Adversaries, the penitentiary in the Old South, the City, the Black Belt and the Upcountry, War and Reconstruction, the Convict Lease System, and the Crisis of the New South.

R.00969 Carroll, L. (1982). Race, ethnicity and the social order of the prison. In R. Johnson and H. Toch (eds.), *The pains of imprisonment* (pp. 181–204). Beverly Hills: Sage.

Contained in this edited book chapter is the author's conclusion that racial tension and hostility is rampant in American society and in prisons as well. Carroll suggests, however, that there are ways to control such hostility in prison including using classification schemes, encouraging black and white inmates to interact, and increasing the number of minority staff.

R.00970 Carroll, L. (1988). *Hacks, Blacks and cons: Race relations in a maximum security prison.* Prospect Heights, IL: Waveland Press.

In this book the author describes race relations in one prison. He analyzes race relations through identification of conditions in prison that are race specific.

R.00971 Chonco, N. R. (1989). Sexual assaults among male inmates: A descriptive study. *Prison Journal 69*(1), 72–82.

Presented in this research article are the results of a case study of 40 violent male and nonviolent maleoffenders in a large midwestern state. The study was conducted to determine the characteristics of the predators, the victims, and the subjects that are not victimized in prison sexual assaults.

R.00972 Ellis, D., Grasmick, H. & Gilman, B. (1974). Violence in prison: A sociological analysis. *American Journal of Sociology 80*, 16–43.

In this article, the authors examine violence in prisons. From a sociological perspective, they identified group behavior variables and then correlated them to violence observed in prisons. The authors focused considerable attention on the relationship between racial conflict and prison violence.

R.00973 Fox, J. G. (1982). *Organizational and racial conflict in maximum security prisons*. Lexington, MA: Lexington Books.

This book is based on the author's study of racial and organizational conflicts in five state maximum-security prisons. The researcher collected attitudinal data, from prison administrators, guards, and inmates, regarding racial conflicts.

R.00974 Giallombardo, R. (1966). *Society of women: A study of women's prison*. New York: John Wiley and Sons.

Contained in this book are the results of an exploratory study of women's prisons afrom a sociological perspective. The author discusses race relations among female offenders.

R.00975 Irwin, J. (1980). *Prisons in turmoil*. Boston: Little, Brown and Co.

The author provides a historical account of the turbulence in American prisons. Irwin suggests that administrative policies and influential social processes have enhanced the turmoil. The author compares the past and present state of prison turbulence and offers solutions for the future. He specifically addresses the problems associated with race relations in offender populations.

R.00976 Jacobs, J. B. (1983). *New perspectives on prisons and imprisonment*. Ithaca, NY: Cornell University Press.

Presented in this book are 12 essays on the present sociological analyses of contemporary American prisons. Included are discussions of race relations in American prisons.

R.00977 Jacobs, J. B. & Grear, M. P. (1978). Drop outs and rejects: An analysis of the prison guard's revolving door. *Criminal Justice Review 2*(2), 57–70.

The authors surveyed 55 former prison guards and determined that employee turnover was a result of organizational and cultural conflicts within the formal organization. One aspect of the cultural conflicts which the authors addressed are racial problems.

R.00978 Kalinich, D. B. (1980). *Power, stability, and contraband: The inmate economy.* Prospect Heights, IL: Waveland.

The author studied the contraband market in a state prison in southern Michigan and analyzed the organizational structure and the informal inmate power structure that facilitates the contraband system. Included is a discussion of the dilemma facing the prison administration in controlling contraband and strategies that may help decrease the contraband flow. The author also discussed the role that race plays in the inmate economy.

R.00979 Kruttschitt, C. (1983). Race relations and the female inmate. *Crime and Delinquency 29*, 577–592.

The author suggests that since the Attica State Prison revolt, criminologists and penologists have been exploring the racial climate in male prisons. Even so, it is suggested that similar empirical studies of female prisons is lacking. As a result, the amount and extent of racial turmoil in female prisons in unknown.

R.00980 McDonald, D. C. & Weisburd, D. (1992). Segregation and hidden discrimination in prisons: Reflections on a small study of cell assignments. In C.A. Hartjen and E.E. Rhine (eds.), *Correctional theory and practice* (pp. 146–161). Chicago: Nelson Hall.

This edited book chapter stems from a study of housing assignments in a large state prison in the northeastern United States. The purpose was to determine the relationship between house assignments and race or ethnicity. The authors wanted to determine if racial or ethnic discrimination existed and explore the implications of such discrimination on prison administrators' decision-making processes regarding housing assignments.

R.00981 Owen, B. (1985). Race and gender relations among prison workers. *Crime and Delinquency 31*, 147–159.

The author examined the impact of affirmative action on correctional management, in particular, the degree to which affirmative action impacted the hiring of racial minorities as correctional guards.

R.00982 Poole, E. & Regoli, R. (1980). Race, institutional rule breaking and disciplinary response: A study of disciplinary decision-making in prison. *Law and Society Review 14*, 931–946.

The authors studied disciplinary decision-making in a medium security prison for adult males. As part of the study the authors developed and tested a discretionary justice model as a disciplinary response method to inmate rule violations. The authors also discussed the relationship between race and inmate rule infractions.

R.00983 Tewksbury, R. (1989). Fear of sexual assault in prison inmates. *Prison Journal 69*(1), 62–71.

In this article the author describes fear of sexual assault among incarcerated male inmates. Accordingly, fear is a psychological factor with greater impact on the normal functioning of individuals and institutions than the actual incidence of sexual assault. Also discussed is the relationship between race and sexual assault in prison.

R.00984 Wright, K. (1989). Race and economic marginality in explaining prison adjustment. *Journal of Research in Crime and Delinquency 26*, 67–89.

The author examined data, from inmates in a New York correctional facility as well as scholarly research, to determine if African American and Caucasian inmates adjust to incarceration in similar ways.

Cases

R.00985 *Brown v. Board of Education*, 347 U.S. 483 (1954)

In this landmark case the Supreme Court struck down the "separate but equal" doctrine, that supported segregation in state institutions.

R.00986 *Washington v. Lee*, 263 F.Supp. 327 (M.D. Ala. 1966), Aff'd per curiam, 390 U.S. 333 (1968)

The Court held that requiring segregation by race in the state, county and city penal facilities in Alabama is unconstitutional in that it violates the Equal Protection clause of the Fourteenth amendment and the Cruel and Unusual clause of the Eighth Amendment.

RECIDIVISM

R.00987 Fabelo, T. & Arrigona, N. (1991). *Uniform recidivism and revocation rate calculation: recommended methodologies for state criminal justice agencies.* Austin, TX: Criminal Justice Policy Council.

All state agencies in Texas had different methods for defining and calculating recidivism or revocation rates. The 71st Texas Legislature mandated the Criminal Justice Policy Council to develop a uniform definition of recidivism and revocation rates. The definition and method of calculation is presented in this book.

R.00988 Hill, J. (1993). *The measurement and reporting of recidivism in the Oregon Department of Corrections.* Draft Memorandum. Salem, OR: Oregon Department of Corrections.

This corrections' memorandum of the Oregon Department of Corrections contains the department's definition of recidivism. Components of the definition are recidivist behavior, length of time an individual will be tracked, and the number of times an offender will be counted. The author reports that the definition must be used in any Department of Corrections offender/program evaluations.

R.00989 Korn, R. R., & McCorkle, L. W. (1966). *Criminology and penology.* New York, NY: Holt, Rinehart and Winston.

The authors of this standard textbook provide a comprehensive discussion and evaluation of available data in criminology and penology. They outline the more important theoretical frameworks in the field. They also discuss some of the common problems associated with the scientific study crime and criminals, for example, recidivism.

R.00990 Maltz, M. D. (1984). *Recidivism.* Orlando, FL: Academic Press.

Provided in this book is a comprehensive overview of recidivism. The author begins by explaining the different definitions of the term and how definitional ambiguity has impacted evaluation studies of recidivism. The second part of the book contains an overview of the methodological problems associated with using recidivism as a measure of correctional program success.

R.00991 Petersilia, J. (1987). *The influence of criminal justice research*. Santa Monica, CA: The RAND Corporation.

The author reviews the impact that the National Institute of Justice (NIJ) has had on the American criminal justice system. She limits her analysis to evaluation of the projects funded by the institute. She concludes that criminal justice policy and practice over the past two decades have been strongly influenced by NIJ funded research. This is especially true of recidivism policies.

R.00992 Petersilia, J., & Turner, S. (1993). Intensive probation and parole. In M. Tonry (ed.), *Crime and justice: An annual review of research* (Vol. 17). Chicago, IL: University of Chicago Press.

The authors report the results an evaluation of a RAND Corporation study of a national intensive supervision demonstration project. The authors found that the project programs were implemented well, especially those focusing on probation and parole officers contacts with the offenders and drug testing. A weakness of the project programs was that the officers were not very successful at increasing offender participation in treatment programs.

R.00993 Waldo, G., & Griswold, D. (1979). Issues in the measurement of recidivism. In L. Sechrest, S. White and E. Brown (ed.), *The rehabilitation of criminal offenders: Problems and prospects*. Washington, DC: National Academy of Sciences.

Provided in this book is an overview of punishment policy. The authors' chapter, in the edited book, specifically addresses some of the more common problems associated with the measurement of recidivism.

R.00994 Wolfgang, M., Sellin, T., & Figlio, R. (1972). *Delinquency in a birth cohort*. Chicago: University of Chicago Press.

This classic work represents the first longitudinal study of juvenile delinquency. The authors examined a cohort of boys, born in 1945 in Philadelphia, Pennsylvania. Data were drawn from school, police, and selective service records. Thirty-five percent of the boys were found to be involved in some form of delinquency while 65 percent were not. The authors also examined other variables to determine why the juveniles were committing delinquent acts. In terms of repeat delinquency, the authors found that the majority of the delinquency was committed by about six percent of the youth. This 'chronic six percent' were characterized as having a recidivism record of having committed four or more delinquent acts .

RECREATION PROGRAMS

R.00995 Gillin, J. L. (1926). *Criminology and penology*. New York: The Century Co.

Provided in this, most comprehensive textbook on criminology and penology of its time, is information on recreation programs in corrections.

R.00996 Hitchcock, H. C. (1990). Prisons: Exercise versus recreation. *Journal of Physical Education, Recreation and Dance* 61(August), 84–88.

An overview of the importance of recreation programs in penal institutions is presented in this article. The author notes the significant legal cases such as *Ruiz v. Estelle, Campbell v. Cauthron,* and *Spain v. Procunier.* A review of case law indicates four major categories of conditions that determine the quantity and quality of Constitutionally required exercise: the size of an inmate's cell, the amount of time per day spent locked in the cell, the overall duration of confinement, and the overall health care delivery system.

R.00997 Hull, J. (1994, April 11). Building a better thug. *Time 143*(15), p. 47.

This news magazine article indicates that across the nation, prisons and jails use weight rooms as incentives for good behavior. However, the Milwaukee County, Wisconsin Board of Supervisors voted to ban weight rooms from their facilities. The rational for eliminating this type of recreation program was due to the fear that the weight lifting programs were making prisoners into physically tougher criminals. This was considered problematic in the handling of inmates while they are incarcerated as well as when they are released.

R.00998 Sharp, J. (1994). *A report from the Texas performance review: Behind the walls – the price and performance of the Texas Department of Criminal Justice.* Austin: Comptroller of Public Accounts.

This legislative report presented to the 73rd Texas Legislature by the Texas Comptroller of Public Accounts is based on a year-long study of the Texas Department of Criminal Justice. The report contains details for a suggested reorganization of the Texas Department of Criminal

Justice that would improve the agency's working relationship with local communities and make it more responsive to Texas taxpayers. The report also outlines shifts in inmate housing patterns that could free up thousands of beds in existing prison facilities.

R.00999 Welch, R. (1991). Arts in prison: Tapping inmates' creativity offers hope, improves security. *Corrections Today 53*(5), 146, 148, 150–152.

An overview of some of the benefits, to both staff and inmates, of inmates' participation in arts and crafts programs in institutional settings is presented in this article.

REFORMATORY

R.01000 Brockway, Z. (1912). *Fifty years of prison service: An autobiography.* Montclair, NJ: Patterson Smith. (Reprinted in 1969).

Contained in this autobiographical book is the famous prison administrator's views on prison reform. A central part of the book is Brockway's experiences during the 25 years he was superintendent of the New York State Reformatory at Elmira. Of particular note is Brockways' perspectives on the indeterminate sentence and education programs as central features of prison reform.

R.01001 McKelvey, B. (1977). *American prisons: A history of good intentions.* Montclair, NJ: Patterson Smith.

Presented in this book is a historical account of the American prison system from 1835 through 1977. The author presents detailed information on changing standards, reform movements, criminological theories, and confrontations in penology. The author discusses the role of the reformatory era in the history of American prisons.

R.01002 Pisciotta, A. W. (1982). Scientific reform: The "new penology" at Elmira, 1876–1900. *Crime and Delinquency 29*, 613–630.

In this study the author reports that although the opening of the Elmira Reformatory in 1876 changed the course of American corrections it did not achieve its aim of individualized treatment, indeterminate sentencing, and parole.

R.01003 Pisciotta, A. W. (1994). *Benevolent repression: Social control and the American reformatory–prison movement.* New York: University Press.

In this book, the author provides a historical analysis of the history of the adult reformatory movement. The primary focus is on the reform efforts of Zebulon Brockway at Elmira Reformatory in New York between 1876 and 1920. A thorough discussion of indeterminate sentencing and educational programs is provided.

R.01004 Rafter, N. H. (1990). *Partial justice: Women, prisons, and social control.* (2nd. ed.). New Brunswick, NJ: Transaction Publishers Rutgers – the State University.

Presented in this book are the results of an examination of women's prisons in the United States from the late 1800s until 1935. The data is derived from a national survey of all institutions that housed only female offenders during the period under study. Prison reports, legislative and archival documents, as well as prison registries in three states were analyzed for demographic and offense data on 4,600 inmates. The author discusses the influence of the reformatory movement to correctional rehabilitation of female offenders.

R.01005 Smith, B. A. (1988). Military training at New York's Elmira Reformatory, 1888–1920. *Federal Probation 52*(1), 33–40.

A discussion of the military training model as a correctional management strategy at Elmira Reformatory is presented in this article. Due to an emergency situation at Elmira, the military training model was introduced as a means to organize and discipline inmates. The author indicates that it persisted beyond the crisis and was incorporated into the organizational structure of the institution.

REHABILITATION ACT OF 1973

R.01006 Baum, E. M. (1984). Handicapped prisoners: An ignored minority? *Columbia Journal of Law and Social Problems 18*, 349–379.

In this article, the author maintains that the courts are filled with cases concerning prisoner rights and discrimination cases regarding handicapped persons in the free world. Even so, the author suggests that little attention has been paid to the rights of physically handicapped prisoners.

R.01007 Cook, T. (1983). The substantive due process rights of mentally disabled clients. *Mental Disability Law Reporter 7*(4), 174–185.

This article, written by a trial attorney in the Civil Rights Division of the

United States Department of Justice, provides an overview of the substantive due process rights of mentally retarded residents of mental institutions based upon the attorney's interpretation of *Youngberg v. Romeo.* In *Romeo,* the Court unanimously recognized that mentally disabled people cannot be deprived of the following liberty interests: reasonable care and safety, freedom from bodily restraint, adequate food, shelter, and medical care, those liberty interests to which convicted criminals are entitled, and adequate training or habilitation.

R.01008 Harvard Law Review (1984). Employment discrimination against the handicapped and Section 504 of the Rehabilitation Act of 1973: An essay on legal evasiveness. *Harvard Law Review 97,* 997–1015.

Contained in this article is an examination of the Rehabilitation Act of 1973. The primary focus in on Section 504, which prohibits discrimination against "otherwise qualified handicapped individuals by any program or activity receiving Federal financial assistance."

R.01009 Khan, A. (1990). Application of section 504 of the rehabilitation act to the segregation of HIV–positive inmates. *Washington Law Review 65*(4), 839–881.

As the number of inmates with HIV infection has grown prison administrators have increasingly housed these inmates in housing units separate from the general population. This may be a violation of Section 504 of the Rehabilitation Act which states that any program receiving Federal financial assistance cannot discriminate against "otherwise qualified" handicapped persons.

R.01010 Robbins, A. (1993). Employment discrimination against substance abusers: The federal response. *Boston College Law Review 33,* 155–209.

The author concludes that the Courts and administrative agencies interpreted the Rehabilitation Act of 1973 (ADA) to include substance abusers in the Act's definition of "individuals with handicaps." Congress ratified this interpretation by including substance abusers in the ADA's definition of "individuals with disabilities."

R.01011 Shumaker, G. M. (1986). AIDS: Does it qualify as a "handicap" under the Rehabilitation Act of 1973? *Notre Dame Law Review 61,* 572–594.

The author argues that Congress clearly intended for the Rehabilitation Act of 1973 to be a flexible and meaningful weapon to fight baseless discrimination against the handicapped by employers. It is further reported that the broad definition of a protected "handicapped individual" can include persons with AIDS. Because no viable statutory or judical barriers exist to such a classification, AIDS should be deemed a handicap for purposes of the Rehabilitation Act of 1973.

REHABILITATION PROGRAMS

R.01012 Allen, H. & Gatz, N. (1974). Abandoning the medical model in corrections: Some implications and alternatives. *Prison Journal 54*(Autumn), 4–14.

The authors propose a re-integrative model as an alternative to the medical model found in corrections. They indicate that even though the medical model has been abandoned, correctional rehabilitation persists. Thus, they advocate the implementation of a re-integrative model for corrections.

R.01013 Bartollas, C. (1985). *Correctional treatment: Theory and practice.* Englewood Cliffs, NJ: Prentice Hall.

In this textbook the author profiles treatment in American correctional facilities. He suggests that a new approach to treatment is needed because nothing new is being done. The treatment models used today are very similar to the previous models used.

R.01014 Bell, R., Conrad, E., & Suppa, R. (1984). The findings and recommendations of the national study on learning deficiencies in adult inmates. *Journal of Correctional Education 35*, 129–137.

The authors report finding from a national study which was conducted to determine learning deficiencies in adult inmates. Their findings and recommendations for developing rehabilitation programs that are inclusive of this group are also discussed.

R.01015 Cullen, F. T. & Gilbert, K. E. (1982). *Reaffirming rehabilitation.* Cincinnati: Anderson Publishing Co.

In this book, the authors criticize the present movement to eliminate treatment or rehabilitation programs from prisons. They analyze their position from two historical perspectives in criminological theory: the classical and positivist schools of criminology, address rehabilitation in relationship to the new justice model, examine problems caused by determinate sentencing, and discuss the effects of new sentencing laws.

R.01016 Cullen, F. T., Skovron, S., Scott, J. & Burton, V. (1990). Public support for correctional treatment: The tenacity of rehabilitative ideology. *Criminal Justice and Behavior 17*(1), 6–18.

The authors examine public support or lack thereof for correctional treatment modalities. The authors suggest that for the past decade or so, scholars and politicians have suggested that citizens have demonstrated little support for correctional treatment.

R.01017 Dinitz, S. (1979). Nothing fails like a little success. In E. Sagarin (ed.), *Criminology: New concerns*. Beverly Hills, CA: Sage.

In this edited book chapter, the author argues that prison reformers have supported changes which are superficial and basically cosmetic. The author states that the reforms used in the past, i.e., self-improvement, social reintegration, and psychological intervention are useless today. Therefore it is suggested that true reforms are needed, but that these reforms must be innovative and new, not just recycled old ideas.

R.01018 Garrett, C. (1985). Effects of residential treatment on adjudicated delinquents. *Journal of Research in Crime and Delinquency 22*(4), 287–308.

The author suggests that the opinion that 'nothing works' in correctional treatment has spilled over to juvenile treatment. Recent trends toward more punitive sanctions are the result of the general dissatisfaction with rehabilitation.

R.01019 Gendreau, P. & Ross, R. R. (1987). Revivification of rehabilitation: Evidence from the 1980s. *Justice Quarterly 4*(3), 349–408.

The authors examined the literature from 1981 to 1987 in order to assess the rehabilitation interventions which were frequently used. The interventions examined included biomedical, diversion, early/family intervention, parole/probation, restitution, and work programs.

R.01020 Glasser, W. (1965). *Reality therapy*. New York, NY: Harper and Row.

Provided in this book is an overview of the therapy technique called Reality Therapy (RT). The author contends that it is an appropriate therapy approach for use with inmates. The components and administration of RT are detailed in the book.

R.01021 Goldstein, A., Glick, B., Irwin, M., Pask-McCarty, C. & Rubams, I.

(1989). *Reducing delinquency: Intervention in the community*. Elmsford, NY: Pergamon.

The authors describe a community based treatment program, Aggression Replacement Training (ART). They provide information on the components and administration of ART. They also indicate that the training program is designed to facilitate positive functioning of youth in the community.

R.01022 Lester, D., Braswell, M. & Van Voorhis, P. (1992). *Correctional counseling* (2d ed.). Cincinnati: Anderson Publishing Co.

Contained in this book are 14 papers in which the authors focus on the philosophical framework for correctional counseling. Such issues as offender classification systems, individual and group treatment methods and the effectiveness of correctional rehabilitation are examined.

R.01023 Maletzky, B. (1991). *Treating the sexual offender*. Newbury Park, CA: Sage.

In this book the author describes a multitude of techniques for treating the sexual offender in both in-patient and out-patient settings.

R.01024 Martinson, R. (1974). What works? Questions and answers about prison reform. *The Public Interest 35*(1), 22–54.

This controversial article stems from the author's evaluation of 231 offender rehabilitation programs. Martinson concludes that very little success, measured in terms of recidivism, has been achieved by offender rehabilitation programs. These conclusions play an integral part in the demise of the treatment model and the enhancement of the 'justice model' in the field of criminal justice.

R.01025 McCorkle, R. (1993). Research note: Punish or rehabilitate. *Crime and Delinquency 39*(2), 240–252.

The author discusses the role of prisons in this research note. In particular, the author considers whether prisons should punish or rehabilitate offenders.

R.01026 Palmer, T. (1992). *The re-emergence of correctional intervention*. Newbury Park, CA: Sage.

In this book the author expands on a previous attack of Martinson's thesis that nothing works in rehabilitation. The author argues, as have others who challenged Martinson's conclusions, that rehabilitation does have merit and should be used in prisons.

R.01027 Redl, F., & Toch, H. (1979). The psychoanalytic perspective. In H. Toch (ed.), *Psychology of crime and criminal justice.* New York: Holt, Rinehart, and Winston.

In this edited book, many of the aspects of the relationship between psychology and the criminal justice system are discussed. In this chapter, the authors examine the relationship between psychology and juvenile delinquency.

R.01028 Rothman, D. J. (1980). *Conscience and convenience: The asylum and its alternatives in progressive America.* Boston: Little, Brown and Co.

Presented in this book is an exploration of the origins and consequences of programs that have dominated criminal justice, juvenile justice, and mental health in the 20th century. The author discusses the similarities between penitentiaries and state mental institutions, demonstrating that both are asylums in the United States. Also discussed is the role of treatment programs.

R.01029 Samenow, S. (1984). *Inside the criminal mind.* New York: Times Books.

The author argues that explanations for criminal behavior based on broken homes, alcoholism, media violence, unemployment, drug addiction, or passionate impulses are not as valid as the explanation that the criminal thinks differently than the average person. The author argues that this is important in the development of effective rehabilitation programs.

R.01030 Yochelson, S. & Samenow, S. (1976). *The criminal personality, Vol. 1: A profile for change.* New York: Jason Aronson.

The authors refute the current theories explaining criminality. They based their description of criminal thinking on 15 years of research, intense therapy, and follow-up studies. They think that the most probable explanation for criminal behavior is that criminals think differently than non-criminals.

RELIGION IN PRISON

R.01031 Dammer, H. R. (1992). *Piety in prison: An ethnography of religion in the* *correctional environment.* Ann Arbor, MI: University Microfilms.

Using participant observation and interviews the author studied the meaning of religion in the correctional setting. The subjects were an active group of religious inmates in two large maximum security prisons for men in the northeast United States. The author discusses his findings and proposes a theory of the meaning of religion in a correctional environment.

R.01032 Evans, K. (1978). Reflections on education in the penitentiary, in Taylor, W. and Braswell, M. (Eds.), *Issues in police and criminal psychology.* Washington, DC: University Press of America.

In this edited book chapter, the author traces the history of educational programs in prisons. Evans describes the relationship between religion and education programs in early penitentiaries.

R.01033 Garland, D. (1990). *Punishment and modern society: A study in social theory.* Chicago: University of Chicago Press.

The author presents an analysis of the way we currently punish offenders in American society and determines that the social meaning of punishment is poorly understood. Society needs to explore the meaning of punishment and find better ways to punish. Such means of punishment should be more closely match our social ideals.

R.01034 Hamm, M. S. (1992). Santeria in Federal prisons: Understanding a little–known religion. *Federal Prisons Journal 2*(4), 37–42.

With the large numbers of Cuban nationals incarcerated in correctional facilities in the United States, correctional personnel need to understand the practice and nature of the Santeria religion.

R.01035 Johnson, B. R. (1984). *Hellfire and corrections: A quantitative study of Florida prison inmates.* Ann Arbor, MI: Microfilms International.

This dissertation is a study of the religiosity-deviance relationship. It is based on data collected from 782 inmates released from 1978 through 1982 from an institution in Florida. Religious variables, religiosity indexes, and institutional adjustment indexes represent the three sets of variables analyzed to determine the impact of religiosity upon institutional adjustment of prison inmates. The researcher concludes that religiosity of prison inmates does not have a statistically significant impact upon inmate institutional adjustment.

R.01036 Smarto, D. (1987). *Justice and mercy.* Wheaton, IL: Tyndale House.

Presented in this book is an overview of the corrections system, its policies and problems, Biblical principles of justice, and the status of the church's ministry. Chapters include the following: individuals in prison ministry, the local church and prison ministry, conversion stories, understanding the prisoner, and Christian prison ministries in America.

RESEARCH IN PRISON

R.01037 Lovell, R. & Kalinich, D. (1992). The unimportance of in-house research in a professional criminal justice organization. *Criminal Justice Review 17*(1), 77–93.

The authors examine the role of and potential for in-house research. They interviewed top administrators, program managers, and research personnel while reviewing documents and project memorandums. Their goal was to determine the role that in-house research plays in policy-making and decision-making of an organization.

R.01038 Lovell, R. & Stojkovic, S. (1987). Myths, symbols and policy making in corrections. *Criminal Justice Policy Review 2*(3), 225–239.

In this article, the authors contend that one important attribute of correctional policy is that it should resolve myths associated with corrections. In fact, the authors suggest that acceptable policy is policy that contributes to growth and organizational enhancement. The authors suggest that research is the basis for sound policy development.

R.01039 Williams, F. P. III, McShane, M. D., & Sechrest, D. (1994). Barriers to effective performance review: The seduction of raw data. *Public Administration Review 54*(6), 537–542.

In this article, the authors argue that in the future, the key to being a successful administrator will be accountability and the management of performance review. The authors suggest that administrators have access to vast amounts of data that they do not effectively use. The authors propose that administrators take advantage of their resources and offer solutions to the problem of interpreting data.

RIOTS

R.01040 Barak-Glantz, I.L. (1985). Anatomy of another prison riot. In M.

Braswell, S Dillingham, and Montgomery, R. (eds.), *Prison violence in America* (pp. 47–71). Cincinnati: Anderson Publishing Company.

The author presents a review of the history and causes of prison riots, with particular attention to three Michigan prison riots in May 1981, and examines means to prevent prison riots.

R.01041 DiIulio, J. J. (1987). *Governing prisons: A comparative study of correctional management*. New York: Free Press.

The author examines the Texas, California, and Michigan correctional systems in order to compare and contrast the management styles and procedures used in these prisons. The author also provides a brief discussion of building tenders as a management strategy employed by the Texas Department of Corrections.

R.01042 Fox, V. (1972). Prison riots in a democratic society. *Police 16*(12), 35–41.

This article contains an analysis of the development patterns in prison riots, including the role of violence in riots. The author also presents the results of a survey of the public's reaction the Attica riot.

R.01043 Kratcoski, P. C. (1988). The implications of research explaining prison violence and disruption. *Federal Probation 52*(1), 27–32.

The author examines inmate violence toward correctional guards by investigating incident reports and inmate records at a Federal and a state correctional institution.

R.01044 Lillis, J. (1994). Prison escapes and violence remain down. *Corrections Compendium 19*(6), 6–21.

This article is based on research in which the author surveyed 41 State correctional systems, the District of Columbia, the Federal Bureau of Prisons, and Canada to determine the incidence of prison escapes and violence for 1992 and 1993. It was found there was not a significant increase from 1992 to 1993. Detailed data is provided.

R.01045 Saenz, A. B. & Reeves, T. Z. (1989). Riot aftermath: New Mexico's experience teaches valuable lessons. *Corrections Today 51*(4), 66–70.

The authors review the lessons learned from the New Mexico prison riot in 1980. They suggest measures for consideration by policy-makers in the development of policy to prevent future riots in correctional settings.

R.01046 South Carolina Department of Corrections. (1973). *Collective violence in correctional institutions: A search for causes.* Columbia, SC: State Printing Office.

This final report of the South Carolina Department of Corrections documents its findings regarding riots in South Carolina prisons.

R.01047 Wicker, T. (1975). *Time to die.* New York: Times Books.

Provided in this book is an eyewitness account of the negotiations between prison authorities and inmates during the riot at Attica Correctional Facility in September, 1971.

BENJAMIN RUSH

R.01048 Bacon, M. H. (1969). *The quiet rebels: The story of the Quakers in America.* New York: Basic Books, Inc.

In this book the author provides a historical analysis of the early years of the persecution experienced by the Quakers as they attempted to settle in New England. The author includes a discussion of Benjamin Rush's influence on the development of American corrections.

R.01049 Hawke, D. F. (1971). *Benjamin Rush: Revolutionary gadfly.* Indianapolis, IN: The Bobbs-Merrill Company.

Provided in this book is a profile of Benjamin Rush, especially his early career. Hawke indicates that Rush, in addition to signing the Declaration of Independence also promoted antislavery and temperance, and advocated educational and medical reform.

R.01050 James, S. V. (1963). *A people among peoples: Quaker benevolence in eighteenth-century America.* Cambridge, MA: Harvard University Press.

In this book, the author examines Quakerism and questions why Quakers became Americans rather than self-isolated sectarians. During the 1700s, Quakerism had the potential to be the largest American denomination, yet it did not fulfill this promise. This book explores the reasons why.

R.01051 McKelvey, B. (1936). *American prisons: A history of good intentions.* Montclair, NJ: Patterson Smith. (Reprinted, 1977).

Contained in this book is a historical account of the American prison system from 1835 through 1977. The author presents detailed information on changing standards, reform movements, criminological theories, and confrontations in penology. The author provides a discussion of the reformatory era in the history of American prisons.

S

SAN QUENTIN PRISON

S.01052 Ashcroft, L. (1993). San Quentin, its early history and origins. *Marin County Historical Society Magazine 17*(Spring), 1–37.

Contained in this article is a historical description of San Quentin Prison. The author provides a review of the institution's history through the following chapters: the first prison, the prison ship, life in the new prison, the State takes over, Estelle's second term, the State takes over again, McCauley returns, the great escape, prison reforms, women in prison, and the modern prison.

S.01053 Davidson, R. T. (1974). *Chicano prisoners: The key to San Quentin*. New York: Holt, Rinehart and Winston.

Presented in this book are the results of a study of prisoners in San Quentin Prison. The author, took the role of participant-observer and conducted an anthropological study of the subculture of prisoners in San Quentin prison. Focusing specifically on the Chicano prisoner, the author examined the factors responsible for the violence inflicted on Chicanos and their lack of participation in prison programs.

S.01054 Duffy, C. (1950). *The San Quentin story*. Garden City, NJ: Doubleday.

In this book the author presents the story of the warden of San Quentin state penitentiary. The author tells of the warden's early days at San Quentin, when the best known prisoner was Tom Mooney and riots and prison breaks were frequent occurrences.

S.01055 Howard, C. (1981). *American Saturday*. New York: Richard Marek Publisher.

Provided in this book is a well researched account of George Jackson's death. The author provides a detailed account of the events that occurred on Saturday, August 21, 1971 when prisoner George Jackson was killed while trying to escape from San Quentin prison.

S.01056 Jackson, G. (1979). *Soledad Brother*. New York: Coward McCann.

This book consists of a collection of letters written by George Jackson to various people including his lawyers, family members and female friends. Jackson was convicted of stealing $70.00 from a gas station and sentenced to a indeterminate sentence of one year to life. While in prison, Jackson killed a correctional officer. These letters chronicle Jackson's life in prison, including his experiences as a political activist.

S.01057 Lamott, K. (1961). *Chronicles of San Quentin: The biography of a prison*. New York: David McKay Company.

This book, presented in journalistic style, represents a historical account of San Quentin prison. The author also provides some insights into the prison world.

S.01058 Owen, B. (1988). *The reproduction of social control: A study of prison workers at San Quentin*. New York: Praeger Publishers.

This book is based on a study of the world-view of San Quentin employees. Data were collected through interviews with 35 employees at San Quentin State Prison. The primary objective of the interview was to measure the employees' world-view, an integral element in institutional social control.

SEARCHES

I. Introduction

Case

S.01059 *Block v. Rutherford*, 468 U.S. 576, 104 S.Ct. 3227, 82 L.Ed.2d 438 (1984)

The plaintiff argued that his due process rights were violated by the jail's policy of denying pretrial detainee contact visits with their spouses, relatives, children, and friends. The Court agreed and ordered that contact visits be allowed for the low risk detainee incarcerated for more than a month.

S.01060 *Hudson v. Palmer*, 468 U.S. 517, 104 S.Ct. 3194, 82 L.Ed.2d 393 (1984)

The plaintiff filed suit against the corrections system alleging that the Fourth Amendment right to privacy over material in ones's had been violated when guards searched the cell. The Court disagreed and placed limitations on inmates' right to privacy in their cells.

II. Strip Searches

S.01061 Braly, M. (1967). *On the yard: A novel.* New York: Penguin.

Portrayed in this book is the daily routine of a California prison. The author also discusses the use of strip searches and their impact on inmates.

S.01062 Shakur, S. (1993). *Monster: The autobiography of an L.A. gang member.* New York: Penguin.

The author describes how he was transformed from a street gangster to an evangelical proponent of Black nationalism while serving time in a maximum security prison in California. He also discusses the dehumanizing effects of strip searches.

S.01063 Summers, W. C. (1991). Conducting strip searches. *The Police Chief* *58*(5), 54–56.

The author discusses the differences between a strip search and a body cavity search. Included is a discussion of conditions the courts consider in their legal evaluation of the reasonableness of strip searches.

S.01064 Toch, H. (1977). *Living in prison: The ecology of survival.* New York: Free Press.

Documented in this book is how men adapt to the stress of living in prison. The author discusses the personal impact that loss of security has on individual inmates.

S.01065 Rauch, W. H., Henderson, J. D., Aiken, E., Benson, C., Lester, D., Fisher, B., Gerard, R. & Levinson, R. (1987). *Guidelines for the development of a security program.* Washington, DC: Superintendent of Documents

Government Printing Office.

This government publication is a manual in which guidelines to be used by correctional personnel in planning security programs for prisons are provided. A primary goal in the development of programs for juveniles and adults is that they are both humane and efficient.

SENTENCES, EXCESSIVE

S.01066 Baker, T. E. & Baldwin, F. N., Jr. (1985). Eighth Amendment challenges to the length of a criminal sentence: Following the Supreme Court "from precedent to precedent." *Arizona Law Review 27*(1), 25–74.

In this article the authors address the following: background history emphasizing the last three Supreme Court decisions on proportionality, an examination of reconciliation and *stare decisis* for an underlying theme, and suggestions for understanding and explaining the proportionality case law.

S.01067 Forer, L. G. (1994). *Rage to punish: The unintended consequences of mandatory sentencing.* New York: W.W. Norton.

In this book the author, a former judge, advocates the abolishment of capital punishment, sentencing guidelines, and mandatory sentencing. The author argues that these practices have not reduced crime, have resulted in crowded prisons, and have been an excessive tax burden to the public.

S.01068 Gallo, C. (1981). *Rummel v. Estelle:* Sentencing without a rational basis. *Syracuse Law Review 32*(3), 803–840.

The author discusses the development of the Eighth Amendment's prohibition against punishment that is grossly disproportionate to the severity of an offense.

S.01069 Hackney, G. D. (1992). A trunk full of trouble: *Harmelin v. Michigan. Harvard Civil Rights-Civil Liberties Law Review 27*(1), 262–280.

In this article the author reviews the *Harmelin* case. In this case the Court held that a mandatory sentence of life imprisonment without parole did not violate the Eighth Amendment ban of cruel and unusual punishment when imposed on a defendant with no prior criminal record, convicted on possession of 672.2 grams of cocaine.

S.01070 Keir, N. (1984). *Solem v. Helm*: Extending judicial review under the cruel and unusual punishments clause to require "proportionality" of prison sentences. *Catholic University Law Review 33*(2), 479–515.

Contained in this law review article is an examination of the Supreme Court's decision in *Solem v. Helm*. In this case the court ruled that punishment, regardless of method used, should be proportionate to the offense committed.

S.01071 Schwartz, C. W. (1980). Eighth Amendment proportionality analysis and the compelling case of William Rummel. *Journal of Criminal Law and Criminology 71*(4), 378–420.

The author argues that the Supreme Court was correct in upholding a life sentence imposed under a Texas habitual criminal statute. The author argues that the Supreme Court's decision to reject Rummel's claim of a Eighth Amendment violation is sound.

S.01072 Theodore, M. H. (1992). *Harmelin v. Michigan*: Is Eighth Amendment proportionality in jeopardy? *New England Journal on Criminal and Civil Confinement 18*(1–2), 231–258.

The author presents a critique of the U.S. Supreme Court's reasoning in *Harmelin v. Michigan* with particular emphasis on the Court's conclusion that Michigan's "drug lifer" law is not in violation of the Eighth Amendment.

Cases

S.01073 *Harmelin v. Michigan*, 501 U.S. ___, 111 S.Ct. 2680, 115 L.Ed.2d 836 (1991)

The Supreme Court rejected the defendant's claim that his sentence was unconstitutionally disproportionate to the severity of his crime. The Court argued that a prison sentence is proportionate when the severity matches the degree of moral blameworthiness of the offender, plus the harm or risk of harm to others that results from the offense.

S.01074 *Hutto v. Davis*, 454 U.S. 277, 103 S.Ct. 703, 70 L.Ed.2d 556 (1982) (per curiam)

The plaintiff alleged that a 40 year prison sentence for possessing with intent to distribute nine ounces of marijuana was a sentence so disproportionate to the crime committed that it constituted cruel and unusual punishment. The Court agreed.

S.01075 *People v. Bullock*, 440 Mich. 15, 485 N.W.2d 866 (1992)

The plaintiff challenged Michigan's mandatory penalty of life without possibility of parole for possession of 650 grams or more of any mixture containing cocaine. The plaintiff alleges this statute constitutes cruel and unusual punishment. The Court denied the plaintiff the right to add this claim to the others challenged in this lawsuit.

S.01076 *Rummel v. Estelle*, 445 U.S. 263, 100 S.Ct. 1133, 63 L.Ed.2d 382 (1980).

The plaintiff challenged the Texas habitual offender statute. Rummel argued that his Eighth Amendment rights were violated when he received a life sentence for obtaining $120 under false pretense, his non-violent felony conviction. The Supreme Court rejected Rummel's claim on the grounds that Rummel knew the consequences of his behavior, that he had been given opportunities to reform and chose not to do so.

S.01077 *Solem v. Helm*, 463 U.S. 277, 103 S.Ct. 3001, 77 L.Ed.2d 637 (1983)

The defendant was convicted of writing a "no account" check for $100. He had three prior conviction for non-violent drunkenness related felonies. He was sentenced as a recidivist and given a life sentence without parole. He appealed on the basis that the sentence was disproportionate to the crime. The Supreme Court found in Helm's favor, deciding that punishment should be proportionate to the offense committed regardless of the method of punishment.

S.01078 *Weems v. United States*, 217 U.S. 349, 30 S.Ct. 544, 54 L.Ed.2d 793 (1910)

Weems was found guilty of falsifying a public record and sentenced to twelve years at hard labor while chained at the ankles and wrists. The Supreme Court found that the sentence received was disproportionate to the crime committed. The Court's decision established the principal that punishment which might not be cruel or unusual under other circumstances is cruel and unusual if it is disproportionate to the offense committed.

SEX OFFENDER PROGRAMING

S.01079 Berlin, F. S. & Krout, E. K. (1986). Pedophilia: Diagnostic concepts, treatment and ethical considerations. *American Journal of Forensic Psychiatry 7*, 13–30.

In this article the authors examine pedophilia. They report on its etiology, manifestations, diagnosis, and treatment. They emphasize clinical and ethical considerations in the treatment of pedophiles.

S.01080 Earls, C. & Quinsey, V. (1985). What is to be done? Future research on the assessments and behavioral treatment of sex offenders. *Behavioral Sciences and the Law 3*, 377–390.

In this article the authors suggest that future research on sex offenders should focus on the assessment and treatment of such offenders. The authors also suggest that assessment methods should be extended and refined, different treatment techniques need to be explored, and long-term follow-up research should be conducted with sex offenders who have been treated with different methods.

S.01081 French, L. (1992). Characteristics of sexuality within correctional environments. *Corrective and Social Psychiatry 38*, 5–8.

According to the author incarceration enhances aberrant sexual behavior. He identifies three classification situations: convicted sex offenders – pedophiles, sex-stress situations, and sex as an associated clinical feature. The author suggests that due to the challenge of both AIDS and hepatitis more research is needed to unravel the complexities associated with the prison milieu of sexual active inmates.

S.01082 French, L. & Vollman, J., Jr. (1987). Treating the dangerous sexual offender: A clinical/legal dilemma. *International Journal of Offender Therapy and Comparative Criminology 31*, 61–69.

In this article, the authors suggest that dangerous sexual offenders pose additional problems for correctional personnel. Dangerous sexual offenders are a problem because of the type of crimes they have committed and the lack of effective clinical treatment to corrected the abnormal sexual behavior.

S.01083 Groth, A. N. & Oliveri, F. (1989). Understanding sexual offense behavior and differentiating among sexual abusers: Basic conceptual issues. In S. M. Sgroi (ed.), *Vulnerable populations: Sexual abuse treatment for children, adult survivors, offenders, and persons with mental retardation, Vol. 2*. Lexington, MA: Lexington Books.

The authors discuss the differences between sexual offenses and sexual deviations and how they relate to the concept of sexual abuse and provide a discussion of how to treat abusers.

S.01084 McFarland, L. (1986). Depro-Provera Therapy as an alternative to imprisonment. *Houston Law Review 23*, 801–819.

In this law review article the author discusses the legal issues associated with the use of Depro-Provera Therapy. The author examines the use of the drug therapy as a condition of probation for a limited classification of convicted sex offenders.

S.01085 Sapp, A. D. & Vaughn, M. S. (1991). Sex offender rehabilitation programs in state prisons: A nationwide survey. *Journal of Offender Rehabilitation 17*, 55–75.

In this article, the authors describe programs and strategies which are used in the rehabilitation of adult sex offenders. The findings are based on data collected from 73 state-operated adult correctional institutions.

S.01086 Spitzer, R. (1987). *Diagnostic and statistical manual* (3rd ed., rev.) Washington, DC: American Psychiatric Association Press.

The *Diagnostic and Statistical Manual* (DSM) contains a listing of psychiatric abnormalities. Mental health professionals use this diagnostic manual when evaluating clients. The manual contains an exhaustive list of psychiatric abnormalities and their attendant characteristics.

S.01087 Whitfield, R. (1987). Treatment of male sexual offenders in a correctional facility. *Journal of Offender Counseling 8*, 2–16.

In this article, the author discusses treatment of male sexual offenders in prison. The author provides background information and treatment perspectives for counselors and psychologists to consider when treating sexual offenders in correctional facilities.

SEXUAL EXPLOITATION IN PRISON

S.01088 Bartollas, C., Miller, S. J. & Dinitz, S. (1976). *Juvenile Victimization*. Newbury Park, CA: Sage.

In this book the authors report on juvenile victimization in juvenile reformatories. The exploitative patterns of staff and inmates is detailed after intensive observations and interviews were conducted in a prototypical juvenile reformatory.

S.01089 Davis, A. (1968). Sexual assaults in the Philadelphia prison setting and sheriff's vans. *Trans–Action 6*, 8–16.

This article is based on a three–month investigation, conducted jointly with the District Attorney's Office and the Police Department, of sexual victimization in the Philadelphia jail. The author reports the number of sexual assaults, physical and psychological characteristics of both victims and the aggressors, and rationales for the assaults.

S.01090 Jones, R. S. & Schmid, T. J. (1989). Inmates' conceptions of prison sexual assault. *Prison Journal 69*(1), 53–61.

The author's data was derived from a ten month participant observation study at a maximum security prison for men. One observer was an inmate and the other was an outsider. The authors found that the way first time inmates define the prison social world is influenced by their imagery of prison sexual assault.

S.01091 Levin, M. G. (1985). Fight, flee, submit, sue: Alternatives for sexually assaulted prisoners. *Columbia Journal of Law and Social Problems 18*, 505–530.

The author reviews sexual assault in American prisons. Included are depravation or a political act?, escaping confinement to avoid sexual assault, litigation strategies, Constitutional challenges, and judicial dismissal. He concludes with two questions; Is it moral or legal to incarcerate people in a manner that consistently allows other inmates to violate inmates and is American society willing to confront the ugly truth of inmate sexual assault?

S.01092 Lockwood, D. (1980). *Prison sexual violence*. New York: Elsevier North/Holland.

In this book, the author explains the psychological impact prison sexual threats and attacks have on inmates. The author also discusses selection of victims, 'target' violence, and the response of staff to sexual violence.

S.01093 Siegal, D. (1992). Rape in prison and AIDS: A challenge for the Eighth Amendment framework of *Wilson v. Seiter*. *Stanford Law Review 44*(6), 1541–1581.

In this law review article, the author provides a detailed description of the sexual assaults committed against Clifton Redman, an eighteen-year-old pre–trial detainee, who was booked into a San Diego detention center. The author then reviews the significant cases which have established precedence with regards to AIDS in an institutional setting.

Cases

S.01094 *People v. Lovercamp*, 43 Cal App. 3d 823, 118 Cal Rptr 110 (1974)

Two female prisoners escaped from the California Rehabilitation Center because they were repeatedly threatened by a group of lesbians who said either "fuck or fight." The women alerted the correctional authorities of this problem but the lesbian group continued to fight them. The women escaped because there was no other way to stop the violence. The Court ruled that the "defense of necessity to escape is a viable defense." The Court quickly delineated five conditions which must be present in order for a defense of necessity to be available.

S.01095 *Smith v. Wade*, 461 U.S. 30, 103 S.Ct. 1625 (1983)

Plaintiff alleged his Eighth Amendment rights were violated when he was harassed, beaten, and sexually assaulted by his cell mates in a Missouri reformatory for youthful first-time offenders. Relief was sought against the guards who worked at the reformatory. Prison guards have "qualified immunity" and as a result the standard of negligence had to be "gross negligence" or "egregious failure to protect." In addition, before punitive damages could be assessed, the petitioner's conduct had to be "a reckless or callous disregard of, or indifference to, the rights and safety of protected" respondents. The District Court found the petitioner liable and awarded compensatory and punitive damages. The Court of Appeals affirmed.

S.01096 *Strokes v. Delacambre*, 710 F.2d 1120 (1983)

Strokes alleged he suffered injuries while being detained in a Louisiana jail for a misdemeanor charge. A jury found that two employees of the jail had violated Strokes constitutional rights. On appeal, the Court affirmed.

SING SING PRISON

S.01097 Lewis, O. F. (1922). *The development of American prisons and prison customs*. New York: Prison Association of New York.

Contained in this book is a historical analysis of the evolution of American prisons. The author includes an extensive presentation on Philadelphia's Walnut Street Prison of 1790 and the New York State Prison of 1796. The Auburn State System is also presented and contrasted with the two former systems. The author discusses the role of Thomas Mott Osborne in the evolution of Sing Sing Prison.

S.01098 McKelvey, B. (1977). *American prisons: A history of good intentions.* Montclair, NJ: Patterson Smith.

Presented in this book is a historical account of the American prison system from 1835 through 1977. The author presents detailed information on changing standards, reform movements, criminological theories, and confrontations in penology. The author discusses Sing Sing's historical significance to American corrections.

S.01099 Trombley, S. (1992). *The execution protocol: Inside America's capital punishment industry.* New York: Crown.

The author visits Missouri's Potosi Correctional Center and follows one death row inmate from his sentencing hearing to his execution.

SITE SELECTION AND CONSTRUCTION OF PRISONS

S.01100 Carlson, K. A. (1992). Doing good and looking bad: A case study of prison/community relations. *Crime and Delinquency 38*(1), 56–69.

In this article the author suggests that prisons are economically good for local communities, often viewed unfavorably by the members of the community, and characterized by poor community relations.

S.01101 Eynon, T. G. (1989). Building community support. *Corrections Today 51*(2), 150–152.

Suggested in this article are ways to get community support for prisons, for example involving the community in correctional management. The community should be invited to participate in the process. Influential local groups should be part of the initiation and operation of community participation programs.

S.01102 Grieco, A. L. (1978). New prisons: Characteristics and community reception. *Quarterly Journal of Corrections 2*(2), 55–60.

In this article the author reports that the number of prisons being built in the United States since 1970 has been steady, with no indication it will slow down. The author also reports on the characteristics of new prisons and the public reaction to them.

S.01103 Houk, W. B. (1987). *Acquiring new prison sites: The federal experience.* Rockville, MD: National Institute of Justice/National Criminal Justice Reference Service.

The process used by the Federal prison system to select and acquire sites for new prisons is explained in this article.

S.01104 Ince, M. (1988). *Impact of a correctional facility on the surrounding community.* Washington, DC: American Planning Association.

In this publication, the author presents the impact correctional institutions have on their adjacent communities. The specific impact variables assessed are crime rate, property values, quality of life, and economy.

S.01105 Krause, J. D. (1992). The effects of prison siting practices on community status arrangements: A framework applied to the siting of California state prisons. *Crime and Delinquency 38*(1), 27–55.

In this article, the author suggests that quality of life among prison facilities and the surrounding communities can be increased through positive relations between correctional personnel and community residents.

S.01106 McGee, R. A. (1981). *Prisons and politics.* Lexington, MA: D.C. Heath and Co.

This book stems from the author's experiences as a correctional administrator. The author conducts a historical analysis of the impact of politics on correctional policy, special attention is directed at prison policy in California.

S.01107 McShane, M. D., Williams, F. P. III, & Wagoner, C. P. (1992). Prison impact studies: Some comments on methodological rigor. *Crime and Delinquency 38*(1), 105–120.

In this article the authors argue that much of the research which was conducted to analyze the impact prisons have on their communities is based on faulty research designs.

S.01108 Rogers, G. O. & Haimes, M. (1987). Local impact of a low-security Federal correctional institution. *Federal Probation 51*(3), 28–34.

In this article the authors present the results of an evaluation of a minimum–security Federal correctional institution in Loretto, PA. The institution, in its second year of operation, is assessed for its economic impact on the surrounding community.

S.01109 Sechrest, D. K. (1992). Locating prisons: Open versus closed approaches to siting. *Crime and Delinquency 38*(1), 88–104.

In this article, the author recognizes that as prison populations increase so does the need to build more prisons. The author examines the goals of selecting prison sites in relationship to public safety and economic concerns of the community.

S.01110 Shichor, D. (1992). Myths and realities in prison siting. *Crime and Delinquency 38*(1), 70–87.

In this article the author recognizes that placing correctional facilities in the community has been debated for a number of years. The author reviews the major arguments for and against this practice.

S.01111 Singer, N. M. (1977). Economic implications of standards for correction institutions. *Crime and Delinquency 23*(1), 14–31.

In this article, the author reports on recommendations made by a 1973 National Correctional Task Force. Three sets of proposals which were designed to comply with standards for correctional institutions are reviewed.

SNITCH

S.01112 Akerstrom, M. (1988). Social construction of snitches. *Deviant Behavior 9*(2), 155–167.

Criminal groups have a norm against snitching but before the snitch can be punished there must be an identification process. This article details how inmates in a Swedish prison try to find out who is a snitch and if they have informed inside or outside the prison.

S.01113 Akerstrom, M. (1989). Snitches on snitching. *Society 26*(2), 22–26.

In this article the author explains how those who are labeled as betrayers cope with the label. The article is based on data collected from 23 male informants in Swedish prisons. The data were acquired through in-depth, tape-recorded interviews which lasted from one to two hours.

S.01114 Clemmer, D. (1940). *The prison community*. New York: Holt, Rinehart, and Winston.

Contained in this book is the results of a classic study of imprisonment from a sociological perspective. The researcher conducted the study in an average American state prison which housed over 2,300 inmates. The author describes the prison subculture, addressing language norms that are specific to the penal setting.

S.01115 Colvin, M. (1992). *Penitentiary in crisis: From accommodation to riot in New Mexico*. New York: State University of New York Press.

In this book, the author discusses the history of control strategies used in the New Mexico Penitentiary. Also discussed is the torture and murder of the institutional snitches by rioting inmates.

S.01116 Giallombardo, R. (1966). *Society of women: A study of women's prison*. New York: John Wiley and Sons.

The results of an exploratory study of women's prisons from a sociological perspective are presented in this book. The author discusses the prisonization process experienced by female inmates.

S.01117 Johnson, E. H. (1961). Sociology of confinement: Assimilation and the prison rat. *Journal of Criminal Law, Criminology, and Police Science 51*, 528–533.

In this article, the author reports the results of a recent study of 50 inmate informants. Johnson divided the prisoner informants into subgroups titled assimilated and unassimilated. He then developed an index from the responses of informants to specific categories. Also considered in the development of the index were the informants' assigned roles and the social environments of their confinement.

S.01118 Kalinich, D. B. & Pitcher, T. (1984). *Surviving in corrections: A guide for corrections professionals*. Springfield, IL: Charles C. Thomas.

The authors present an interpretation of the dynamics and problems that challenge institutional corrections professionals.

S.01119 Marquart, J. W. & Crouch, B. M. (1984). Coopting the kept: Using inmates for social control in a southern prison. *Justice Quarterly 1*, 491–509.

In this article, the authors report on the 'building tenders' in a Texas maximum security prison. The data were collected over an 18 month period through participant observation. The authors describe the building tenders, the elite inmates in the Texas prison system, who were used by the system to maintain order among the other prisoners. One of the building tender's responsibilities was to provide information about other inmates to the administration.

S.01120 Marquart, J. W. & Roebuck, J. B. (1985). Prison guards and snitches. *British Journal of Criminology 25*, 217–233.

In this article the authors provide a profile of the prison snitch. They describe the process used to recruit inmates, the information gathered, the amount and type of payment, and how this process maintains social order in the prison. They base their conclusions from data collected in a Texas maximum security prison.

S.01121 Morris, R. (1983). *The devil's butcher shop: The New Mexico prison uprising.* New York: Franklin Watts.

In this book the author traces the development of the riot at the New Mexico State Penitentiary in Santa Fe. His data sources include a report of the Attorney General, official documents, eyewitness statements, and reports from the penitentiary intelligence office.

S.01122 Priestley, P. (1980). *Community of scapegoats: The segregation of sex offenders and informers in prisons.* Oxford, England: Pergamon.

In this book, the author analyzes Rule Forty-Three which allows for the voluntary separation of sex offenders, informants, and petty criminals from the general prison population for their own protection. Data were collected by a welfare officer employed at Shepton Mallet Prison in England between 1966 and 1968. The author also discusses the necessity for placement of snitches in protective custody.

S.01123 Roebuck, J. B. & Smith, R. A. (1993). The Atlanta riot: A study in identity and stigma management. In N. K. Denzin (ed.), *Studies in symbolic interaction* (pp. 239–269). Greenwich, CT: JAI Press.

In this edited book chapter, the authors describe the infamous Atlanta riot. Many researchers have analyzed the Atlanta riot on the basis of problems associated with the riots including overcrowding, poor food, inmate control, political activism, racial strife, and disturbances. However, no one has offered a clear and concise reason for the prison riot. These authors reanalyze the Atlanta riot and suggest specific causes. The author discusses the role of snitches in prison riots.

S.01124 Stojkovic, S. (1986). Social bases of power and control mechanisms among correctional administrators in a prison organization. *Journal of Criminal Justice 14*, 157–166.

Contained in this article are the results of research conducted by the author where the social bases of power and control mechanisms among correctional administrators were analyzed. Data were collected from administrators in a maximum security male correctional facility in a large midwestern state to determine the social bases of their power. The relationship of snitches and administrators' power and control was also analyzed.

S.01125 Sykes, G. M. (1958). *Society of captives: A study of a maximum security prison*. Princeton, NJ: Princeton University Press.

This book is based on a classic study of a maximum security prison from a sociological perspective. The researcher examined the prison's organizational dysfunctions and their subsequent effects, for example, the prisonization of inmates.

S.01126 Vandivier, V. (1989). Do you want to know a secret? Guidelines for using confidential information. *Corrections Today 51*, 30, 31, 73.

This article contains basic guidelines regarding the use of confidential information by corrections personnel. The author provides guidelines in order to limit lawsuit losses that stem from inappropriate use of confidential information in the disciplinary process.

S.01127 Williams, V. L. and Fish, M. (1974). *Convicts, codes and contraband: The prison life of men and women*. Cambridge, MA: Ballinger.

Presented in this book is an overview of the inmate economic system. The authors examine the relationships between prison hustling and inmate careers in both women and men's prisons.

S.01128 Wilmer, H. A. (1965). The role of the 'rat' in the prison. *Federal Probation*

29, 44–49.

The author discusses the role of the 'rat' in prisons. A 'rat' is an informer or snitch. This article provides an overview of the dynamics of using inmates as informants.

Cases

S.01129 *Wolff v. McDonnell*, 418 US 539, 94 S.Ct. 2963, 41 L.Ed.2d 935 (1974)

In this 6-to-3 decision, the Court held that the due process clause of the 14 Amendment provides inmates with procedural protection if they are facing a loss of good time or confinement because of an institutional disciplinary action. Some of the specific procedural requirements are, advance written notice of charges, written statement by fact finders explaining the findings, and opportunity to call witness and present case.

STATEVILLE

S.01130 Jacobs, J. B. (1977). *Stateville: The penitentiary in mass society*. Chicago: The University of Chicago Press.

The author provides a detailed, historical account of Stateville, a maximum security prison in Chicago, Illinois. An analysis of the relationship between the prison and the outside world is presented. Also examined are the conflicting roles of custody and treatment.

SUICIDE

S.01131 Albanese, J. S. (1983). Preventing inmate suicides: A case study. *Federal Probation 47*(2), 65–69.

In this article the author concludes that for short-term offenders, better screening at intake and using something other than standard razor blades will decrease inmate suicides, attempted suicides, and self-destructive behavior.

S.01132 Anno, B. J. (1991). *Prison health care: Guidelines for the management of an adequate delivery system*. Rockville, MD: National Institute of Justice/National Criminal Justice Reference Service.

This manual on correctional health care provides correctional administrators with management guidelines for prison health delivery systems. It is based on the most recent research literature, case law, standards of national prison and medical organizations, and experts on correctional health care.

S.01133 Camp, G. M. & Camp, C. G. (1992). *The corrections yearbook: Adult correction, 1991*. South Salem, NY: Criminal Justice Institute.

The authors present the results of a survey of the State and Federal adult correctional agencies in the United States and the Correctional Service of Canada.

S.01134 Charle, S. (1981). Suicide in the cellblocks. *Corrections Magazine 7*(4), 6–16.

This article contains a discussion of inmate characteristics and circumstances associated with inmate suicides.

S.01135 Lillis, J. (1994). Prison escapes and violence remain down. *Corrections Compendium 19*(6), 6–21.

A report on prison escapes and violence in 41 State correctional systems, the District of Columbia, the Federal Bureau of Prisons system, and Canada for 1992–1993.

S.01136 Moran, T. (1988). Experts: Inmate suicides hard to stop. *Houston Chronicle*, July 6, B1.

This newspaper article describes the suicide of J.R. McConnell who electrocuted himself in the Harris County Jail. According to the article, 32 suicides had occurred in county jails in Texas during the current year bringing the suicide rate to 156 per 100,000 population. The suicide rate in Texas jails is eleven times greater than the state's overall suicide rate of 13.6 per 100,000. According to a local jail administrator, someone determined to kill himself cannot be stopped.

S.01137 National Commission of Correctional Health Care. (1987). *Standards for health services in prisons*. Chicago: National Commission on Correctional Health Care.

A revision of the 1979 standards for the qualitative and quantitative measurement of prison health care delivery systems. These standards are the basis for accrediting such systems.

T

TECHNOLOGY

T.01138 Latessa, E. J., Oldendick, R. W., Travis, L. F., Noonan, S. B. & McDermott, B. E. (1988). *Impact of technology on adult correctional institutions*. Washington, DC: National Institute of Corrections.

Contained in this report is the results of an examination of technology in the prison work environment. The authors collected survey data from 117 correctional institutions in 46 departments of corrections. The research surveys contained questions about various aspects of technology.

T.01139 Travis, L. F., Latessa, E. J. & Oldendick, R. W. (1989). The utilization of technology in correctional institutions. *Federal Probation 53*(3), 35–40.

The authors examine the state of technology in correctional facilities. Their analysis was based on survey data collected from 117 correctional institutions in 46 departments of corrections.

TREATMENT PLANS

T.01140 Andrews, D. A. & Bonta, J. (1994). *The psychology of criminal conduct*. Cincinnati: Anderson Publishing Co.

The authors present a "general psychology of criminal conduct" theory that is interdisciplinary in regards to individual differences in criminal activity and makes a distinction between accounting for that variation and accounting for variation in aggregated crime rates.

T.01141 Baird, S. C. (1981). Probation and parole classification: The Wisconsin model. *Corrections Today 43*(3), 36, 38–41.

In this article the author provides an overview of the Wisconsin probation and parole classification system. The evaluation of the system is based on a 24 month assessment. The researcher provides an outline of each component in the classification system.

T.01142 Cullen, F. T. & Gilbert, K. E. (1982). *Reaffirming rehabilitation.* Cincinnati: Anderson Publishing.

In this book, the authors criticize the present movement to eliminate treatment or rehabilitation programs from prisons. They analyze their position from two historical perspectives in criminological theory: the classical and positivist schools of criminology. They also address rehabilitation in relationship to the new justice model, to problems caused by determinate sentencing, and to the effects of new sentencing laws.

T.01143 Motiuk, L. L. (1993). Where are we in our ability to assess risk? *Forum on Corrections Research 5*(2), 14–18.

Assessment techniques are more effective than they were in the recent past and the new integrated Offender Intake Assessment System will soon provide a means for comprehensive, integrated, and systematic assessments.

TRUSTY

T.01144 Clemmer, D. (1940). *The prison community.* New York: Holt, Rinehart, and Winston.

Presented in this book are the results of a classic study of imprisonment from a sociological perspective. The researcher conducted the study in an average American state prison which housed over 2,300 inmates. The author describes the prison subculture, addresses language norms that are specific to the penal setting, and discusses the role of prisoner trusty.

T.01145 Cloward, R. A., Cressey, D. R., Grosser, G. H., McCleery, R., Ohlin, L. E., Sykes, G. M. & Messinger, S. L. (1960). *Theoretical studies in social organization of the prison.* New York: Social Science Research Council.

The authors present studies that explore the nature, organization, and goals of the penal system and its effect on the groups with which it is involved. One of the underlying themes in this book is that prisons cannot effectively treat inmates when the community and society demands that this same institution provide custody and punishment.

T.01146 DiIulio, J. J., Jr. (1987). *Governing prisons: A comparative study of correctional management*, New York, NY: Oxford Press.

Contained in this book is a comprehensive overview of prison management. The author comparatively explores prison management in three state correctional systems, Texas, California, and Michigan. Chapters in the book contain discussions of governability of prisons, quality of life in prison, (3) correctional philosophy and leadership, correctional change, and the prison as a constitutional government.

T.01147 DiIulio, J. J., Jr. (ed.). (1990). *Courts, corrections, and the Constitution: The impact of judicial intervention on prisons and jails*. New York, NY: Oxford Press.

Presented in this edited book are submissions from fourteen academic and practicing social scientists and lawyers on judicial intervention in prison and jail administration. Detailed case studies of judicial intervention in state prison systems in Texas, Georgia, West Virginia, New Jersey and in the New York City jails are presented. The contributors provide a review of the research literature on intervention.

T.01148 McWhorter, W. L. (1981). *Inmate society: Legs, half-pants and gunmen, a study of inmate guards*. Saratoga, CA: Century Twenty One Publishing.

An overview of the role of 'trusty' in the Mississippi prison system from the Reconstruction period through 1972 is presented in this book. The author explains the role of trusty as it relates to the prison society.

T.01149 Sykes, G. M. (1958). *Society of captives: A study of a maximum security prison*. Princeton, NJ: Princeton University Press.

This book is based on a classic study of a maximum security prison from a sociological perspective. The researcher examined the prison's organizational dysfunctions and their consequent effects, for example, the prisonization of inmates. The inmate social structure, including the trusty, is also discussed.

Cases

T.01150 *Gates v. Collier*, 349 F.Supp 881 (N.D. Miss. 1991)

This case involved an inmate class action suit brought against the Superintendent of the Mississippi State Penitentiary at Parchman, Mississippi, the parole board, and the Governor of Mississippi. The plaintiffs allege their constitutional rights were violated by the methods of the new prison administration. The prohibition against cruel and unusual punishment is applicable to the State of Mississippi through the Due Process Clause.

T.01151 *Ruiz v. Estelle*, 503 F. Supp. 1265 (S.D. Texas, 1980), Cert. denied, 103 Ct. 1438

This case, brought by inmate Ruiz, became the most comprehensive civil action in the realm of correctional law. The plaintiff alleged that the Texas Department of Corrections (TSC) had unconstitutionally exposed prisoners to physically deteriorated, dangerous, and overcrowded conditions, the court concurred. Throught this case the courts also addressed the TDC's use of Building Tenders (inmate trusties) in the supervision of other inmates.

U

UNIONS

I. Correctional Officers

U.01152 Christianson, S. (1979). Corrections law developments: How unions affect prison administration. *Criminal Law Bulletin 15*(3), 238–247.

Unionization of correctional officers is the focus of this article. Unionization is discussed as it relates to prison administration. The role of judicial intervention is also discussed.

U.01153 Fox, J. G. (1982). *Organizational and racial conflict in maximum--security prisons*. Lexington, MA: D. C. Heath.

The author presents the results of a study that examined the attitudes of prison administrators, guards, and inmates in five maximum-security prisons with particular emphasis on the nature and scope of organizational and racial conflict.

U.01154 Lombardo, L. X. (1981). Occupational stress in corrections officers: Sources, coping strategies, and implications. In S. E. Zimmerman and H. D. Miller (eds.), *Corrections at the crossroads: Designing policy* (pp. 129–149). Newbury Park, CA: Sage Publications.

The author reports on occupational stress and mechanisms for alleviating such stress among correctional officers. The 1976 research was based on interviews conducted with a randomly selected sample of 50 corrections officers employed at an Eastern state maximum security prison.

U.01155 Potter, J. (1979). Guards unions: The search for solidarity. *Corrections Magazine 5*(3), 25–35.

The author examines the new militancy of prison guards in light of the problems associated with prison unions. New York, Massachusetts, and California are the primary focus on the research.

U.01156 Smith, B. & Sapp, A. (1985). Fringe benefits: The hidden cost of unionization and collective bargaining in corrections. *Journal of Police and Criminal Psychology 1*(2), 33–39.

The authors report the results of a questionnaire that was mailed to the 50 state correctional systems assessing whether employees received 35 specific fringe benefits. The independent variable examined was unionization of correctional employees. Results indicated that unionized corrections employees have an advantage in fringe benefits.

II. Inmates

U.01157 Berkman, R. (1979). *Opening the gates: The rise of the prisoners' movement.* Lexington, MA: Lexington Books, D.C. Heath and Co.

In this book, the author reports on the political activism of the 1960s, how it extended into prison life. The author assesses maximum security prisons to evaluate politicism in the context of the prisoners' movement.

U.01158 DeGraffe, L. J. (1990). Prisoners' unions: A potential contribution to the rehabilitation of the incarcerated. *New England Journal of Criminal and Civil Confinement 16*(2), 221–240.

In this article the author presents an overview of inmate unions in prisons and discusses the impact of the unions on rehabilitation and collective bargaining practices.

U.01159 Huff, C. R. (1974). Unionization behind the walls. *Criminology 12*(2), 175–194.

In this article unionization of prison inmates is analyzed. The author examines such issues as the history of the movement, the goals and reasons for inmate unions, legal issues, and the reactions of prison officials to inmate unions.

U.01160 Ward, D. A. (1972). Inmate rights and prison reform in Sweden and Denmark. *Journal of Criminal Law, Criminology and Police Science* *63*(2), 240–255.

In this article the author presents an evaluation of prison reform in Sweden and Denmark. The author presents data on the general characteristics of prisons as well as a discussion of inmate unions.

V

VIOLENCE

V.01161 Beard, J. A. (1994). Using special management units to control inmate violence. *Corrections Today 56*(5), 88–91.

The Special Management Unit Program, of the Pennsylvania Department of Corrections, is designed to provide a high level of security and control for seriously disruptive and violent inmates and focuses on restoring these inmates to the general population.

V.01162 Bowker, L. H. (1980). *Prison victimization.* New York: Elsevier.

In this book the author provided the reader with a thorough discussion of the many facets of prison victimization. In particular, the author reviews the physical, economic, psychological, and social harm experienced by staff and inmates in prison. The author also discusses the way prison violence victimizes those that punish and those who are punished.

V.01163 Bowker, L. H. (1982). Victimizers and victims in American correctional institutions. In R. Johnson and H. Toch (eds.), *Pains of imprisonment* (pp. 63–76). Newbury Park, CA: Sage Publications.

In this edited book chapter the author describes the major kinds of physical, psychological, economic and social prison victimization patterns and intervention strategies to decrease such victimization.

V.01164 Braswell, M., S. Dillingham, & R. Montgomery (eds.). (1985). *Prison violence in America*. Cincinnati: Anderson.

Contained in eleven chapters of this book are articles that address prison violence from several perspectives. The authors describe some of the more common types and causes of prison violence. They also offer prevention and coping strategies for administrative consideration.

V.01165 Ekland–Olson, S. (1986). Crowding, social control, and prison violence: Evidence from the post-Ruiz years in Texas. *Law and Society Review 20*, 389–421.

In this article the author examines two explanations for prison violence, crowding and social control. The crowding model emphasizes that confusion and tension found in overcrowded prisons leads to violence. The social control model asserts that violence is the result of the social order found in prisons.

V.01166 Fleisher, M. S. (1989). *Warehousing violence: Frontiers of anthropology* (Vol. 3). Newbury Park, CA: Sage Publications.

This article was based on research that was conducted to determine a more cost effective method for management of violent offenders. Data were collected through long-term participant observation in a maximum security institution and open-ended interviews.

V.01167 Larsen, N. (1988). The utility of prison violence: An a-causal approach to prison riots. *Criminal Justice Review 13*(1), 29–38.

Contained in this article is an examination of current explanations for prison violence. The author analyzed riots that occurred between 1952 and 1980 in various institutions. Based on the findings, the author proposes an a-causal approach to prison disturbances.

V.01168 Love, B. (1994). Program curbs prison violence through conflict resolution. *Corrections Today 56*(5), 144, 146–147.

In this article the author highlights the conflict resolution program at a state correctional institution in Pennsylvania. Outlined is how the prison can have better communication between staff and the inmates and how to use conflict resolution to resolve problems.

V.01169 McCorkle, R. C. (1992). Personal precautions to violence in prison. *Criminal Justice and Behavior 19*(2), 160–173.

This article is based on data collected in a questionnaire from 300 inmates in a Tennessee State prison. The objective was to determine the different types and prevalence of precautions used to avoid personal violence in prison. Social correlates were examined as well. It was determined that passive avoidance was used by the more fearful, older and isolated inmates. More aggressive approaches were used by the younger inmates who had longer histories of incarceration.

V.01170 Rideau, W. (1992). The sexual jungle. In W. Rideau and R. Wikberg (eds.), *Life Sentences: Rage and survival behind bars*. New York: Time Books.

This edited book consist of a collection of works by prisoners in the Louisiana State Maximum Security Prison at Angola. Addressed in this chapter is an overview of sex in prisons and its relationship to violence.

V.01171 Roberg, R. and Webb, V. (1981). Violence in prison: Its extent, nature and consequences. In R. Roberg and V. Webb (eds.), *Critical issues in corrections*. St. Paul, MN: West.

This edited book consist of a collection of articles in which the authors discuss critical issues in contemporary corrections. In the sited chapter the authors focus specifically on violence in prisons.

V.01172 Scharf, P. (1983). Empty bars: Violence and the crisis of meaning in the prison. *Prison Journal 63*(1), 114–124.

Addressed in this article is the purpose of prisons. The author assumes that the rehabilitative model has somewhat failed and askes the question, what is the purpose of prisons?

V.01173 Steinke, P. (1991). Using situational factors to predict types of prison violence. *Journal of offender Rehabilitation 17*(1/2), 119–132.

This study was conducted in a medium security California State prison in a unit with 500 men who had some psychiatric or behavior problems during incarceration. The investigator tested the prediction that when the occurrence of an infraction happened certain situational variables could be identified as predictors of whether this infraction included an individual act of violence.

V.01174 Wright, K. N. (1991). The violent and victimized in the male prison. *Journal of Offender Counseling Services and Rehabilitation 16*, 1–25.

In this article the author discusses the violent offender and the victimized offender in prisons. From an examination of inmate records and self-reports, Wright concludes that those victimized are the "lambs" within the institution, i.e. those who lack the sophistication and experience to cope with institutional life.

VISITATION

V.01175 American Correctional Association. (1965). *Manual of correctional standards* (rev. ed.). Laurel, MD: American Correctional Association.

Contained in this manual is an explanation of the standards of the American Correctional Association. Of particular interest are acceptable objectives, organization, functions and operations for state correctional systems.

V.01176 Dickinson, G. E. (1984). Changes in communication policies. *Corrections Today 46*(1), 58–60.

Presented in this article is an evaluation of communication policies in prisons. The author found that visitation rules and correspondence policies were becoming more liberal and more relaxed.

V.01177 Glaser, D. (1965). *The effectiveness of a prison and parole system*. New York: Bobbs-Merrill.

The author examines the prison and parole systems in the United States. The research has three broad objectives, to determine the failure rates for different types of offenders, to identify the determinate that relate to reversion, and to determine what programs are best suited to reduce recidivism. A strong family bond/family support was found to be negatively correlated to recidivism.

V.01178 Holt, N. & Miller, D. (1972). *Explorations in inmate-family relationships. Research report no. 46*. Sacramento, CA: California Department of Corrections.

Contained in this report are the results of an examination of inmate-family relationships in California prisons. Specifically, the type and prevalence of inmate-family relationships are explored. In addition, the impact these relationships have on inmate behavior is examined. It was determined that strong inmate-family relationships was a predictor of inmates' successful reintegration.

V.01179 Krantz, S. (1983). *Corrections and prisoners' rights in a nutshell* (2nd ed.). St. Paul, MN: West.

Discussed in this reference book is a brief overview of the correctional process, from pretrial diversion to release from prison. The book also contains an overview of prisoners' rights and emerging correctional law. Laws relating to visitation are also discussed.

V.01180 Shafer, N. E. (1989). Prison visiting: Is it time to review the rule? *Federal Probation 53*(4), 25–30.

In this article the author examines visiting policies and practices in long-term adult prisons. Most of the visiting policies reflect a concern for security and order. The author suggests that the policies and procedures be re-examined to determine how to ensure a successful visit.

V.01181 Shafer, N. E. (1994). Exploring the link between visits and parole success: A survey of prison visitors. *International Journal of Offender Therapy and Comparative Criminology 38*(1), 17–32.

The authors examined the relationship between prison visiting and success on parole. Data were collected from 364 visitors at two U.S. male adult prisons. The author focused on the frequency of visitation and the duration of visitations over the entire prison sentence. Family variables were also examined. The author suggests that other variables need to be addressed before one can assess the relationship between visitation and parole.

Cases

V.01182 *Lynott v. Henderson*, 610 F. 2d 340 (5th Cir. 1980)

The plaintiff sued federal prison officials alleging that they had violated his constitutional rights largely by the discriminatory application of the prison's visitation regulations. The court found that the plaintiff lied about his marital status, and therefore, the denial of visitation was not unconstitutional.

V.01183 *Payne v. District of Columbia*, 253 F.2d 867 (D.C.Cir. 1958)

The plaintiff filed suit asking that the prison be required to allow conjugal visitations with husbands and that private accommodations be provided during the visitation process. The court dismissed the complaint.

V.01184 *Pell v. Procunier*, 417 U.S. 817, 94 S.Ct. 2800, 41 L.Ed.2d 495 (1974)

The Supreme Court ruled that prisoners do not lose their First Amendment rights with incarceration. However, they do not have the right to face-to-face communications with news people so long as alternative channels of communication (such as use of mail) remain open and no discrimination in terms of content is involved.

V.01185 *Polakoff v. Henderson*, 370 F. Supp 690 (N.D.Ga. 1973)

The plaintiff contends that constitutional rights were denied because other similarly situated and classified inmates were afforded the opportunity for conjugal visits and he was not. The case was dismissed.

V.01186 *Procunier v. Martinez*, 416 U.S. 396, 94 S.Ct. 1800, 40 L.Ed.2d 224 (1974)

This case dealt with the issue of censorship of nonlegal correspondence. The Supreme Court held that prison mail censorship is constitutional if two criteria are met. Censorship must be directly related to the security, order, or rehabilitation of the prison and the restrictions must not be greater than necessary to satisfy the particular government interest involved.

V.01187 *Rowland v. Wolff*, 336 F. Supp 257 (D.Neb 1971)

The prisoner contends his rights were violated because he was denied visitation with his sister after it was alleged that his sister "passed" the prisoner a weapon. The court maintained that it will not interfere in matters shown to involve discretionary internal administrative decisions made by officials of the penal complex.

V.01188 *Saxbe v. Washington Post Company*, 417 U.S. 843, 94 S.Ct. 2811, 41 L.Ed.2d 514 (1974)

The Supreme Court reversed the lower court and upheld blanket prohibitions against reporters' interviews with prisoners.

V.01189 *Souza v. Travisono*, 498 F. 2d 1120 (1st Cir. 1974)

The inmates at the Rhode Island Adult Correctional Institutions argued that denying prisoners access to law students serving as agents of the Inmate Legal Assistance Program was unconstitutional. The court agreed but did not extend the access to mundane legal matter, e.g., prisoner divorces.

V.01190 *Tarlton v. Clark*, 441 F. 2d 384 (5th Cir. 1971)

The prisoner alleged his constitutional rights were denied when he was not allowed to have sexual relations with his wife. The court denied the appeal. The inmate also wanted the parole board to document why he was not paroled. The court ruled that the prisoner does not have a right to cross-examine parole board members. The Court also refused to become involved in the function and operation of the parole board.

V.01191 *Walker v. Pate*, 356 F. 2d 502 (7th Cir. 1966)

The plaintiff's principal complaint was that the Warden had discriminated against him by preventing his wife and daughter from visiting him while he was in confinement. The court ruled that both could visit and in fact prison regulations encouraged such visitation; however, the wife was confined in a female correctional institution and the daughter lived in another state.

VOCATIONAL PROGRAMS

V.01192 Boston, G. R. (1986). Seeds of hope: Prison garden program at Rykers Island. *Corrections Today 48*(8), 104.

Detailed in this article is a description of a new prison garden program sponsored by the Horticultural Society of New York. In Project Greenworks inmates learn a marketable skill by raising vegetables. Volunteers from the Horticultural Society teach the courses that are open to 16-to-20 year-old inmates. According to department officials the greenhouse instruction contains elements of math and science.

V.01193 Hershberger, S. L. (1987). Vocational education: Preparing for life outside. *Corrections Today 49*(5), 128, 130–132.

Contained in this article is a discussion of vocational training and its relationship to preparing an inmate for life outside of the institution. A plan for a college-credit vocational curriculum, instruction, and administration is described for the penitentiaries in New Mexico.

V.01194 Lattimore, P. K., Witte, A. D. & Baker, J. R. (1990). Experimental assessment of the effect of vocational training on youthful property offenders. *Evaluation Review 14*(2), 115–133.

In this article the authors present their findings on the implementation and evaluation of one vocational training program for youthful property offenders. The Sandhills Vocational Delivery System (VDS) program was offered at two North Carolina male correctional facilities. The authors report the results of the evaluation of that program.

V.01195 Mitchell, A. (1981). Dawn of solar training. *Corrections Magazine 7*(5), 41–45.

A discussion about various state and federal vocational training programs in prisons is presented in this article. Programs such as the solar heating technology program are used to provide practical experience to inmates so they can get a job once they are released from the institution.

V.01196 Schumacker, R. E., Anderson, D. B. & Anderson, S. L. (1990). Vocational and academic indicators of parole success. *Journal of Correctional Education 41*(1), 8–13.

This article is based on an examination of vocational and academic training as predictors of successful reintegration. In this study, the authors compare adult prison releasees who had vocational or academic training with those from a control group who did not have any vocational or academic training.

V.01197 Simon, R. J. & Landis, J. (1991). *Crimes women commit: The punishments they receive.* Lexington, MA: Lexington Books.

In this book, the authors examine the types of crime women commit and the subsequent punishment they receive. Using criminal justice and demographic data from the last 25 years, the authors examine the relationship between the social, economic, and environmental lives of women and the types and frequency of crimes they commit. The authors found that many female inmates do not have a vocation or job training. As a result, vocational programs for female offenders are recommended.

V.01198 Storck, C. (1985). Standardizing vocational training. *Corrections Today 47*(5), 44–45.

In this article the author discusses the New York Correctional System and its large inmate population. Reported are recommendations for improvement from a series of committees who examined the New York Vocational Training Programs in correctional institutions. The overall goal of the committees was to establish new vocational programs with standardized curricula, institutional materials, and records.

V.01199 Zumpetta, A. W. (1988). Full-time vocational training in corrections: Measuring effectiveness vs. appearance. *Journal of Correctional Education 39*(3), 130–133.

For this research article the author examined full-time vocational training programs at two correctional facilities in Pennsylvania in order to apply four management principles to the training. The principles include planning, organizing, actuating, and controlling.

VOLUNTEERS

I. Citizens

V.01200 Gladwin, B. (1993). Taconic warden finds volunteers have much to offer women inmates. *Corrections Today 55*(5), 88–93.

Contained in this edition of *Corrections Today* are articles in which the role of volunteers in corrections is addressed. This particular article stems from a New York warden's evaluation of volunteer work. The warden discusses the more salient benefits of volunteers in female correctional institutions.

V.01201 Harris, L. and Associates. (1969). *Volunteers look at corrections.* Washington, DC: Joint Commission of Correctional Manpower and Training.

This publication is based volunteers' perceptions of their work in prisons. The subjects, randomly selected from lists of volunteers in various correctional institutions, were interviewed by the researchers. The volunteers indicated that they work in prisons because they view their work as making a contribution to the staff and offenders. They also view their work as beneficial and identify a need to help others as one of the main reasons for volunteering.

V.01202 Hawk, K. (1993). 4000 BOP volunteers are committed to working within the federal system. *Corrections Today 55*(5), 72–75.

In this edition of *Corrections Today* articles about the roles of citizen volunteers in corrections are presented. In this article the author discusses the 4,000 volunteers who work in the United State Federal Bureau of Prisons. The author describes the kinds of services provided by volunteers.

V.01203 Moses, M. (1993). New program at women's prison benefit mothers and children. *Corrections Today 55*(5). 132–135.

Presented in this edition of *Corrections Today* are articles about the roles of citizen volunteers in corrections. In this article the author discusses a new program, initiated at a women's prison, that provides opportunities for mothers and children to visit.

V.01204 Ogburn, K. (1993). Volunteer program guide: Starting and maintaining your program. *Corrections Today 55*(5), 66.

Contained in this edition of *Corrections Today* are articles about the roles of citizen volunteers in corrections. In this article the author provides tips and suggestions for developing and maintaining volunteer groups in correctional settings.

V.01205 Scheier, I., Berry, J. L., Cox, M. L., Shelley, E., Simmons, R., & Callaghan, D. (1972). *Guidelines and standards for the use of volunteers in correctional programs*. Washington, DC: U.S. Department of Justice.

This report is based on a national study of volunteer programs in correctional settings. It provides guidelines and standards for the development and operation of volunteer programs in both adult and juvenile facilities.

V.01206 Winter, B. (1993). Does corrections need volunteers? *Corrections Today 55*(5), 20–22.

Contained in this edition of *Corrections Today* are articles about the roles of citizen volunteers in corrections. In this article the author discusses the need for volunteers in a correctional setting.

II. Inmates

V.01207 Boudin, K. (1993). Participatory literacy education behind bars: AIDS opens the door. *Harvard Educational Review 63*(2), 207–232.

The author, an inmate in Bedford Hills Correctional Facility, details her experiences in the literacy program at Bedford Hills. Instead of a curriculum that emphasizes workbook based reading skills, the author advocated a literacy program that is more relevant to inmates' lives and experiences.

V.01208 Hendricks, T. (1992). Shock, it works. *The Conservationist*, September-October, 44–47.

In this article the author analyzes the effectiveness of New York State's shock incarceration program. Also discussed are the contributions of the inmate volunteers and the necessary role they play in the program.

V.01209 McDonald, D. C. (1986). *Punishment without walls: Community service sentences in New York City.* New Brunswick, NJ: Rutgers University Press.

Contained in this book is an overview of the impact of community service sentencing in New York City. The Vera Institute initiated community service sentencing programs in three New York City courts between 1979 and 1981. The author evaluates the impact of the community service sentencing program for chronic property offenders.

V.01210 U.S. Department of Justice. (1992). *State of the bureau, 1992.* Sandstone, MN: Federal Bureau of Prisons.

Conatined in this agency report is an overview of the development and operations of correctional institutions in the Federal Bureau of Prisons (BOP). The author discusses BOP strategies for maintaining safe working conditions and suggests ways that the BOP can assist state and local correctional facilities. One of the issues discussed is the role of volunteers in correctional institutions.

V.01211 Wheeler, W. L. (1993). Volunteers: Corrections unsung heroes. *Corrections Today 55(5), 136, 139.*

In this article, the author describes an experimental project that is now a permanent program in 19 Connecticut correctional facilities. The project began in 1992 when the Recreation Director responded to an ad in the newspaper asking for volunteers to make quilts for AIDS/HIV babies. Over 800 quilts have been made by Connecticut inmates. One inmate is quoted as saying, "when I get home next year I will make my one year-old son a quilt."

W

WALLA WALLA, WASHINGTON STATE PENITENTIARY

W.01212 Camp, C. G. & Camp, G. M. (1988). *Management strategies for combating prison gang violence. Part II. Combating violent inmate organizations at the Washington State Penitentiary at Walla Walla: A case study.* Rockville, MD: National Institute of Justice.

Contained in this report are management strategies for controlling prison gang violence. It is based on first hand observations and analyses of responses to prison gang violence by five correctional facilities in Washington and Illinois. The researchers discuss solutions for consideration by correctional administrators. Walla Walla is one of the institutions that contributed prison gang data for the present research.

W.01213 Cardozo-Freeman, I. & Delorme, E. P. (1984). *The joint: Language and culture in a maximum security prison.* Springfield, IL: Charles C. Thomas.

This book is based on research conducted at Washington State Penitentiary at Walla Walla. The researchers collected data through taped interviews with inmates to test the hypothesis that language shapes and is shaped by culture. Inmates' language was analyzed to determine what prisoners' think, feel, and value.

W.01214 Elli, F. (1966). *The riot.* New York: Coward-McCann, Inc.

This non-fiction book is a novel about a prison riot in a state penitentiary.

W.01215 Farrington, K. & Parcells, R. P. (1991). Correctional facilities and community crime rates: Alternative hypotheses and competing explanations. *Humboldt Journal of Social Relations 17*(1 and 2), 17–127.

In this research article the authors report the results of their examination of the relationship between the presence of a prison in a community and the patterns of crime in that community.

W.01216 Hoffman, E. & McCoy, J. (1981). *Concrete Mama: Prison profiles from Walla Walla.* Columbia, MO: University of Missouri Press.

In this book is a brief history of prisons, including prisons in the United States and Washington State in particular. Profiles of 10 inmates, 1 visitor, and 1 correctional officer at Walla Walla State Prison in Washington State are presented. The author also provides photographic and narrative information in each case profile.

W.01217 Stastny, C. I. & Tyrnauer, G. (1982). *Who rules the joint? The changing political culture of maximum security prisons in America.* Lexington, MA: Lexington Books.

Presented in this book are the results of an extensive study of the struggle for power at Washington State Penitentiary at Walla Walla. The researchers conduct a historical examination of the struggle for power among conflicting groups, for example, prisoners, guards, wardens, governors and legislators, judges, outside community influences, and professionals.

W.01218 Tyrnauer, G. (1981). What went wrong at Walla Walla? *Corrections Magazine 7*(3), 37–41.

An evaluation of participatory management at Walla Walla state penitentiary in Washington State is presented in this article. The author indicates that administrators approved an experiment in inmate self-governance. The author discusses reasons why the experiment was not successful.

W.01219 Tyrnauer-Stastny, G. and Stastny, C. I. (1977). Changing political culture of a total institution: The case of Walla Walla (WA). *Prison Journal 57*(2), 43–55.

In this article the authors discuss inmate self-government and other reforms featured at the Washington State Penitentiary at Walla Walla.

WALNUT STREET JAIL

W.01220 Foulke, W. P. (1855). Remarks on the penal system of Pennsylvania, particularly with reference to county prisons. *Pennsylvania Journal of Prison Discipline and Philanthropy 10*(2).

Addressed in this pamphlet about county prisons in Pennsylvania are some of the important radical reforms in structure, discipline, and administration. Highlighted in the pamphlet are the defects of the present system. Details are also provided on provisions of law, motivations for compliance, and advantages compliance.

W.01221 Irwin, J. (1985). *The jail: Managing the underclass in American society.* Berkeley, CA: University of California Press.

Presented in this book are the results of the author's study of county jails in San Francisco, California. The author focuses on pretrial prisoners and the pretrial process. A major finding is that jails are used to manage offensive people, those who are detached and disreputable, instead of those who commit crime. The author provides a brief review of the Walnut Street Jail.

W.01222 Johnston, N. (1973). *A brief history of prison architecture.* New York: Walker and Company.

Provided by the author of this book is a brief history on prison architecture. The author points out that before an architect can design a prison, the architect must have a realistic understanding of the pressures and consequences of the group living in the institution. The author provides a brief review of the Walnut Street Jail.

W.01223 Pigeon, H. D., et al. (1944). *Principles and methods in dealing with offenders.* State College, PA: Pennsylvania Municipal Publications Service.

The authors present a manual for the in–service training course offered by the Public Service Institute of Pennsylvania for public employees in the correctional and penal fields. The subjects covered include the police, detention, the courts, probation, release procedures, behavior of the delinquent, treatment of individual offenders and casework as a means of treatment.

W.01224 Takagi, P. (1975). The Walnut Street Jail: A penal reform to centralize the powers of the state. *Federal Probation 39*(4), 18–25.

This author takes a radical approach in examining prison reform. Using the Walnut Street Jail as a model, and explaining how it became a prison, the author suggests that this reform was done to increase state power as a response to a fiscal crisis.

W.01225 Teeters, N. K. (1937). *They were in prison: A history of the Pennsylvania Prison Society, 1787–1937*. Philadelphia, PA: John C. Winston.

This book is a chronicle of the Pennsylvania prison system. The author discusses the main differences between the Auburn and Pennsylvania systems. This reference book contains excerpts from the prison's records.

W.01226 Teeters, N. K. (1955). *The cradle of the penitentiary: The Walnut Street jail at Philadelphia, 1773–1835*. Philadelphia, PA: Pennsylvania Society.

In this book, the author provides a historical account of the development of the Walnut Street Jail in Philadelphia. The author examines the reforms that lead to the jail becoming a prison. The time period examined is 1773 to 1835.

WARDENS

W.01227 Bartollas, C, & Miller, S. (1978). *Correctional administration: Theory and practice*. New York: McGraw Hill.

Contained in this book is an overview of correctional administration. The authors discuss correctional management practices and the theories upon which they are based.

W.01228 Cullen, F. T., Latessa, E. J., Burton, V. S., Jr., & Lombardo, L. X. (1993). The correctional orientation of prison wardens: Is the rehabilitative ideal supported? *Criminology 31*, 69–92.

This article stems from a national study which was conducted to determine how wardens view rehabilitation. The authors collected data from wardens in 375 state and federal institutions. The authors found that wardens remain supportive of rehabilitation: however, they place primary emphasis on maintaining custody and institutional order.

W.01229 Cullen, F. T., Latessa, E. J., Kopache, R., Lombardo, L. X., & Burton, V. S., Jr. (1993). Prison wardens' job satisfaction. *Prison Journal 73*, 141–161.

This article stems from a national study which was conducted to determine wardens' level of job satisfaction. Data were collected from wardens in

375 state and federal correctional institutions. The authors found a high level of job satisfaction among the research sample.

W.01230 DiIulio, J. J. Jr. (1991). *No escape: The future of American corrections.* New York: Basic Books.

The author provides a detailed overview of American corrections. Presented are suggestions for improving jails and prisons from a management perspective and a review privatization of community-based corrections.

W.01231 DiIulio, J. J. Jr. (1987). *Governing prisons: A comparative study of correctional management.* New York: Free Press.

Provided in this book is a comprehensive overview of prison management. The author comparatively explores prison management in three state correctional systems, Texas, California, and Michigan. Chapters in the book contain discussions of governability of prisons, quality of life in prison, correctional philosophy and leadership, correctional change, and the prison as a constitutional government.

W.01232 Jacobs, J. (1977). *Stateville: The penitentiary in mass society.* Chicago: University of Chicago Press.

The author provides a detailed, historical account of a Stateville maximum security prison in Chicago, Illinois. Jacobs analyzed the relationship between the prison and the outside world. Also examined are the different roles of custody and treatment.

W.01233 Lunden, W. A. (1957). The tenure and turnover of state prison wardens. *American Journal of Corrections* (Nov/Dec), 14–15, 33, 34.

Several issues are addressed in this article including: the tenure of state prison wardens, the turnover of state prison wardens, the revolving-door wardens, and reasons for changes in wardens. The researcher concludes that almost two-thirds of the 612 wardens in 66 state prisons and reformatories in 41 states held their office for four years or less, and about one-fourth for five to nine years. The evidence shows that more than one-third of the turnovers in state prison wardenships were due to political changes in the state administration.

ENOCH COBB WINES

W.01234 Barnes, H. E., & Teeters, N. K. (1943). *New horizons in criminology.*

New York: Prentice-Hall, Inc.

This book consist of a comprehensive discussion of crime, criminals, punishment, and prisons. The authors also offer suggestions for future reforms in the repression of crime and the treatment of criminals. They provide information on the role played by Enoch Cobb Wines in the evolution of penology.

W.01235 Bentham, J. & Wines, E. C. (1991). Jeremy Bentham and Enoch Wines discuss the privatization of corrections. *Journal of Contemporary Criminal Justice* 7(1), 60–68.

This article is a reprint of the observations made by Jeremy Bentham and Enoch Wines. The observations made by Bentham stem from letters, which constitute the Panopticon Papers, which were written by Bentham in Russia in 1787. The observations made by Enoch Wines, who became secretary of the New York Prison Association in 1862, address the privatization of prisons.

W.01236 Clear, T. R. & Cole, G. F. (1994). *American corrections* (3rd ed.). Belmont, CA: Wadsworth.

Provided in this textbook is a review of the historic problems in corrections, the evolutionary changes that have resulted in contemporary corrections, and current issues in corrections, for example, incarceration trends, capital punishment, and surveillance of inmates in the community. The authors also acknowledge the many contributions of Enoch Cobb Wines to corrections.

W.01237 Eriksson, T. (1976). *The reformers: An historical survey of pioneer experiments in the treatment of criminals.* New York: Elsevier.

This book consist of a historical review of experiments in correctional treatment reform. The researcher provides information on the major reform efforts in Europe and the United States from the 16th century to the present.

W.01238 Wines, E. C. & Dwight, T. W. (1867). *Report on the prisons and reformatories of the United States and Canada.* Albany, NY: Van Benthuysen and Sons' Steam Printing House.

The authors visited and studied the prisons and reformatories of the northern 18 states and Canada in 1866. The authors discovered many deficiencies such as prisons being part of the political machinery of the state, the incarceration of youths with hardened criminals, and the lack of positive rehabilitation and reward. The authors presented their findings and recommendations to the New York Legislature in 1867.

W.01239 Wines, F. H. (1910). *Punishment and reformation: A study of the penitentiary system.* New York: Crowell. (Reprinted 1919).

This book, complied from a series of lectures the author gave at the University of Wisconsin in the 1890s, chronicles the changes in law that reflect a reformatory approach to criminals during the nineteenth century. Examples of issues discussed are what constitutes crime, retribution and punishment, mental facors and delinquency, treatment programs, inmate self-government, and predictions for the future.

WOMEN INMATES

I. History

W.01240 Dobash, R., Dobash, R. & Gutteridge, S. (1986). *The imprisonment of women.* New York: Basil Blackwell.

These authors maintain that prisons for females have been shaped and maintained because of patriarchal assumptions about the nature of female criminals. Correctional policies found in women's prisons in Great Britain from the 18th century to present are analyzed to inform the reader about influences that affect the way female institutions are managed.

W.01241 Feinman, C. (1983). An historical overview of the treatment of incarcerated women: Myths and realities of rehabilitation. *The Prison Journal 63*(2), 12–26.

The author provides a historical overview of the types of treatment that are available to incarcerated women. The author maintains that rehabilitation programs for incarcerated women have continued to be designed around the traditional role of the female in society with little consideration for the socioeconomic background of the inmate or the neighborhood to which the female offender will return.

W.01242 Freedman, E. B. (1981). *Their sisters' keepers: Women's prison reform in America, 1830–1930.* Ann Arbor: The University of Michigan Press.

The author examines the involvement of women reformers in the women's prison movement and the changing relationships between these reformers and the female criminals. Beginning with an analysis of white middle class women's attitudes toward female prisoners in the nineteenth century and concluding with a look at the work of early twentieth century women criminologists and penologists, the author provides an excellent overview of women's role in the women's prison movement.

W.01243 Lekkerkerker, E. C. (1931). *Reformatories for women in the U.S.* Gronigen, Netherlands: J.B. Wolters.

The author is a Dutch student of criminology who gathered data and materials during a two year visit to the United States. This study represents an extensive study of the problems associated with the care and treatment of incarcerated women.

W.01244 Rafter, N. (1985). *Partial justice: Women in state prisons, 1800–1935.* Boston: Northeastern University Press.

This book consists of results of an examination of women's prisons in the United States from the late 1800s until 1935. The data is derived from a national survey of all institutions that housed only female populations during the period under study. Prison reports, legislative and archival documents as well as prison registries in three states were analyzed for demographic and offense data on 4,600 inmates. The author discusses the influence of the reformatory movement to correctional rehabilitation of female offenders.

W.01245 Strickland, K. (1976). *Correctional institutions for women in the U.S..* Lexington, NY: Lexington Books.

Contained in this book is the author's examination of correctional institutions for females in the United States. An overview of the facilities is presented.

II. Current Issues

W.01246 American Correctional Association. (1990). *The female offender. What does the future hold?* Washington, DC: St. Mary's Press.

This publication stems from a Task Force study of female offenders. The Task Force was assembled by the American Correctional Association to study female offenders. The study was conducted to determine the implication of increases in the crime rate for women and the correctional needs of this increasing population.

W.01247 Bureau of Justice Statistics. (1992). *Prisoners in 1991*. Rockville, MD: National Institute of Justice/National Criminal Justice Reference Service.

According to this government report an analysis of official records from the Federal and State correctional systems reveal that the number of inmates has reached record numbers.

W.01248 Fletcher, B., Dixon-Shaver, L., & Moon, D. (1993). *Women prisoners: A forgotten population*. Westport, CT: Praeger.

The results of a longitudinal study of individual and institutional factors that promote recidivism in females are reported in this book. Data on female inmates were derived from two Oklahoma prisons through the use of surveys, interviews and field observations. Inmates, staff, and institutional records, provided the necessary data.

W.01249 Moyer, I. (1992). *The changing roles of women in the criminal justice system*. Prospect Heights, IL: Waveland Press, Inc.

In this book, the author examines the changing roles of women (practitioners and offenders) in the criminal justice system. The author applies conflict theory to the slow, but progressive, changes in the role of the female offender and female professionals in the criminal justice system. Other essays in the book reflect the feminist paradigm. The author also incorporates race, ethnicity, and international data when available in the discussion of women in the criminal justice system.

W.01250 Muraskin, R. & Alleman, T. (1993). *It's a crime: Women and justice*. Englewood Cliffs, NJ: Prentice-Hall.

Contained in this edited book is a series of articles focusing on females in the criminal justice system. Many topics are presented including feminist theory and a historical overview of women's issues. Women in the criminal justice system, including corrections and law enforcement, abortion, drugs, AIDS, and women as victims of violence are other issues that are also addressed.

W.01251 Rafter, N. (1990). *Partial justice: Women, prisons and social control*. New Brunswick, NJ: Transaction Books.

Provided in this book are the results of an examination of women's prisons in the United States from the late 1800s until 1935. The data is derived from a national survey of all institutions that housed only female populations during the period under study. Prison reports, legislative and archival documents as well as prison registries in three states were analyzed for demographic and offense data on 4,600 inmates. The author discusses the influence of the reformatory movement to correctional rehabilitation of female offenders.

Cases

W.01252 *Glover v. Johnson*, 478 F.Supp. 1075 (1979)

This case is based on a class action suit challenging the disparities of Michigan's programs for female inmates. The court fleshed out in some detail what is required to meet the demands of the Equal Protection Clause. Women have a constitutional right to "parity of treatment" with men in the programs made available to them.

W.01253 *Todaro v. Ward*, 431 F.Supp. 1129 (1977)

The basis of the present case is general health care in prison. There is no discussion of particular health care needs of women in this case.

WORK PROGRAMS

W.01254 Auerbach, B., Sexton, G., Farrow, F. & Lawson, R. (1988). *Work in American prisons: The private sector gets involved.* Washington, DC: National Institute of Justice.

Contained in this government report is a description of the historical, as well as, current developments in private-sector prison industries. Primary emphasis is place on the prohibitions against prison industry, analyzing costs and benefits, and suggestions for future strategies.

W.01255 Burger, W. E. (1982). More warehouses or factories with fences? *New England Journal of Prison Law 8*(1, Winter), 111–120.

In this article, the author suggests that prison industry can accomplish dual objectives. It can provide training to inmates and leads to subsequent employment while lightening the load of maintaining the prison system.

W.01256 Dwyer, D. C. & McNally, R. B. (1993). Public policy, prison industries, and business: An equitable balance for the 1990s. *Federal Probation 57*(2, June) 30–36.

The authors provide a historical and contemporary review of the role of prison industries in American prisons. Several work models are discussed.

W.01257 Flanagan, T. & Maguire, K. (1993). A full employment policy for prisons in the United States: Some arguments, estimates, and implications. *Journal of Criminal Justice 21*, 117–130.

In this article, the authors advocate for a policy of full employment in prisons. They examine current employment policies in prisons in the United States and offer a number of work models while discussing the implication of dramatically increasing prisoner employment.

W.01258 Greiser, R. C. (1989). Do correctional industries adversely impact the private sector? *Federal Probation 53*(1), 18–24.

In this essay, the author responds to common complaints or myths proliferated in the private sector concerning prison industry.

W.01259 Hawkins, G. (1983). Prison labor and prison industries. In M. Tonry and N. Morris (eds.), *Crime and justice: An annual review of research* (Vol. 5) (pp. 98–103). Chicago: University of Chicago Press.

In this edited book chapter, the author addresses the barriers to prison work and industry. The principle of less eligibility seems to be the top barrier to such programs.

W.01260 Schaller, J. (1982). Work and imprisonment: An overview of the changing role of prison labor in American prisons. *The Prison Journal 62*(2), 3-12.

In this article, the author provides a historical account of the changing role of prison labor in American prisons. The reasons for lack of prison industry seem to focus on economic concerns and a lack of prison policy advocating prison industry.

WORK-RELEASE PROGRAMS

W.01261 Busher, W. (1973). *Ordering time to serve prisoners*. Washington, DC: U.S. Government Printing Office.

Discussed in this report are work release program concepts and a methodology for planning and implementing such programs.

W.01262 Champion, D. J. (1990). *Probation and parole in the United States*.

Toronto: Merrill Publishing Company.

The text is about adults and juveniles who have been convicted of criminal offenses and have been adjudicated as delinquent and the agencies and personnel who monitor these offenders. It is difficult to distinguish between probation and parole because many of the programs for both overlap and many of the people that supervise these individuals supervise both probationers and parolees.

W.01263 Jones, M. *(1982). Report on the Virginia Work Release Program.* Rockville, MD: National Institute of Justice/National Criminal Justice Reference Service Microfiche Program.

The author reviews the current literature on work release nationwide and provides specific information about Virginia's work release population trends, facilities, selection process, and earnings.

W.01264 McCarthy, B. R. & McCarthy, B. J. (1984). *Community-based corrections.* Monterey, CA: Brooks/Cole.

The authors review community based corrections in relationship to the larger system of corrections and how they apply specifically to certain offender groups.

W.01265 McCarthy, B. R. & McCarthy, B. J. (1991). *Community-based corrections* (2d ed.). Monterey, CA: Brooks/Cole.

This book is an extensive sourcebook on alternatives to prisons, i.e., community-based corrections. The authors provide a comprehensive review of the different types of community-based alternatives.

W.01266 Rothman, D. J. (1980). *Conscience and convenience: The asylum and its alternatives in progressive America.* Boston: Little, Brown and Co.

This book consists of an exploration of the origins and consequences of programs that have dominated criminal justice, juvenile justice, and mental health in the 20th century. The author discusses the similarities between penitentiaries and state mental institutions, demonstrating that both are asylums in the United States. Also discussed is the role of treatment programs.

Y

YOUTH IN PRISON

Y.01267 Barnes, C. W., & Franz, R. (1989). Questionably adult: Determinants and effects of the juvenile waiver decision. *Justice Quarterly 6*, 117–135.

Contained in this article is the results of a study of juvenile waiver decisions. The authors conducted a study on 206 waiver motions filed between March, 1978 and December, 1983 in a large metropolitan county in Northern California. The authors examined as the independent variables demographic characteristics and legal and organizational determinates to ascertain the reason for the waivers. These same variables were used as control variables when the authors examined the severity of the sentence.

Y.01268 Bishop, D. M, Fraizer, C. E., & Henretta, J. C. (1989). Prosecutorial waiver: Case study of questionable reform. *Crime and Delinquency 35*, 179–210.

In this article the authors examine the controversial automatic waiver of juveniles from juvenile court to adult court. This kind of waiver, known as prosecutorial waiver, is set out in state statutes which provide the prosecutor with complete authority for the waiver decision.

Y.01269 Butts, J. & Connors–Beatty, D. J. (1993). *The juvenile court's response to violent offenders: 1985–1989.* Washington, D.C.: U.S. Department of Justice.

Provided in this report is a historical account of the juvenile court and its response to violent crime and violent juvenile offenders for the period

1985 to 1989.

Y.01270 Champion, D. J., & Mays, G. L. (1991). *Transferring juveniles to criminal courts: Trends and implications for criminal justice*. New York: Praeger.

This book is an excellent source on how juveniles get transferred into adult court. The authors describe the different types of transfers and the frequency in which the transfers are used.

Y.01271 Forst, M., Fagan, J., & Vivona, T. S. (1987). Youths in prison and training schools: Perceptions and consequences of the treatment-custody dichotomy. *Juvenile and Family Court Journal 40*, 1–14.

This article is based on a comparison of youth in prison versus youth in juvenile facilities. The authors compare two groups of juveniles, one group (n=81) who were incarcerated in adult facilities and the other group (n=59) who were held in custody in secure juvenile training schools. Those juveniles detained in training schools gave more positive evaluations of the treatment and training programs, general services, and institutional personnel than those incarcerated in adult prisons.

Y.01272 Houghtalin, M., & Mays, G. L. (1991). Criminal disposition of New Mexico juveniles transferred to adult courts. *Crime and Delinquency 37*, 393–407.

Provided in this article are the results of a study of juvenile transfers to adult court in New Mexico. The authors found that transferring juveniles to adults courts appears to be a rare phenomenon in New Mexico.

Y.01273 McConnell, E.H. & Barnhill, E.M. (1997). Juvenile waiver in Georgia: Senate Bill 440, Paper presented to the Academy of Criminal Justice Sciences, Louisville, KY: March 14.

In this study the researchers examined the impact of Georgia's mandatory waiver of juveniles to felony court when committing specific crimes, also referred to as the seven deadly sins. An analysis of the data indicated the following incarceration outcomes: African American males who commit robberies or homicides account for the largest percentage of juveniles in prisons for adults, Caucasian males who commit homicides or sexual assaults account for the second largest number of incarcerated juveniles, while the fewest that are incarcerated are females who have been convicted of robberies or homicides. The researchers conclude that the greatest impact of Senate Bill 440 is its ability to shape the public's perception that violent juveniles are being harshly punished.

Y.01274 McShane, M. D., & Williams, F. P. III (1989). The prison adjustment of juvenile offenders. *Crime and Delinquency 35*, 254–269.

In this study, the authors examined two groups of inmates. One group contained juveniles who committed their crimes before age 17 and were tried as juveniles (n=55). The other group, who committed their crimes between the ages of 17 and 21, were tried as adults (n=91). The authors found that the juvenile offenders were twice as likely as their adult counterparts to have trouble adjusting to incarceration. Trouble adjusting was measured in terms of failure to work or earn good-time credit.

Y.01275 Rubin, H. T. (1989). The juvenile court landscape. In A.R. Roberts (ed.), *Juvenile justice: policies, programs, and services*. Chicago: Dorsey.

Contained in this edited book are many discussions of juvenile delinquency issues, from both historical and contemporary perspectives. The focus of this particular chapter is on juvenile court processes, i.e., waivers.

INDEX

About the Compilers

ELIZABETH HUFFMASTER McCONNELL is Associate Professor of Criminal Justice, Chair of the Criminal Justice Department, and Director of the Criminal Justice Graduate Program at Charleston Southern University, Charleston, South Carolina.

LAURA J. MORIARTY is Assistant Dean, College of Humanities and Sciences, and Associate Professor, Department of Criminal Justice, at Virginia Commonwealth University, Richmond, Virginia.